75TH ANNIVERSARY

PORSCHE 356

GORDON MALTBY

FOREWORD BY GRANT LARSON

PAGE 1: Ferdinand Porsche, left, and his son Ferdinand Anton (Ferry) in 1937. PAGE 2: The U.S. was Porsche's largest market in the 356 era, and in 1955 the "Continental" coupe was introduced for America. It is shown here in the capital of America's heartland, Chicago. THIS PAGE: The Speedster—that most iconic of Porsche 356s—celebrated 50 years in 2004 at an event in Monterey. A special course was set up through the DelMonte forest to remember the Pebble Beach Road Races where Porsches were introduced to thousands of California sports car fans.

CONTENTS

FOREWORD BY GRANT LARSON

Growing up in Wisconsin, my father owned a few unusual German cars. Unfortunately, a Porsche was not one of them, but rather the likes of a DKW Junior or an NSU Prinz—which at least had an air-cooled rear engine. A neighbor kid's father had a 356, a gray coupe tucked back in the corner of a dark garage, which gave it an element of mystery. I thought my dad's cars were cool, but this little bathtub-shaped Porsche was something special. Just standing close and looking at it made it even more intriguing.

In getting my first car, the groove at the time was muscle cars. And what I couldn't own, I would draw, which eventually led me down the path of becoming a designer. In my twenties, my taste began to change and became more refined. A Porsche became my new dream car. That admiration also spiked my interest in automotive and design history—finding out how these wonderful shapes came to be.

In studying the design of Porsches, it became clear that the 356 laid the groundwork and the form language for nearly all models that succeeded. But it did not begin with the first Porsche in 1948, nor even the VW Beetle. It goes further back to the beginnings of Porsche as a consultant to other manufacturers. The Porsche engineering firm was established in 1931 at the height of a worldwide financial crisis, their first shot at going totally against the wind. Shortly thereafter several vehicles were developed under the hand of designer Erwin Komenda and his team such as the Wanderer Typ 8 and the Zündapp Typ 12 in 1932, the NSU Typ 32 in 1934, and of course the VW Beetle and the Typ 60K10 car for the Berlin-Rome race. A visual overlap or "morph" of all these vehicles together would later result in the basic form of the 356.

It goes without saying that the 356 paved the path for the 901 as well as all 911s thereafter. We speak today of "brand identity," and it is this unmistakable appearance over several decades that has survived the test of time. When you look at the details, there is a distinct side window graphic DLO or "daylight opening." The narrow cabin and wide shoulders, low front bonnet, and round headlamps provided the Porsche identity that would be developed and cultivated with minimal deviation over the years.

But what is it that makes a car so timeless and so iconic? The answer is quite simple: a proven concept combined with top engineering, wrapped in a beautiful, functional shape. In the 356 the idea of "form follows function" is in full swing. The 2+2 seating configuration with a rear-mounted engine resulted in the fastback roofline. With rear seats easily converted into additional luggage space, the Porsche developed an everyday-use identity. Beginning with the 356, Porsche has not followed the trends of any decade, but instead has relied on instinct and intuition, remaining true to core beliefs.

When I began as a designer for Porsche in 1989, I worked alongside the clay modelers and sculptors who had shaped not only the first 911 but also the later 356s. When you come to work for Porsche, you usually stay for your entire career. This gave me additional insight as to how the company works. Early on, when I was working on prototypes to succeed the air-cooled 993, Ferry Porsche looked at my model and said, "Don't make the front fenders so low; you need them to help you direct where the car is going." After this project—along with the four-door, front-engine 989—was shelved in 1991, the idea of resurrecting the company with the parts-sharing 996 and 986 Boxster was in the works. My interest in Porsche history eventually led me to apply some of the DNA of the 550 and especially the 718 RSK to the new Boxster.

The success of the company, starting with the 356, can be attributed to the effort, passion, and vision of one man: Ferry Porsche. Developed in the rubble of war-torn Germany with limited materials, and sold for the same price as a Cadillac, the 356 was Porsche's second successful attempt at going against the wind. Now that is a success story.

I personally have three 356s in my garage: my ultimate lifelong-dream car 1956 Speedster; a long-term T1A beehive lightweight coupe project; and my very first Porsche, a 356SC, which has effortlessly taken me from Stuttgart up to England, and down to Gmünd. And back. Its sportiness and usability have really been proven during these trips, not to mention its reliability. Which leads me to wrap it up in one sentence: once you develop a solid concept, there is no reason to deviate from it.

The Auto Union racers designed by Ferdinand Porsche in the mid-1930s were the pinnacle of race car engineering, competing in Grand Prix, land speed contests, and hillclimbs. Driver Hans Stuck was instrumental in the cars' creation and also drove them to hillclimb wins, becoming European Mountain Champion three times. Here his son Hans Joachim Stuck pilots a Typ A on the Klausen Pass in Switzerland, honoring his father and the cars which once dominated the highest echelons of racing. Design elements of these exotic racers would make their way into Porsches twenty years later.

FERDINAND PORSCHE'S AMAZING HALF CENTURY

Carinthia. The mellifluous sound of the name is perfectly matched by the beauty and charm of this mountainous region of southern Austria. The Eastern Alps extend rocky fingers between forested valleys, where lakes gather spring meltwater and rivers transport it all the way to the Black Sea. One of these rivers, the Malta, begins its journey bounding over waterfalls and through a scenic valley some 45 kilometers from and 1,000 meters above the small town of Gmünd. In the early twentieth century, the river provided water and power for a sawmill just outside the town's center. By 1944, while World War II still raged, Willi Meineke's sawmill and lumberyard was appropriated for another, more important use. Although Gmünd could be considered an Austrian backwater, it was specifically this "middle of nowhere" attribute that made it extremely valuable when events some 500 kilometers to the northwest called for a reckoning.

In contrast to the bucolic scenes around the Austrian Malta valley, in Germany's cities Royal Air Force bombers conducted night raids and the U.S. Army 8th Air Force bombed during the day. Stuttgart was a major rail hub and home to Daimler-Benz, a Bosch plant, and the SKF bearing factory, among

Gmünd, shown in an old postcard, was a sleepy Austrian village far from the war's turmoil.

Workers test the first Porsche, built in the crude sheds at Willi Meineke's lumberyard in 1948.

many others. In the Stuttgart suburb of Zuffenhausen was the recently built headquarters of Dr. Ing. h.c. F. Porsche KG. The company had been formed by Ferdinand Porsche in 1931, and by 1944 it had almost six hundred employees, many working in the large three-story brick building on Schwieberdinger Strasse. There, designers, engineers, and draftsmen created plans for numerous projects, most commissioned and underwritten by the German military. In the lower-level workshops the plans were brought to life as prototypes, then tested and developed.

Porsche's work on everything from boat motors to rockets and tanks had not escaped the notice of Allied intelligence. Zuffenhausen was north of the city center and escaped most of the huge attacks, but in a stroke of bad luck, a single small bomb made its way through a wall and into the cellar of Porsche's building, destroying a complete archive of company plans and records.

That event finalized a decision that had been under consideration for months: to move the staff and business operations to a safe haven away from the bombing. Porsche tasked his thirty-four-year-old son, Ferdinand Anton Ernst (known as Ferry), to find a suitable location and organize the move. The family already owned an expansive lakefront property in Austria, and an adjacent flying center there would allow space for equipment storage and some development work. Another location was needed, however, to provide both engineering space and housing for the staff, along with a shop area for mechanical work. Ferry Porsche was familiar with the small town of Gmünd, and although the military authorities in Stuttgart had ordered the company to move to Czechoslovakia, he lobbied instead for his native Austria. Much of the Stuttgart contingent moved there during 1944, bringing machine tools, drawing boards, and their families, in some cases. The existing lumberyard buildings were crude and cramped, and more had to be built to accommodate the group, but work continued on designs for military projects even though Germany's prospects for victory were dimming by the day.

When in May 1945 the victorious Allies reached the rural valleys of southern Austria, they found mostly farmers and cows. They had not expected to see the draftsmen working in rough sheds outside the town of Gmünd, who were no mere pencil pushers but rather talented engineers who had created some of the most sophisticated mechanical devices the world had yet seen. With the new peace, however, weaponry design gave way to more immediate needs, and the company—whose list of successful projects now numbered well over three hundred and whose reputation was known around the world—concentrated on plebian items such as water pumps and winches.

Porsche's sabbatical in the Malta valley would continue for several years, and while sequestered in Gmünd, Ferry Porsche guided his staff on a mission to do something the company had never done during its many years of designing automobiles for others: build a car that could be called a Porsche. During the winter of 1947 drawings were made for a midengined two-seater, a sporting, aerodynamic runabout that was simple and yet modern. Using components from the Volkswagen "people's car" the company had created before the war, by June 1948 the 356th design project of the Porsche firm drove out along the mountain roads near Gmünd wearing seven distinct letters on its nose: P-O-R-S-C-H-E. The first Porsche had been born in Carinthia.

IN THE BEGINNING

The story of the Porsche company begins before the turn of the twentieth century, a full fifty years before Porsche 356 #001 was conceived. Ferdinand Porsche was born in 1875 in Bohemia, now Czechia. Maffersdorf (now part of the city of Liberec) was a prosperous burg with a textile and carpet mills, a spa, a brewery, and, at Tandvalska Street 38, the home and workshop of tinsmith Anton Porsche. Anton's second son, Ferdinand, was expected to follow in the family plumbing business and train as

Young Ferdinand was expected to follow in his father's plumber footsteps, but he emphatically chose another path. In 1902 he was at the wheel of a Lohner-Porsche gasoline and electric hybrid vehicle in front of his family's home in Maffersdorf. His father, Anton Porsche, and his brother are seated at the rear.

a metalworker to someday lead the company. When electricity came to the local textile mill, however, the teenager became fascinated with the new technology, spending much time there as the equipment was installed. It was a turning point from which he would never look back.

Experimenting at home with batteries caused his father to angrily denounce Ferdinand's foolish waste of time, but his mother proved the cooler head and convinced her husband to allow their son to study the new technology—but only after he had finished his daily work. He commuted to nearby Reichenberg for evening classes, an exhausting but exciting experience for the young man. He later installed electric lighting in the family home. Although Ferdinand's father could not recognize his potential, others did: the owners of the textile mill saw an inquiring mind and encouraged his parents to allow him to go to Vienna at eighteen. They were instrumental in finding a position for him there at Vereinigte Elektrizitäts-AG Béla Egger, a leading producer of electrical lighting and power transmission products.

At Béla Egger's firm, Ferdinand was assigned to the test department, where he showed promise. Starting from the lowest rung of the ladder, he became head of the test department by 1898, having learned from everything going on around him, plus part-time study at Vienna's Technical University. VE-AG at the time was working with Ludwig Lohner, the owner of a long-established carriage-making business in the city. Lohner correctly saw a trend toward motorized vehicles and made an agreement to develop an electric carriage with VE-AG. He came to appreciate Porsche's ability to sort out the issues that continually cropped up, and in 1899 he hired the twenty-four-year-old to lead a new venture building Lohner electric vehicles in another section of Vienna. Using battery power, Porsche's design for a Lohner "electric phaeton" used a steerable wheel hub that was itself a specially designed electric motor. It was a sensation at the 1900 Paris Exhibition, bringing sales success with Lohner's well-heeled traditional customers and in commercial use as taxis.

Although electricity was at the heart of Porsche's interests, automobiles and competition became very important. A race near Berlin in September 1899 was the first example of a credo that would much later be synonymous with his own company's sports cars: "Racing improves the breed." With three passengers aboard, he drove the first VE-AG/Lohner electric car over 40 kilometers, up and down hills. He won the race by 18 minutes; only half the field even finished.

As new chief engineer at Lohner, a milestone for Porsche was his Semper Vivus ("Always Alive") hybrid of 1900, whose gas engines drove a generator that could power hub motors or recharge a battery pack. It was a huge, heavy, solidly sprung carriage that took skill to drive but was state-of-the-art. Innovations were coming at a fast and furious rate, and these System Lohner-Porsche vehicles engendered many patents for Lohner and its prolific engineer. Porsche also developed and promoted the gas/electric Mixte carriages, driving one in the Exelberg hillclimb in the Vienna woods to a new record time and a class win in April 1902. Later that year he was at the wheel of a Mixte-drive Lohner-Porsche beside Archduke Franz Ferdinand, who was leading military maneuvers. Having been drafted into service, Ferdinand Porsche was wearing the uniform of a reserve infantryman. It is ironic that Porsche, who had little interest in politics and was anything but the military type, would in future years be immersed in both worlds. The young man was at the wheel that day in recognition of his designing the automobile they were riding in, and no one knew the machine better. He was peppered with questions from many of the top brass and aristocracy. It was hoped that the military would be inclined to use the Mixte-drive system in their vehicles, as it was already being used for fire equipment and buses in Vienna. However, in spite of lengthy bouts of show-and-tell by Porsche with some of the highest-ranking Dual Monarchy military men, no subsequent orders came.

ENTER MR. MERCEDES

A successful Viennese insurance agent and stock trader named Emil Jellinek was the Austrian counsel general in Nice, on the French Riviera. His enthusiasm for automobiles knew no bounds, and he was influential enough to have Stuttgart's Daimler-Motoren create a "car of the future" for him, named after his daughter Mercedes. Selling and racing it against Porsche's Lohner Mixte cars, he was impressed by the competition. Soon, however, as gasoline engines steadily improved in power and reliability, the bloom was off the electric-car rose. Lohner began to phase out production of his electric automobiles.

In 1906 Jellinek took over Austro-Daimler in Weiner Neustadt, south of Vienna, and hired the then thirty-one-year-old Porsche as chief engineer to run the operation, a huge responsibility as well as a tremendous opportunity. In his personal life, Porsche and his wife, Alois (née Kaes), had had a

DER SIEGER Herr Porsche auf österr. Daimler mit **Continental-Gleitschutz**

A period postcard touts the 1910 Prinz-Heinrich-Fahrt winner—on Continental tires. Porsche always took advantage of promotional partnerships.

daughter, Louise, in 1904. In September 1909, while Ferdinand was driving in a race, a son would be born at home. The child was named after his father with the middle name Anton, after his grandfather. He would be known through his life as Ferry.

By 1908 Jellinek was finished with being a car builder, retiring to his diplomatic and social circles. Porsche and his Austro-Daimler business partner, Eduard Fischer, plodded ahead, determined to prove their products in the crucible of racing. In 1910 Prinz Heinrich, brother of Kaiser Wilhelm II and admiral of the German High Seas Fleet, staged a trial for automobiles, a multiday long-distance run for production cars. Porsche designed a streamlined body that he called a "tulip" and installed a four-cylinder overhead-camshaft engine of 5.7 liters built specifically for the race. It may be considered the first homologated Porsche ever. Ten examples were built and entered, earning a one-two-three finish with the winner driven

Crew members pose with Porsche-designed WWI artillery tractors. Porsche's children Louise and Ferry stand atop the fenders at right.

An early airplane engine undergoes testing as Ferdinand Porsche (dark suit and binoculars) poses with his compatriots.

Count Alexander "Sascha" Kolowrat-Krakowsky, left, poses with one of the "Sascha" racers he entered in the 1922 Targa Florio. Designer Ferdinand Porsche and son Ferry are on the right.

by Ferdinand himself with Aloisia as a passenger. Accolades came from all quarters, providing excellent publicity for Austro-Daimler.

Located close to military installations, Austro-Daimler was well situated to benefit from army contracts. While automobile design continued, Porsche also turned his attention to the new flying machines. From 1908 his engines were fitted to airframes and tested extensively, with good results. In 1911 a six-cylinder of 13.9 liters began a series of engines that were powerful enough to set altitude records by 1913. Some of the craft these engines powered were made by Lohner, who had shifted from autos to aeros. By the time the First World War was well underway, Austro-Daimler's six was something of the gold standard of inline airplane engines. Reliable and sturdy, it was used in observation, bombing, and fighter planes; one of the most famous was the German Albatros D.III flown by Manfred von Richthofen, the Red Baron. For a period, Porsche's airplane engines helped the

Central Powers dominate the skies. Also in use or testing were a 30-liter V-12 for flying boats, a W-9, and even a Mixte-drive airplane engine, all rendered moot by the war's conclusion.

In 1908 the Austro-Hungarian Empire's army had defined its needs to move heavy arms, and Austro-Daimler responded with four-wheel-drive artillery "tugs" to pull large weapons over rough terrain. In 1913 the first "Land Train" went into service. A generator vehicle produced electric current, delivered by cable to motors on alternate trailer cars, powering the main engine's wheels along with trailer unit wheels. Highly maneuverable and powerful, the B Zug, or B Train, was superseded by the C Zug in the last years of the war. Scores of these trains survived the war and were later used by the Wehrmacht through 1945.

In the years after World War I ended, few new ideas were brought to fruition as inflation and political strife collapsed the Austrian economy. Although Porsche had been awarded an honorary doctorate (*Doktor Ingenieur* honoris causa, or Dr. Ing. h.c.) by Vienna's Royal Technical Institute in 1917, just two years later he was struggling to keep his workers busy. A rare highlight of these years was when a wealthy film producer and auto enthusiast, Count Alexander "Sascha" Kolowrat-Krakowsky, commissioned a light, small-displacement racer for the Targa Florio race in Sicily. Of the four cars that ran, two topped the 1,100cc class, one driven by Alfred Neubauer. However, this triumph was soon overshadowed when banker Camillo Castiglioni, who now controlled Austro-Daimler, moved to oust Porsche from the company in early 1923. A young engineer (and Porsche protégé) named Karl Rabe took over.

Out of work for just a matter of weeks, Ferdinand Porsche was hired by Daimler-Motoren Gesellschaft in Stuttgart. The move from his native Austria to Germany was not difficult for the senior Porsche, but in his autobiography, Ferry recalled not only a cultural shift but the runaway inflation that affected everyday life. "When I went daily to my private school, I normally took along several million marks with me so that I could buy my ticket for the streetcar ride. After a short time, though, I was compelled to walk home because the cost of a streetcar ticket had risen by so many million marks that I could no longer carry enough money." The family was comfortable, however, with a new villa on Feuerbacher Weg overlooking Stuttgart. Ferdinand would bring home a variety of Daimler cars, which his son—who would not be of legal age to hold a license until 1927—often drove surreptitiously. "At one time or another I had driven just about every car my father had brought home to our garage," Ferry later wrote. His sister, Louise, was likewise an avid driver and took part in rallies and competitions—she was old enough.

At DMG, Ferdinand Porsche designed 2.0-liter entries for the Targa Florio and Coppa Florio in Sicily in 1924, winning

Porsche's Daimler-Benz SS models were supercharged for both street and racing.

both races and much acclaim in the racing world. In 1926 a merger with Benz and Cie. began, giving added responsibility to Porsche as the technical director of the new firm Daimler-Benz AG. Supercharging was applied to high-end production cars and sporting versions alike. The models K (Kurz, "short wheelbase"), S (Super), and SS (Super Sport) were purchased by wealthy men, some of whom used them in competition. While Daimler had had a racing program before his arrival, Porsche stepped up the pace. His SSK model of 1927 (Super Sport Kurz) won major races from Argentina to Italy and England. One of its successful drivers was a young German named Adolf Rosenberger.

Following a well-established pattern, at Daimler-Benz Porsche applied his seemingly boundless curiosity, energy, and talent to a wide range of projects for airplanes, boats, and tanks for the military. The creations he brought to life at the company would carry on for years, but, alas, the designer himself would not. In 1928 a long-simmering disagreement with Hans Nibel, who had been chief designer at Benz, deteriorated into a shouting match and led to Porsche's departure.

For the 1924 Targa Florio, Porsche (center with light coat) designed small 2.0-liter racers, shown here before transit to Sicily, where they dominated. A normal-size street car is at left.

Porsche initiated a legal claim against Daimler-Benz, handled by a lawyer named Anton Piëch of Vienna, who was newly married to Louise. He had time to weigh the options for his next employment and accepted an attractive offer from Steyr-Werke in Steyr, Austria, in January 1929. Hired to polish the maker's image and expand its offerings, Porsche created both a luxury prototype, the eight-cylinder Austria, and a middle-market (but advanced) six-cylinder auto, called the Typ 30. After the global economic crash of 1929, however, Steyr's output dropped from almost five thousand units in that year to twelve in 1930. Its main shareholder bank collapsed and ended up under the control of Camillo Castiglioni, the same financier who had given Porsche a pink slip at Austro-Daimler seven years before. Porsche opted out of his three-year contract in April 1930 and began to reflect on what his next move would be.

Ferry had followed his Stuttgart schooling with an apprenticeship at Bosch, and when his father moved to Steyr, he had stayed with his sister in Vienna and received a diploma from the Vienna Technische Hochschule. He was well positioned to enter the world he loved—the world of cars.

Having worked for other companies for three decades, the fifty-six-year-old Ferdinand looked back on all of his designs that had enriched and brought prestige to those firms and provided them with ongoing income through patents and licenses. He had been handsomely compensated and had developed nurturing relationships with his peers in the industry. He knew everyone. And everyone knew him, or at least knew of him. With this high profile it was time, he felt, to start his own company—to continue as a designer but no longer be beholden to corporate boards or accountants.

THE PORSCHE COMPANY

In December 1930 a new organization opened an office in Stuttgart, where many of the subcontractors and suppliers to the automotive industry were located. The following spring the firm was incorporated as Dr. Ing. h.c. F. Porsche GmbH. Partners with Porsche were son-in-law Anton Piëch and racer Adolf Rosenberger, who was also a wealthy steel vendor and brought needed financial backing to the firm. On the team they assembled were talented men Porsche had known well and worked with: Karl Rabe, designer Erwin Komenda, and Ferry Porsche, just twenty-one but already well versed in the automobile industry.

On paper, the new company promised to do well. The economy, however, was at a low ebb, and commissions came from only some of the lesser German firms, themselves struggling to survive. A numbering system was instituted for projects, and the first one—for the Wanderer company—was designated 7, apparently to make it seem like the company was busier than it actually was. Prototypes were built by Reutter Karosserie, also in Stuttgart. Project (*Typ*) number 9 (1932) was a beautifully streamlined sedan for Wanderer, badged as a Horch; only a prototype was built, but it served as a company car for Ferdinand Porsche for years afterward. A project for motorcycle maker Zündapp was designated Typ 12, a rear engined "everyman's car." It was canceled when cycle sales took off in 1933. A similar project for the NSU motorcycle company produced the Typ 32, a precursor to the Volkswagen. Other commissions followed—mostly for component design—but the American Depression had also affected Europe. Times were tough.

The Porsche villa on Feuerbacherweg above Stuttgart was not only home but a maintenance and staging area for prototypes. From left: The Fiat 500 Topolino was probably being assessed. The Typ 9 Wanderer was a streamlined sedan used by Porsche as a personal car for several years. Compare its lines to the more conventional sedan at right. The Typ 32 was designed for motorcycle maker NSU with an air-cooled rear engine and torsion bar suspension. This steel-bodied version of Komenda's design was built by Reutter, a forerunner to the VW design.

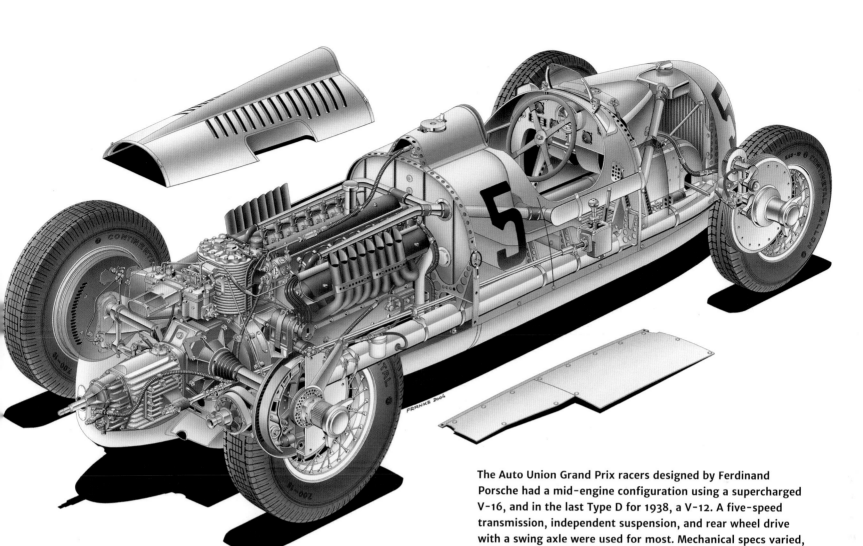

The Auto Union Grand Prix racers designed by Ferdinand Porsche had a mid-engine configuration using a supercharged V-16, and in the last Type D for 1938, a V-12. A five-speed transmission, independent suspension, and rear wheel drive with a swing axle were used for most. Mechanical specs varied, as did body shape. Aerodynamic and streamline versions were used to set land speed records. It was in one of these that German hero Bernd Rosemeyer lost his life while attempting to set a record on a German autobahn in 1938. Below he is seen taking to the track before a Grand Prix event.

Early VW prototypes are seen in the courtyard of the Porsche villa in Stuttgart.

In Germany, political change was in the air. Adolf Hitler became chancellor in January 1933, and only twelve days later he opened the Berlin Auto Show in a plain dark suit with a momentous speech. Stating his intention to deregulate Germany's automotive industry and build a nationwide highway system, he added a plan to dominate international motorsport. Executives of Daimler-Benz hung on his every word, as they were well positioned to build the race cars he envisioned. It looked like a lock for that company, at least until a meeting on March 10. A new firm, Auto Union, had been formed from distressed carmakers Audi, Horch, DKW, and Wanderer. An executive there arranged a meeting with Hitler, hoping for a race car—building program that would support the company's thousands of workers. Ferdinand Porsche was there, as was famous driver Hans Stuck. It was a lengthy presentation by Porsche that resulted in the decision to divide the effort (and money) between Daimler-Benz and Auto Union. Porsche the salesman had scored a huge win, mostly because Hitler the auto enthusiast had admired him for years.

The Auto Union racers, Typ 22, were designed in Stuttgart by a Porsche "division" called High-Performance Vehicle Construction Ltd. (HFB) and built at the Horch plant in Zwickau in eastern Germany. Chassis and suspension were by Karl Rabe and the V-16 engine by Josef Kales. Construction and testing took place in the winter of 1933–1934, and beginning that summer the midengined P-Wagen (P for Porsche) racked up wins as Typ A, B, C, and later, a V-12 Typ D. Top drivers such as Stuck, Tazio Nuvolari, and Bernd Rosemeyer used them to win hillclimbs, land speed records, and Grand Prix circuit races. Through 1939 these Auto Union "Silver Arrows," along with their counterparts from Mercedes-Benz, fulfilled Hitler's dream of dominating the highest echelons of motorsports.

While the Auto Union contract brought gains for Dr. Ing. h.c. F. Porsche GmbH, the firm's commercial director and financial backer, Rosenberger, was a Jewish man and saw Hitler's rise for what it was. The government's "Aryanization" program forced him out of the Porsche firm in 1933, and two years later he was arrested and briefly detained. With little assistance from Porsche during a dangerous time, he moved to France in November 1935, and then England, for some time representing Porsche's patent interests in those countries. Porsche had reimbursed him only his initial investment, and they severed ties in 1938. In 1940 Rosenberger moved to America and became Alan Robert, and brought a case against

A new headquarters for the Porsche group was built in Zuffenhausen, with offices and a lower-level workshop.

Porsche for compensation in 1950, receiving a modest amount and a new Volkswagen. He died in Los Angeles in 1967. Upon his departure from the company in 1933, his investments and position were replaced by Baron Hans von Veyder-Malberg, a seasoned veteran of auto racing, design, and manufacturing and a longtime acquaintance of Ferdinand Porsche.

Another of Hitler's ideas came to Porsche via Jakob Werlin, the chancellor's automotive consultant. At a meeting in fall 1933, Hitler explained to Porsche his concept of an auto for the common man of Germany: large enough for a family, economical, and, most important, priced under 1,000 marks (at the time, around $400; today, just over $9,000). He had specific ideas about its design, envisioning a rear-wheel-drive diesel, but Porsche was charged with providing a white paper on the idea. In March 1934 at the Berlin Auto Show, one year after his speech about autobahns and race cars, Hitler was in full military dress, and the huge hall was awash in swastika banners. His opening speech announced the development of a small affordable automobile, a "*Volksauto*" for the masses. It was to be produced as a collective product by German car manufacturers. Ostensibly, German firms would compete for the production work, but the design contract went to Porsche (with an inside track) in June,

and work began in earnest immediately. The project was given the Porsche design project number 60.

Recent Typ numbers in the design office had been a mix of interesting but single-purpose creations: motorcycle engine (55), airplane engine (57), truck suspension (59). Typ 60, however, had the scale and potential to encompass ongoing variations and adaptations, although no one at the time could imagine how numerous and wide-ranging they would be. For Dr. Ing. h.c. F. Porsche GmbH, this government contract was the very essence of job security. Drawings were made at the Stuttgart offices at 24 Kronenstrasse, and the prototypes were assembled in the garage of the Porsche villa on Feuerbacher Weg.

The "people's car" did not spring fully formed from Ferdinand Porsche's imagination. Other designers in other countries had similar ideas, and it's certain there was some cross-pollination. But although it was not just a German concept, in that country it had the full backing of the government. Another idea was to mechanize German farmers. In 1937 plans were begun for another of Hitler's requests, a "people's tractor" that resulted in the Typ 111 through 113, precursors to a series that would be quite popular in the 1950s and 1960s.

The first Typ 60 prototypes were built in late 1935, the bodies made by hand at Daimler-Benz's Sindelfingen shops. Engineer Franz X. Reimspiess convinced Ferdinand Porsche to use his "E" engine. The car's components, along with drivetrain and suspension parts, were farmed out to area specialists. Heading up testing for the new car was Ferry Porsche, who was twenty-five years old when the project began. Changes and improvements (including some deletions) took place as these *Versuchwagen* (test cars) racked up the kilometers and new, improved prototypes were built. V1 was a wood and steel sedan, V2 a convertible, and in 1936 three suicide-door V3 test cars hit the road. By 1937 a final design for the all-steel body was reached, and Reutter in Stuttgart built three cars in this configuration. Thirty more Sindelfingen-built cars covered almost 3 million kilometers. Reutter built two more series of test cars in 1938 and 1939, and finally, small-scale production started in 1941 at the new plant in Fallersleben.

Reutter's shops on Augustenstrasse in Stuttgart were at capacity by 1937, so a new body factory was built in Zuffenhausen, a northwestern suburb of the city. The following year the Porsche firm moved to a new home across the street. The contracts to design the people's car brought prosperity to the company, and its new three-story headquarters featured much-needed management space, studio areas for designers, and lower-level shops for mechanical work to bring designs to life. Cooperation between Porsche and Reutter, now neighbors, increased with the proximity.

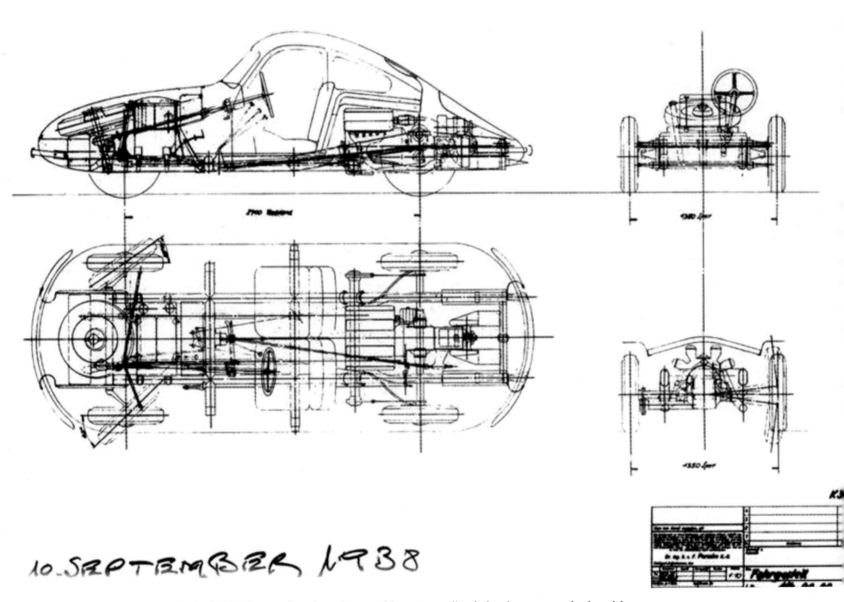

10. SEPTEMBER 1938

The Typ 114 concept had a ladder frame of oval steel covered by a streamlined aluminum coupe body, with seating for two. A five-speed transmission with limited slip at the rear drove the rear wheels through flexible shafts, mounted on swing axles, which pivoted from transverse torsion bars à la VW. A VW-like suspension was used as well in front. A V-10 engine, mounted just behind the seats, was 1.5-liter displacement with aluminum heads and block and six main bearings. Dual overhead cams were shaft and bevel gear driven, opening large valves to hemispherical chambers and domed pistons. These were fed by triple carbs on each bank. A front radiator was initially planned, but a final drawing showed a radiator just ahead of the engine.

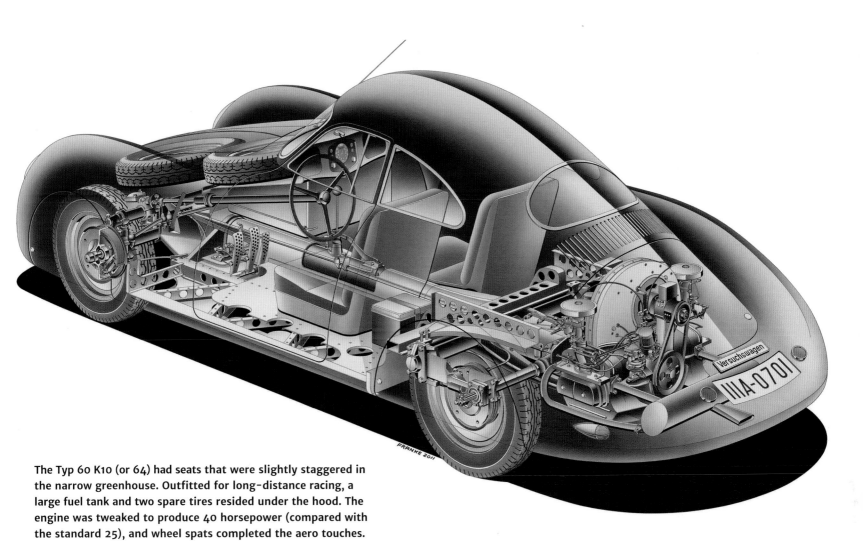

The Typ 60 K10 (or 64) had seats that were slightly staggered in the narrow greenhouse. Outfitted for long-distance racing, a large fuel tank and two spare tires resided under the hood. The engine was tweaked to produce 40 horsepower (compared with the standard 25), and wheel spats completed the aero touches.

A program was soon initiated whereby workers could save for a Volkswagen by buying coupons each week or month. When the coupon books were filled, a new car would be theirs. But although the plant was operational by 1940, no VWs would ever be delivered to German workers.

A PORSCHE VW SPORTWAGEN

Several variations on the Volkswagen theme were created. A right-hand-drive car (Typ 66), postal van (68), panel van (81), and others were approved by the government. A proposed aluminum-bodied, 1.5-liter "sport" version (Typ 64) was not, however, as the idea was found to be out of keeping with the practical nature of the automobile. A back-burner idea instead came to the fore: Ferdinand Porsche and his designers revisited a long-considered idea to produce a Porsche car, something designed and produced by their own company. The Volkswagen would provide a perfect basis, although a larger engine and an aerodynamic body would give it a sporting demeanor. The government turned down that idea as well owing to a prohibition about selling "state" parts to private firms. A Porsche car could not be based on VW components—at least not at this moment.

In 1938, however, the idea of a creating a Porsche was still on Ferdinand's mind. It evolved into a midengine, water-cooled sports coupe, given the number 114 and informally called the F-Wagen. Although the first Porsche Typ 114 never got beyond the paper stage, its shape would soon appear in another form, and its mechanical layout would be used years later.

Professor Porsche (center) inspects the not-yet-complete KdF plant in 1938. He was one of four principal general managers of Volkswagenwerk GmbH.

The idea of a "sporting VW" was not dead, either. Politics led to the creation of a very special Volkswagen meant to promote the brand and bolster the ties between Germany, Austria, and Italy. Also in 1938 the ONS (National Sporting Authority) sanctioned an 800-mile race between Berlin and Rome, partly on the new autobahn and partly on closed roads. The event was to be run by the NSKK (National Socialist Motor Corps) and its leader, Adolf Hühnlein. Propaganda was the name of the game, and the race, set for September 1939, would coincide with the production of the first VW. What better way to sell the coupon books that Germans would fill to buy a car?

Though the Typ 64 had been turned down as a Porsche, the company was now given the green light to create much the same kind of vehicle to participate in the race as a VW. It was called the Typ 60 K10 (tenth VW body style), and three cars were ordered.

In late 1938 work resumed on a basic VW chassis, lightened and reinforced. Erwin Komenda drew a slippery aluminum body that resembled a VW, taking many cues from the Typ 114. Unfortunately, the two cars completed never had their date with destiny in 1939, although one would survive to race many years later. In the meantime, a third was built and the car's ability to maintain 90 miles per hour made it useful later as wartime transportation for Ferdinand and his driver, Josef Goldinger.

THE PEOPLE'S CAR BECOMES A REALITY

As the KdF-Wagen design matured, a means of producing it was decided upon. Kraft durch Freude (Strength through Joy), the National Socialist organization designed to promote the

On May 26, 1938, the Führer laid the cornerstone for the KdF plant at Fallersleben. Ferdinand Porsche was a guest of honor, and Ferry Porsche drove Hitler to the train station in a VW cabriolet.

party to all Germans through sport and travel, added car sales in 1938. Its parent organization, the German Labor Front (DAF), collected German laborers' dues. Recognizing that the new car could not be produced for 1,000 reichsmarks or less at existing auto plants, the DAF took over the project and built a new dedicated Volkswagen factory at Fallersleben in north-central Germany at a huge cost—partly met using its member dues. Ferdinand Porsche was appointed codirector, with Bodo Lafferentz and Jakob Werlin, to run the plant.

Adolf Hitler was presented with the first official KdF-Wagen as the factory cornerstone was laid on May 26, 1938. A coupe, a convertible, and a canvas-top sunroof (the latter two hastily built by Reutter) were on display. Ferdinand Porsche was on hand, and Ferry Porsche drove Hitler to the train station afterward. The huge factory, patterned somewhat after Ford's

River Rouge plant in Detroit (which Ferdinand and Ferry had toured in 1937), had rail and canal access, with room for expansion along with a planned "worker's city" named KdF Stadt to house the thousands of employees—a self-contained industrial colossus.

But the first cars had no sooner started to roll off the line than production had to pivot to military efforts. War had come with Germany's invasion of Poland in September 1939.

THE VOLKSWAGEN AT WAR

As the blitzkrieg began, Ferdinand Porsche was turning sixty-four years old, with an incredible career already behind him. In addition to being in charge of designing, building, and running

A VW military staff car (foreground), Kubelwagen, and Schwimmwagen are shown in the rear courtyard of Porsche Werk I.

the new VW plant, he was also needed at the Stuttgart design offices, at meetings in Berlin, and all around Germany. He was a busy man.

Mobility for the military was a pressing need, so Porsche presented a prototype (Typ 62) of a VW-based open-sided four-seater, with rounded features similar to the original sedan. Although it performed well enough, it was deemed not "military looking." Porsche responded with a new boxlike body that had flat corrugated panels and removable side doors. Simple arched fenders were outboard of the body. More in line with the army's wishes, it was well received, but a glaring flaw was its ground clearance. A novel solution was a reduction gearbox at the rear wheels, which raised the axles from the wheel hubs and allowed the final gearing to be reduced, so that in gear near idle the vehicle could be paced by marching troops. A new Typ number, 82, was given, and the vehicle was accepted in late 1939.

Although the Kübelwagen (Bucket Car) was rear-wheel drive, it carried a limited-slip differential made by ZF. The Auto Union Grand Prix cars had used this "jelly bean" diff, and Porsche engineers would apply it to many more creations over the next few decades. Work was also done on a four-wheel-drive version (design study, Typ 86; prototype, Typ 87). By late 1940 the Kübelwagen had still not gained large-scale acceptance by the army brass, but after snowy winter campaigns in Russia and hot sandy action in North Africa, Wehrmacht soldiers became believers—as did their superiors soon afterward. One thousand were built by the end of 1940, and production would reach over fifty thousand by war's end.

Other variations on the Typ 82 theme included an amphibious light vehicle based on a modified Typ 87 whose doors and apertures were all sealed. Its poor balance and performance in water were not a surprise, but it gave the engineers a baseline for what would work. Karosserie Drauz helped design a body that could function well in water, although it was an ugly duckling in the dry. Testing of this Typ 128 went on through 1940, and with a shortened wheelbase, the vehicle's water entry and exit were improved. In autumn 1941 Ferry Porsche drove the new Typ 166 Schwimmwagen to Hitler's Wolf's Lair retreat in northern Poland for a viewing by military officials. With approval from the very top, over fourteen thousand would be produced.

The VW engine underwent much experimentation by the Porsche staff. An oil cooler inside the fan shroud was added. The Typ 115 in 1939 used supercharging and overhead camshafts. Changes to pistons, larger intake valves, multiple carburetors, hemispherical heads, and even sleeve valves were tried in order to find a balance between more power and reliability. There were five-speed gearboxes and diesel engines, and even projects involving wood, coal, or other fuel gas generation for the engines.

The VW engine designed by Reimspiess went through several stages of development for different purposes, but its basic configuration became the Porsche engine of the 1950s.

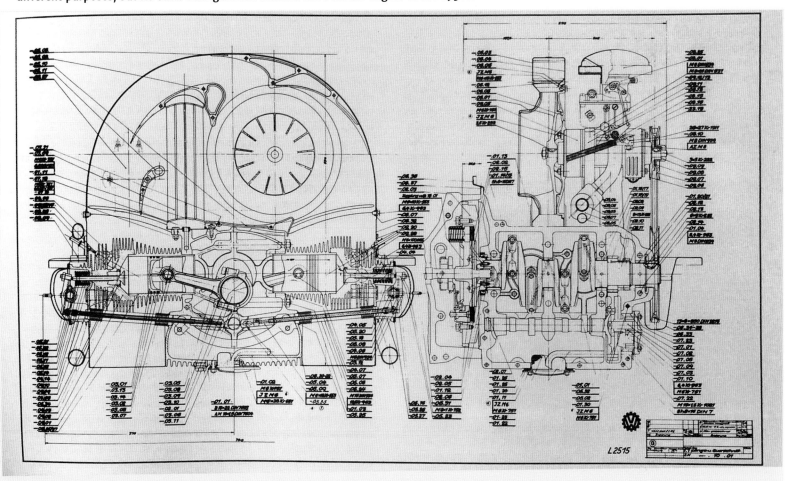

Schwimmwagens undergo development in the ground-level workshop of Werk I.

EXPERIMENTS IN ARMOR

During five years of war, Porsche's plate was full with military projects. Having years of experience with armor and heavy weaponry, Ferdinand Porsche was appointed head of the Reich's Armour Commission. An air-cooled V-10 prototype (Typ 100), essentially a scaled-up version of the Typ 114 sports-car engine, was developed for use in a new tank. Twin units would drive generators to power the 30-ton Typ 101 "Tiger." It was built in only limited numbers, as a competing design was chosen for production. A further adaptation of the design resulted in the Typ 130 tank destroyer of 1943, a rolling

artillery unit that became known as the Ferdinand. Other tank designs that came from the company's drawing boards included an exotic X-16 air-cooled diesel engine (Typ 212), which pioneered the use of turbocharging.

A fitting capstone to Porsche's career as a tank designer began in March 1942, but more than two years would pass before Hitler's idea of a "rolling pillbox" would come to fruition, and then only as a prototype. The Maus (Mouse), Typ 205, was a 188-ton behemoth carrying a 128mm canon, with armor up to 240mm thick. Power came from a Daimler-Benz 44.5-liter

TOP RIGHT: The rough buildings at Karnerau outside Gmünd, where most of the Porsche organization spent the last war year and five more in peacetime. **BELOW:** When Porsche's Tiger tank design was not put into production, some hundred existing built chassis were repurposed for a long-range tank destroyer named "Ferdinand." It carried an 88mm antitank gun. Later versions were renamed Elephant.

V-12 aircraft engine driving a generator and electric motors. Two prototypes were built, and in testing the giants proved to be extremely maneuverable. They were never used in combat and at war's end were captured by the Russians.

At the Fallersleben plant, the KdF-Wagen was conspicuous in its absence. The huge facility was put to use building war matériel such as the Kübelwagen, Junkers bomber parts, V-1 missile wings, and Teller antitank mines. By 1944 over half of the workers there were Soviet POWs, concentration-camp prisoners, or other forced laborers. The plant had been administered until 1943 by Anton Piëch, who consulted regularly with his father-in-law. To his credit, Ferdinand Porsche made requests to top military officials for better treatment, especially nutrition, for workers. By early 1945 production had slowed to a crawl as bombing raids destroyed significant portions of the plant. In Stuttgart, the Porsche firm had also moved out of the path of the bombers, and in late 1944 most were ensconced outside Gmünd. Work continued there, but by the spring of 1945 it was mostly waiting for the war to end, and no one was sure what would happen then.

AN AUSTRIAN INTERLUDE

In Zuffenhausen, Germany, in mid-1944 the movement of Porsche men and machines to safe havens in Austria was well underway. The danger from bombers was all too real; the Reutter Karosserie Werk II complex across the street from Porsche had been heavily damaged, and its main factory in Stuttgart also suffered bombing in December. While inspecting that wreckage, company head Albert Reutter and his chief executive were killed by falling debris. The Porsche Werk headquarters in Zuffenhausen remained intact but emptied as managers, engineers, and craftsmen took their drawing boards and machinery to Gmünd. Other items went to Zell am See for storage near the Porsche villa and farm there.

At the 2018 356 International Meeting in England, three Gmünd coupes were on display, each meticulously restored, befitting their place in history as the original vision of Ferry Porsche and Erwin Komenda.

The Porsche staff moved from their Zuffenhausen headquarters, which was covered in camouflage netting and roof paint, to the bucolic valley of Gmünd, Austria. This vehicle is a Typ 175 Radschlepper Ost four-wheel-drive military tractor for the Eastern Front.

Ferry Porsche had been able to avoid what surely would have been the demise of the company—a move to the east instead of south to Gmünd. He later wrote:

> In the early part of 1943, because the heavy bombing of Stuttgart was increasing in intensity, the military control people ordered us to move to Czechoslovakia. We were to take all our machines and engineers to this new location. . . . [W]e did not by then need a crystal ball to figure out how the war was going to end, and in Czechoslovakia, when the time came, we would be surrounded by enemies, presumably bitter and implacable.

> I therefore applied to the high command in Salzburg and asked them if they might have some other place for us . . . The answer was favorable; there were two possible places left open to us. One was the glider school at Zell am See, near my farm, and the other a sawmill in Gmünd, Carinthia.

Ferry's prescience and his further efforts to secure the Austrian sites with local leaders allowed the company to divide its physical assets between Zuffenhausen, Zell am See, and Gmünd, the last of which had no rail line nearby.

While some employees stayed in Zuffenhausen, many others worked at outlying sites, and as the war came to a close in April and May of 1945, there was a migration of workers in the general direction of their homes in Germany and Austria. When the Allies took control, they divided Germany into zones controlled by France, England, the United States, and Russia. Similarly, in Austria four zones were established, with Gmünd in the British zone and Zell am See in the American. Adding to the complication, Vienna was divided into another four zones,

The entrance at Gmünd retained the name of the lumberyard so as not to draw attention to the engineering work going on inside. It was changed to Porsche Konstructionen after the war ended.

within the Russian sector of Austria. As the entire Porsche family gathered at the sixteen-bedroom Zell am See estate that spring, they were reasonably comfortable, although crowded. "Our problem during that waiting period was not of physical hardship," Ferry wrote, "but of psychological suspense, not knowing what was going to happen next."

What happened next was a visit by Major Franzen, an American, and Lieutenant Colonel Reeves, a Brit. Both were knowledgeable automobile men who knew and respected Ferdinand Porsche's work. Having arrived in Zuffenhausen to question the Porsches, they were directed to Zell am See. Their job was to inspect and analyze the firm's archived work—and prevent it from falling into Russian hands. Toward that end a guard detail of American soldiers was set up. The officer in charge soon confiscated the contents of the wine cellar, and his troops entertained themselves by driving vehicles stored at the nearby glider school. One of these was a Typ 64 (one other Typ 64 was at Gmünd), which they converted to an open car for joyriding and eventually ruined the engine. This abuse could be tolerated, and the interrogation was not unpleasant, but things got worse soon enough.

INTERROGATION AND JAIL

In early summer Ferdinand Porsche was ordered to appear for questioning at Schloss Kransberg near Frankfurt, driven there by his longtime chauffeur, Josef Goldinger. Others at the facility, code-named "Dustbin," included Wernher von Braun and Albert Speer, the latter of whom testified that Ferdinand "never wore a uniform and never made any effort to join a party," according to Ferry's recollections. Ferdinand Porsche was cooperative, and the Allies created an exhaustive intelligence report covering most design and development projects during the war. On September 11, 1945, he returned to Austria with travel restrictions. That same day the British allowed Porsche KG to proceed on tractor designs with gas and diesel engines, Typ 312 and Typ 313. It was a significant recognition, which the Americans shared, that peaceful industrial pursuits would benefit Germany (and Austria).

At the end of July 1945 Ferry Porsche and several of his engineers had also been arrested. The men were shifted from one overcrowded makeshift lockup to another, caught up in a tide of detainees that included Nazi officials, suspected war criminals, and common miscreants. Only a few days after they were finally released in early November and returned to Zell am See, a French contingent arrived there to discuss the idea of Ferdinand Porsche working in France to develop a new people's car for that country.

Marcel Paul, a French communist who had been imprisoned by the Nazis, was now French minister of industrial production and had a vision of claiming the entire Fallersleben VW plant (now called Wolfsburg) for France as war reparations. His emissary Lieutenant LeComte brought father and son to the German town of Baden-Baden near the French border to discuss the idea of Ferdinand Porsche doing for France what he had done for Germany's KdF ten years earlier. The idea presented a challenge and was not unappealing to the elder Porsche, ever the engineer. The French produced a contract, and the Porsches returned to Zell am See to consider it. In December Ferdinand, Ferry, Anton Piëch, and Ferdinand's nephew Herbert Kaes returned to Baden-Baden, hosted by the French at a hotel. With a change of players on the French side, however, negotiations stalled and the Porsche contingent decided to leave. Marcel Paul feted them at a farewell dinner on December 15, and shortly afterward, in a surprise move, they were arrested. The charges were many, revolving around mistreatment of French workers, expropriation of equipment to Germany from French auto plants, and forced labor in France and Germany. Many abuses had indeed taken place, but Ferdinand Porsche, the pragmatist, had been on the side of keeping French managers and workers out of Gestapo jails and at work in the plants. Jean-Pierre Peugeot led the accusers, demanding his pound of flesh in the form of German manufacturing equipment and punishment for the men he deemed war criminals.

The people's-car idea, based on the VW (modified to make it look "French"), had reached French industry leaders, who saw such a plan as a direct threat to their postwar prosperity. They had moved to neutralize the threat—namely, Ferdinand Porsche. "Plainly," Ferry Porsche wrote, "the French auto industry was trying to make out that my father was to blame for everything. In fact they were looking for any excuse at all to prevent the VW project from coming to France."

Yes, it's a Porsche. The company's main business in Gmünd was designing and manufacturing water turbines, winches, and other farm equipment, plus repairing VWs.

There was little to be done for the men, who were held in an ex-Gestapo prison. After a month Ghislaine Kaes was able to bring baskets of food to his uncle by bribing the guards. The seventy-one-year-old Ferdinand was hospitalized briefly with gallbladder problems, adding to the family's concern.

In March 1946 Ferry was released but immediately held 30 kilometers south at a hotel in Bad Rippoldsau. Some factions in the French government were still pursuing the idea of a Gallic people's car, and he was charged with moving the plans along. The internment was not difficult, but he refused to do any work for Marcel Paul's scheme while his father was still imprisoned. Finally, in July 1946 Ferry was released to return to Austria.

Ferdinand and Anton Piëch were moved to Paris in early May, ostensibly to work with Renault on the people's car, and were caught up in an internecine crossfire between French factions. "While this was going on," Ferry wrote, "my father kept asking for a fair trial and for his freedom. He tried to explain to his captors that if they really wanted him to design a new car and plan a new factory and after that proceed to the manufacturing stage, it would be absolutely essential for him to regain his freedom. The request fell on deaf ears." In mid-February 1947 Porsche and Piëch were moved to a freezing prison in Dijon. They waited for months in separate unheated cells while the magistrate received testimonies, which all showed that the men should no longer be held.

Meanwhile, in summer 1946 after a reunion with his family in Zell am See, Ferry Porsche had returned to the works in Karnerau, outside of Gmünd, where he discovered a problem. "During my absence and imprisonment," he wrote, "much of the equipment we had brought to Gmünd from Stuttgart had disappeared, either by appropriation or theft." Chief engineer Karl Rabe was in charge of the operation, and much of the work for the almost two hundred employees involved repair of Kübelwagen cars and other mechanical pursuits. In the "production hall," handcarts, winches, water turbines, and other agricultural implements were made, catering to locals whose farms were on steep slopes, far from electricity. On the drawing boards in the design building were plans for wood, charcoal, coal, and "indigenous fuel" generators to power internal combustion engines in place of gasoline. It was a far cry from the heyday of Auto Union Grand Prix cars, but an old connection would open a path leading back to racing—through Italy.

THE ITALIAN JOB

Karl Abarth was born in Vienna a year before Ferry Porsche. An engineer and avid motorcycle racer, he had married Anton Piëch's secretary, fled to Slovenia during the war, and later moved to Merano, Italy. There he made contact with a former Porsche employee from Vienna, Rudolf Hruska, who had worked in the VW program and on armored projects. In correspondence with Louise Piëch, Ferry Porsche, and later Karl Rabe, it was agreed by

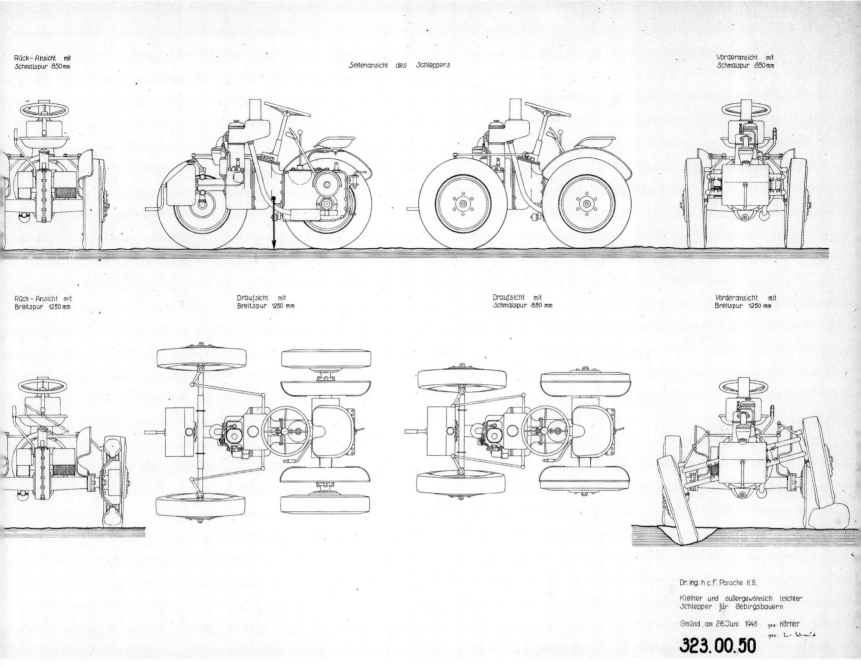

Rück-Ansicht mit
Schmalspur 850 mm

Seitenansicht des Schleppers

Vorderansicht mit
Schmalspur 850 mm

Rück-Ansicht mit
Breitspur 1250 mm

Draufsicht mit
Breitspur 1250 mm

Draufsicht mit
Schmalspur 850 mm

Vorderansicht mit
Breitspur 1250 mm

Dr. ing. h.c.F. Porsche K.G.

Kleiner und außergewöhnlich leichter
Schlepper für Gebirgsbauern

Gmünd, am 28.Juni 1946 gez: Körner
                        ges: L. Schmid

323.00.50

Part of the Cisitalia agreement was for Porsche to design a unique small tractor, something that was already on the books, with an adjustable track and articulated front axle.

all parties that Abarth (who changed his first name to Carlo to fit his new home country) and Hruska become representatives in Italy for the Porsche design firm, now called Porsche Konstruktionen GmbH. Another familiar figure then stepped into this scenario: former Auto Union driver Tazio Nuvolari. Having become acquainted with Abarth, Nuvolari was eager to see a rebirth of Formula 1 racing and enthusiastic about the idea of the Porsche firm designing a car for that class. In September 1946 an agreement was reached in which Porsche would undertake the design; a timeline was set, and it was understood the car would be built in Italy. All that remained was to fund the project.

The next link in the chain was Count Giovanni Lurani, a racer, engineer, politician, and well-connected racing administrator. On behalf of Abarth and Hruska he contacted Piero Dusio, a dynamic industrialist and former soccer player and racer who in 1944 had formed a racing team as part of his Consorzio Industriale Sportiva Italia, or Cisitalia. Dusio's textile company had made a wartime fortune supplying uniforms to the Italian army, and he now had dreams of being an automobile manufacturer and entering the top echelon of racing. Presented with the idea of the prestigious Porsche firm creating such a car, he was intrigued. Along with Abarth and Hruska, a draft contract was created in December 1946 for the design of a Grand Prix racer (Typ 360) and a sports

Ferdinand Porsche visits with a local hunter at Zell am See. Cars of any kind were in short supply in Austria, and war-surplus Kubelwagen and even Schwimmwagen were put to use. Maintaining them brought extra income to the Gmünd and Zell am See workers.

Supercharging and available 4-wheel drive would have made the Typ 360 a formidable threat in Formula 1 racing, but without money for development, it had little chance. Two copies of the grand prix car were built. The second was never completed, but later mostly assembled from parts for the Donington Museum in England.

car (Typ 370). On a more practical level, a small tractor and a water turbine (Typ 323 and Typ 285) were also included in the deal; both designs were already underway. On February 3, 1947, a final contract was signed. Part of the agreement was that Abarth would become the Cisitalia racing director, an income and position that would pave the way for his future automotive career. (One milestone in that career would come a decade later with production of another Italian-styled Porsche, the Carrera GTL.)

RAISING BAIL FOR A RETURN

The 1947 contract was a happy event for the Porsche family, but their patriarch was still imprisoned. Dusio and his now partners Abarth and Hruska had many connections in the racing world, including in Italy and France. Both travel and movement of funds were easier for the Italians, and through their connections an arrangement was made to transfer 1 million French francs—part of the design contract fee—to the

French authorities as "bail." The long and torturous effort to free Ferdinand Porsche and Anton Piëch finally bore fruit with their release on August 1, 1947.

A lot had happened while the old professor was away. At Gmünd, work on the Cisitalia Typ 360 Formula 1 racer design was well underway when he visited. Ferry recalled his father looking at the plans and telling him, "Had I received this order, I would have gone about it in the same way as you have done." That comment is not surprising, since there were clear echoes of the Typ 114 Porsche sports car, which was never built, as well as the Auto Union P-Wagen, which was built and had a triumphant career in Grand Prix racing. Dusio hoped the same for his Cisitalia, but the design and development period stretched on, as did the costs.

There were snags at every turn, beginning with the fact that the occupying forces considered the Porsche firm to be a German company, which not only made travel difficult and finance complicated but required that any new projects be vetted by the British to ensure there were no military applications.

Ferry Porsche explained to the Allied authorities in Klagenfurt, Austria, that the company principals—he and sister Louise—were both Austrian, and the same freedoms given to Austrian firms should apply to Porsche Konstruktionen GmbH, which the pair had established on April 1, 1947. "If we cannot obtain this, then we will have to transfer our activities to Italy," he told them. The authorities acquiesced.

RACING INNOVATION, SPORTS-CAR INSPIRATION

Having been granted sixteen months to produce a car, Porsche sent detailed drawings from Gmünd to Turin, where Cisitalia mechanics made components and assembled the car under the supervision of consultant Robert Eberan von Eberhorst, who had worked on the Auto Union cars. The entire package had a low

Rudge-Whitworth 17-inch central locking wire wheels were mounted. Fuel saddle tanks held 100 liters, and the weight distribution shifted only 2 percent as they emptied. An oil tank and cooler were in the nose.

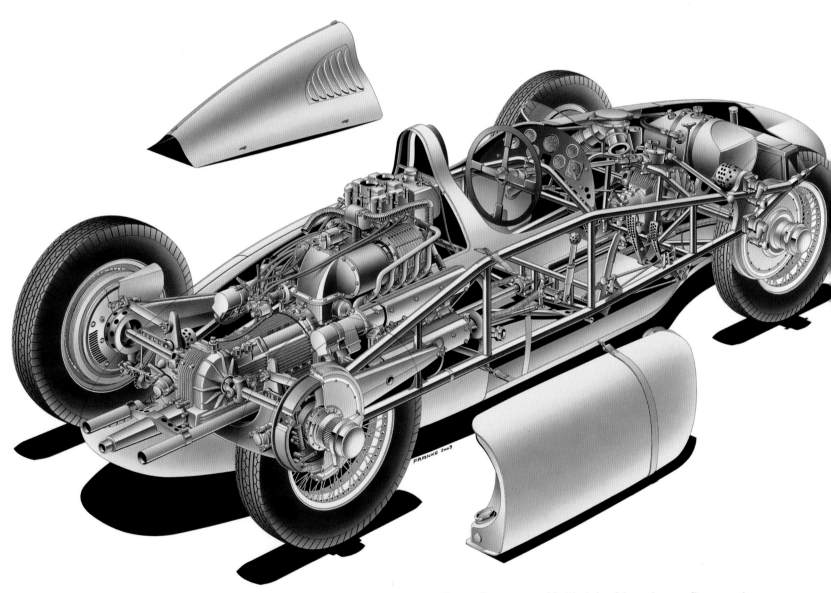

The engine, mounted behind the driver, drove a five-speed synchronized sequential gearbox at the rear. A separate driveshaft running forward powered the front wheels when engaged by the driver through a cockpit lever. A stiff space frame of chrome moly steel tubes carried the mechanicals within two longitudinal rails, and mounted outboard, amidships, were the fuel tanks.

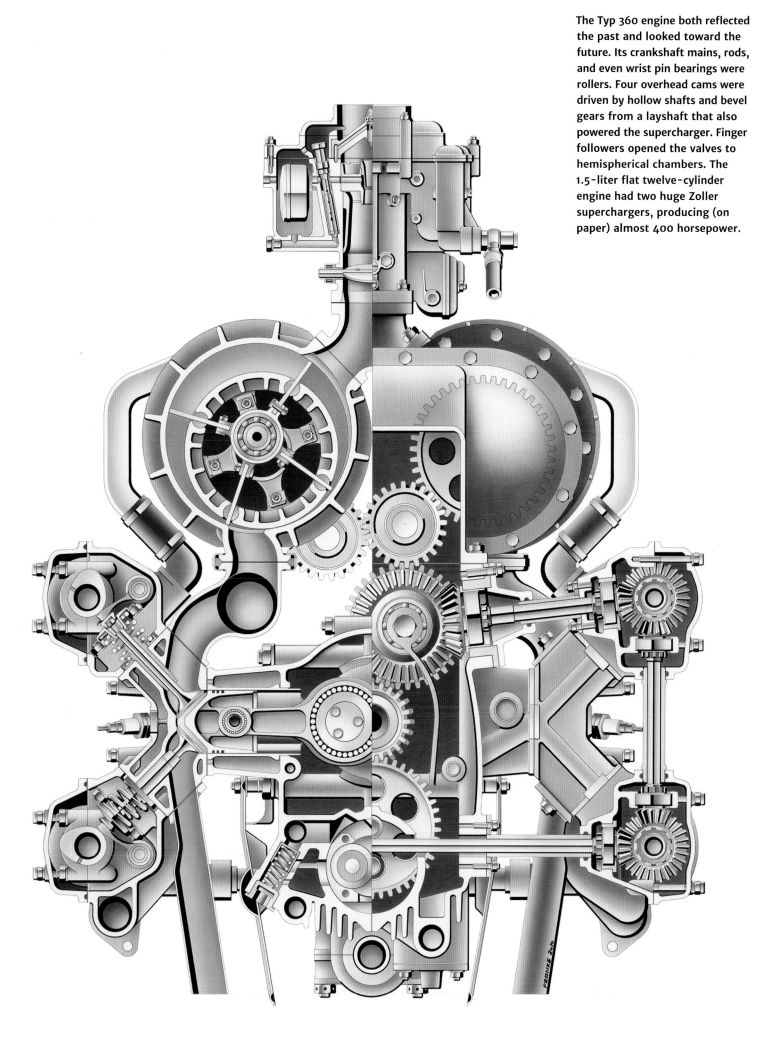

The Typ 360 engine both reflected the past and looked toward the future. Its crankshaft mains, rods, and even wrist pin bearings were rollers. Four overhead cams were driven by hollow shafts and bevel gears from a layshaft that also powered the supercharger. Finger followers opened the valves to hemispherical chambers. The 1.5-liter flat twelve-cylinder engine had two huge Zoller superchargers, producing (on paper) almost 400 horsepower.

drag coefficient and was quite attractive—every bit the state-of-the-art machine that Dusio expected from the Porsche firm.

What he didn't expect was the difficulty, time, and money required to make the racer a reality. Dusio's successful 1946 D46 open-wheeled racer was based on Fiat components, which were fairly simple and plentiful, and the Porsche Typ 360 was magnitudes more complex. Its cost bore heavily on Cisitalia's bottom line, at a time when Dusio was also developing his own sports car, the 202. That car, a beautiful modern coupe design in aluminum by Pinin Farina over a space frame, made waves both at auto shows and at the 1947 Mille Miglia, where Tazio Nuvolari drove a roadster version to a class win. Despite the victory, the burden of becoming a carmaker became too much, and by 1949 Cisitalia was in receivership and Dusio was in Argentina; there, he regrouped to join another company, Autoar, supported by Juan Perón. The single completed Typ 360 went there in 1950, and when Grand Prix rules changed in 1952, its fate was sealed. Ten years later, while in Argentina for the 1960 Grand Prix, Huschke von Hanstein saw the car for sale and bought it for Porsche. It was shipped to Germany in a container marked "Porsche" to simplify (not to say circumvent) customs requirements. For the first time it was in Germany, and it is now in the Porsche Museum, wearing the name Cisitalia on its nose.

Dusio's Cisitalia 202 was a sensation, although only 170 were ever made. It was significant in the Porsche saga, however: Ferry, Karl Rabe, and their engineers took note of the car's success not only for its modern design, with integrated fenders and sensuous

The Cisitalia 202 was built in coupe and cabriolet form, handmade for both road and race. The car has been recognized as a milestone design by Pinin Farina and was an inspiration for the 356.

lines, but for its use of modified Fiat mechanicals. The immediate result of this was to make the Typ 370 Cisitalia sports car a moot point. Ferry Porsche described that Cisitalia concept: "For this new model we planned a flat-six engine, rear mounted and featuring a torque convertor. The transmission would be located below the engine, allowing a more even weight distribution." In the end, however, it all came to nothing more than "a complex set of technical drawings."

ABOVE: The proposed Cisitalia Typ 370 only ever made it to the small model stage, but it showed promise as an aerodynamic body with distinct Komenda touches. Its engine was an air-cooled 2.0-liter eight.
RIGHT: The Typ 370's eight-cylinder engine showed sophisticated ideas, such as a gear-driven angled fan. It never got beyond initial drawings.

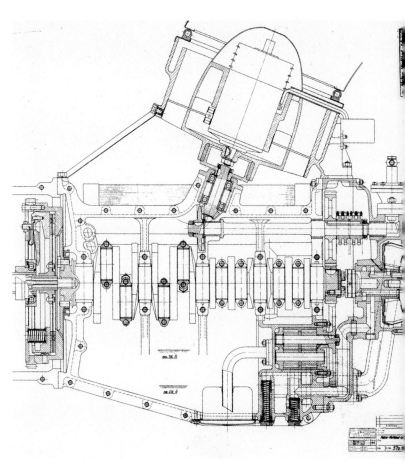

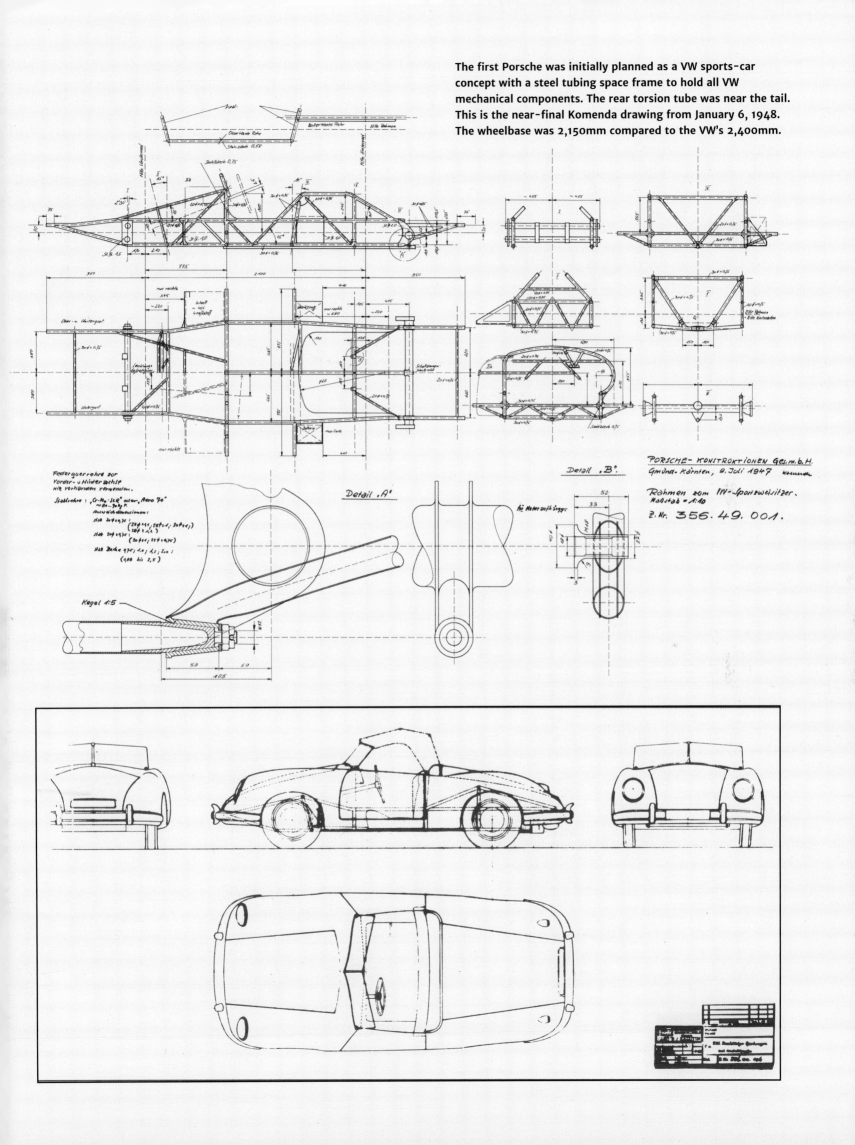

The first Porsche was initially planned as a VW sports-car concept with a steel tubing space frame to hold all VW mechanical components. The rear torsion tube was near the tail. This is the near-final Komenda drawing from January 6, 1948. The wheelbase was 2,150mm compared to the VW's 2,400mm.

BUILDING A VW-CONCEPT SPORTS CAR

The 202 showed the wisdom of building a modern and attractive sports car using familiar, available mechanical parts. For the Porsche group, such a project would mean parts from the Volkswagen. Although the idea of a Typ 114 reprise was appealing—a real Porsche sports car—building that 1938 design would take more resources than available. Instead, a simpler idea took life on the drawing boards in summer 1947. Erwin Komenda conceived a space frame, tailored to use VW suspension parts and accept a VW engine and transmission, albeit turned with the trans at the rear. The Porsche team reasoned that a VW sports car would positively influence the public's opinion of the spartan people's car. It was also seen as a way to open doors to closer relationships, and contracts, with Volkswagen. Careful to acknowledge the car's VW underpinnings, a midengine configuration would reflect one of Porsche's most triumphant designs: the Auto Union Grand Prix cars.

Body designs to clothe this frame began soon after. The earliest Komenda drawings in July 1947 showed front fenders that protruded while the rear fenders lacked definition. Further drawings from the same period are closer to the final car. The definitive shape was drawn in January 1948. The chassis was completed and testing began, sans body, in March.

In April a new hire joined the two body craftsmen already at Gmünd. Panel beater Friedrich Weber has gained legendary status in Porsche history as the expert metal shaper who would disappear periodically to refresh himself at a local beer hall. In spite of his erratic behavior, he was a master, and his work was key to the production of this first Typ 356 and later cars. At the end of his first month the car was built and ready for testing. Letters spelling out "Porsche" were added to its nose over the silver paint, and it took to the roads around Gmünd, including a drive with Ferry at the wheel and Ferdinand accompanying him. Test drives by others in the company garnered favorable reports and saw few breakdowns.

Porsche #356-001 was inspected and issued a road permit by the Kärnten provincial government on June 8, 1948, and a week later received license plate K-45-286. The first postwar race in Austria was on July 1: the "Race around the Hofgarten" in Innsbruck, where Ferry Porsche introduced his Porsche coupe—the remaining Typ 64, which had been updated by Pinin Farina in Italy, with a "Porsche" script added to the nose. Herbert Kaes drove #356-001 on a demonstration lap. Racing that day was an Austrian named Otto Mathé, an acquaintance of the Porsche family, who we can assume had a good look at both Porsches. The roadster was then driven to Bern, where the Swiss Grand Prix was being held at Circuit Bremgarten on July 4. Press coverage was intense that day. Although Italian makes dominated the racing, the new Austrian car garnered much attention. Engineer Max Troesch made a glowing report in the English magazine the *Motor*: "All enthusiasts both in Switzerland and elsewhere are bound to follow the fortunes of this new venture with great interest, and from my brief test run I feel sure that the car will live up to its famous name."

The smooth lines of 356-01, now in the Porsche Museum, have aged well over seventy-five years.

TOP: A plan view shows the aero shape and slightly forward placement of the cockpit, necessary to accommodate the engine and transmission unit. Slots along the rear deck are a stylistic (and only marginally effective) way of getting cooling air to the engine. The lid hinged from the rear, giving modest access to the engine and a spare tire.
BOTTOM: An obvious problem with a space frame is difficult access over the frame tubes, here covered in carpet.

THE LIFE OF P1: PORSCHE 356-001

The first Porsche roadster was a milestone, but to the Porsche men at Gmünd it was just a car to be sold, and they had a willing buyer in Rupprecht von Senger, for 7,000 Swiss francs—even before it was completed in 1948. Sold on to a Mr. Heinz later that year, it was quickly resold to Peter Kaiser at a modest profit. Kaiser raced the car but somehow felt it having the name Porsche on its nose was a liability, so he rearranged the letters (sort of) to spell "PESCO." No longer competitive by 1951, he sold the car to AMAG in Zurich, the official Swiss importer, for 5,000 Swiss francs. Some of the aluminum seams were opening, and it was generally showing its (three-year-old) age.

Rosemarie Muff was the next owner that same year, according to historian Phil Carney. Before 1951 was over, she had sold it to Hermann Schulthess of Zurich for 3,000 Swiss francs. Driving over the Saint Gotthard Pass, six nuns in a larger vehicle crashed into the roadster, pushed it into another car, and damaged both ends. Back at AMAG for repair, it was "modernized" front and rear to resemble the production Porsches of the time. (This may be when the front and rear bumpers were removed.) Schulthess took the car to Porsche in Zuffenhausen in 1952 to have new brakes and a 1,500cc engine installed and entered rallies in 1953.

A Zurich baker named Igoria became the next owner. He had spotted the car at AMAG's repair shop and took a fancy to the open two-seater. He talked Schulthess into a trade for his own 1300 coupe. The next day a disappointed Igoria wanted to cancel, but Schulthess would not renege; he was happy to get rid of #001. The car remained unused and deteriorating in Igoria's garage until Franz Blaser, a mechanic from Laachen, saw it there on his way to work. He bought the tired little roadster and tried to restore it completely.

In 1958 Richard von Frankenberg brought the archetype Porsche home to Stuttgart. He had approached Schulthess, intending to buy the first Porsche for the factory, was referred to Blaser, and got the roadster in exchange for a new 356 Speedster. In the small display area that then constituted Porsche's "museum," #356-001 wore an ivory paint scheme with curvy red accents front and rear, sharing space with some potted plants.

By 1975, in time for the hundredth anniversary of Ferdinand Porsche's birth, Porsche #001 was once again silver and more closely resembled its original appearance. In 1982 it was shipped

ABOVE: In the early 1950s the car was returned to the factory where it was updated with a new engine and brakes. The one-piece rear deck retained the rows cooling small slots and original taillights.
LEFT: 356-001 now has a place of honor at the new Porsche museum next to the Cisitalia Grand Prix car.

n the Porsche "museum" in the 1960s it was displayed in white with
ed stripes, the body much the same as it had been, sans bumpers.

In contrast to the royal treatment 001 receives these days, in 1982 it was casually trailered around California by club members.

to America for the Monterey Historic Races, where Porsche was to be the featured marque at the August event. Upon arriving at the Culver City, California, Porsche and Audi dealership, it was decided a visit to the June 20 Porsche Club of America (PCA) parade would also be good. With no plan to get the car there, some local PCA members stepped up. Ron Ramage and a friend put the car on an open trailer, wrapped some blankets around it, and headed for the Reno parade, with an overnight stay at a cheap motel. Ron returned to LA on Sunday after the parade to find the dealership closed. He stopped at some friends' home, where the car was uncovered and photographed (one photo made a *Porsche Panorama* cover in 1988). At the Monterey event, #001 was on display at the DoubleTree Inn as part of the 356 Registry West Coast Holiday, staged by local club members. Porsche officials took a leisurely approach to security, but at least they didn't leave the ignition key in it.

In 1998 it was on its way to Laguna Seca Raceway again for its fiftieth birthday bash. The car was damaged in transit and missed its own party but was sent home and repaired, once again, in Germany.

Porsche #356-001 has appeared around the world in the ensuing years and remains a centerpiece of the Porsche Museum when not traveling. It was restored again for Porsche's seventieth anniversary, proudly wearing an aluminum "A" on its tail for its birthplace, Austria.

In 1957 it appeared at the Merano, Italy, Porsche meeting. Additional rear lights were in place, and the rear deck was now two pieces with a grille, addressing the cooling deficiencies of the original design. Bumpers were long gone, but stripes were now in vogue. The following year it was purchased by Porsche.

ABOVE: The KdF plant, at the town now called Wolfsburg, survived the war, though with heavy damage. It nearly didn't survive some immediate postwar wrangling for control by its Allied captors.

RIGHT: Under stewardship of the British occupation forces, production resumed as quickly as possible, providing work for thousands and transportation for the British army. Major Ivan Hirst is at the wheel of this milestone VW in March 1946.

The **1000**th VOLKSWAGEN built during MARCH 1946 coming from Assembly Line

Heinz Nordhoff had been an engineer at Opel, learning American production methods. He was initially barred from postwar work in the American sector, but the British recruited him to take over at VW on January 1, 1948. In this 1954 photo he congratulates Ferry Porsche on the thousandth Porsche built, a milestone he helped achieve.

GOLIATH REAWAKENS

In the last months of the war, the Volkswagen plant at "KdF Stadt" had continued to produce war matériel, though heavy air-raid damage slowed work. Wooden airplane drop tanks, Junkers aircraft wings, Teller mines, and bazookas were made, among other things, mostly by forced laborers. The one thing that had never been built was the civilian KdF-Wagen, or people's car, for which the plant had been constructed. More than sixty-six thousand Typ 82 Kübelwagen and other variants were built during the war, with the last fifty rolling off the line on April 10, 1945. The next day American troops began a liberation of the plant and city. The Americans brought a semblance of order to the ensuing chaos and over the next month organized a workforce of some two hundred people who constructed 133 Kübelwagen for U.S. troops' use. The British took over occupation of the area on June 5, and in August they ordered twenty thousand sedans be built for use by the British military. Just after Christmas 1945 production of the Typ 1 "Beetle" began.

A twenty-nine-year-old British major, Ivan Hirst, was put in charge as senior resident officer of the British military government. By March 30, 1946, production reached one thousand vehicles a month. Over ten thousand were built by the end of 1946, and more than eight thousand employees worked at the plant, which turned a profit. The following winter, however, events exacerbated the already challenging conditions: severe weather and coal shortage and metal shortages caused the plant to close until March 1947.

A VW distributor network was put in place in 1947 with the Pon company in the Netherlands purchasing five cars as the first export customers. At the end of the year, British managers conducted a critical evaluation of the car and created an improved "export model." On January 1, 1948, former Opel manager Heinz Nordhoff became general director of Volkswagenwerk GmbH. By the end of that year nearly 20,000 Beetles had been built. In October 1949 British authorities turned over trusteeship to the German federal government, and the state of Lower Saxony took over its administration. That year, 46,154 cars were produced, and VW's future looked rosy.

In fall 1948 a significant positive development took place when discussions between Ferry Porsche and Heinz Nordhoff netted a contract between VW and Porsche, with Porsche to serve as ongoing consultant engineers and providing a sliding-scale royalty for each Volkswagen built, replacing the original payment of DM 1 per car. Porsche would now have direct access to VW parts and spares, and any planned Porsche sports car could be sold and serviced through VW dealers. In addition, an agreement was put in place the following spring that designated a new Porsche company, Porsche Salzburg, as official VW importer to Austria. It was to be headed by Louise and Anton Piëch along with cousin Herbert Kaes. One contract provision prevented Porsche from designing any kind of economy car between 1.0 and 1.6 liters for another company, but this restriction, it was felt, was well worth the trade-off. The agreements would bring much-needed stability to Porsche's operations.

FROM ROADSTER TO COUPE

While some Porsche engineers decamped to Wolfsburg to work on VW designs, production of a new Porsche sports car continued at Gmünd. While the 356 roadster was being introduced to the motoring world with much acclaim, a more practical design was already on paper, still using VW components but built in coupe form to allow year-round use. The handling drawbacks to the midengine roadster's leading-arm rear suspension were evident, and the new design reverted to VW's engine layout. Swapping the engine to the rear also allowed room for luggage behind the seats. A space frame would be impractical for serial production, and the VW body-on-platform design was not sufficiently stiff. Erwin Komenda convinced Ferry Porsche and Karl Rabe that even though Porsche lacked large presses, simple sheet-metal brake equipment in the Gmünd workshops could produce a welded origami structure of boxed section sheet steel, a self-supporting chassis for the body.

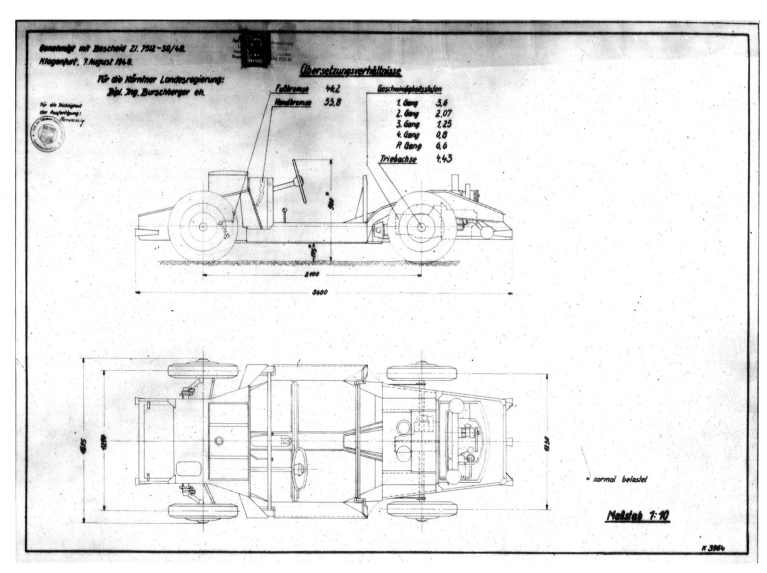

Komenda's chassis for the 356/2 used the standard VW engine layout on a 2,100mm wheelbase. Box-section longitudinal members provided enough strength for a coupe or cabriolet.

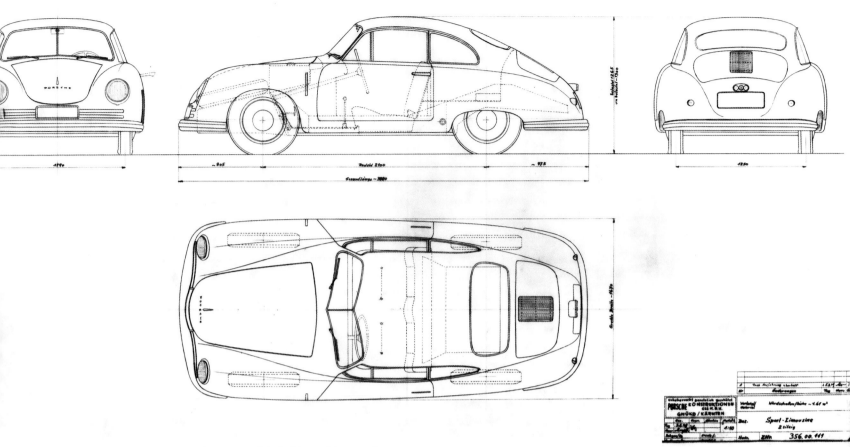

Komenda designed the body in relatively quick fashion. This was the
final iteration of several ideas.

The chassis could be driven without a body, as it
was for testing around Gmünd.

A chassis was built to Komenda's drawings, fitted with VW
suspension, engine, transmission, and controls, and tested on the
nearby roads. His designs for the coupe's body evolved through
a few drawings, guided by Ferry Porsche. Ferry wrote:

> The styling of the 356 was influenced by my own ideas. In
> fact, I was responsible for this model, and the whole concept
> was the product of my own technical "feeling." For example,
> I prefer an open-wheeled race car in which the driver can
> see exactly where he is putting his front wheels. Obviously,
> in production cars the open-wheel concept would not work .
> . . I compromised by designing the front fenders in such a
> manner that although the whole assembly was in one unit,
> the driver would still have a good idea of where his front
> wheels were . . . we gave the Porsche front fenders a shape
> of their own, making them quite distinctive from that of the
> hood.

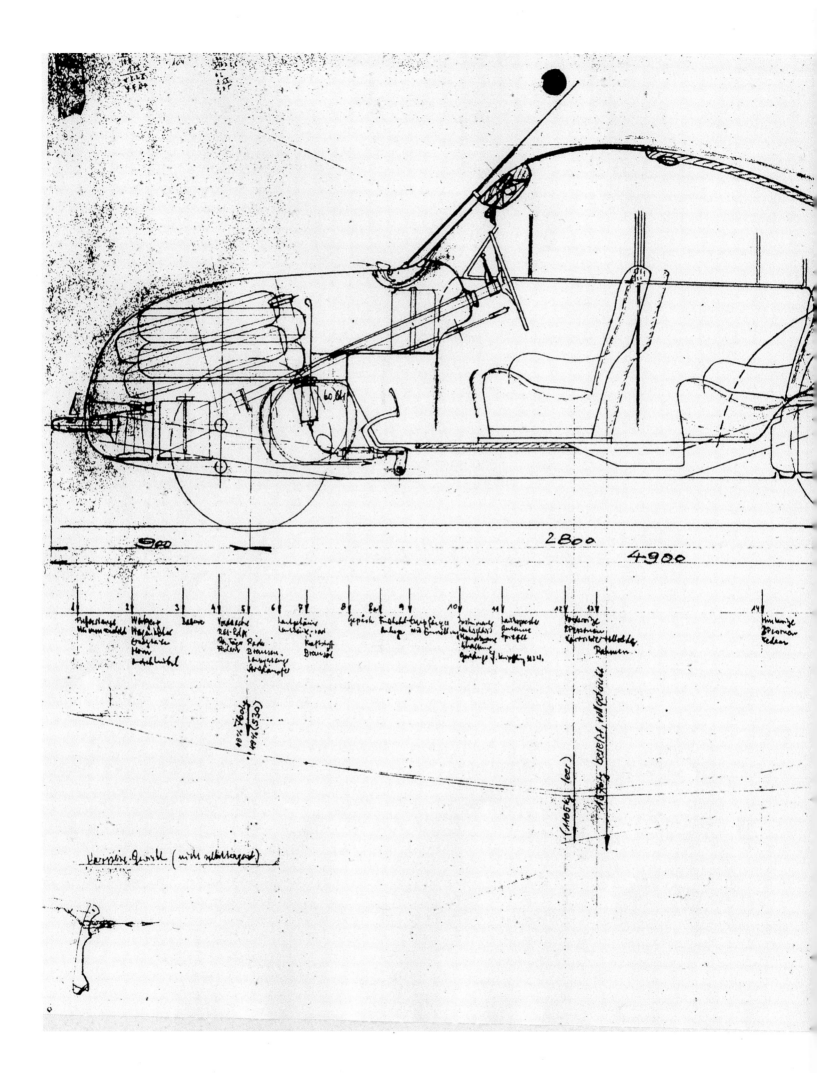

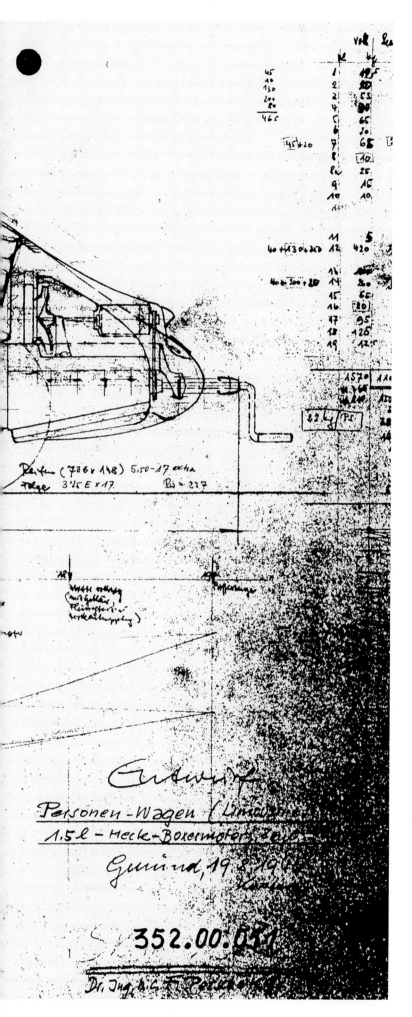

FUNDING PRODUCTION WITH SWISS FRANCS

When the first coupe was completed in August 1948, it and the next four planned cars had already been sold to a Swiss gentleman who was instrumental in their creation. Rupprecht von Senger has been variously described as an engineering draftsman, head of an advertising agency, and later an architect in Zurich. He had contacted the Porsche group in summer 1946 about designing an automobile, a plan that progressed to the stage of giving it a project number (Typ 352) and creating plans for a sophisticated engine. A drawing of the proposed body was made, but after an initial investment by the client, the ambitious project stalled. Von Senger remained intrigued with the company's abilities, however. He followed with interest the development of the "Sport Roadster," and as the first 356/2 coupe neared completion in spring 1948, he agreed to buy five cars.

Aside from the sales, which would be made in hard currency outside Austria, von Senger would also be a key player in providing raw material such as aluminum and heavy mechanical components through Switzerland, one of the few gateways available for such supplies. Ferry Porsche explained, "Even in 1948 we could not get our hands directly on any Volkswagen parts and we had very little aluminum left. However, since the Wolfsburg factory had already begun exporting Beetles to Switzerland, we were able to obtain a useful supply of spares, including engines, which were routed back to us at Gmünd by Von Senger.

"In return," Ferry added, "we appointed him representative for Porsche cars in Switzerland."

Von Senger, however, was not the answer to all the problems confronting the automaker in Gmünd. Although he circulated among the wealthy and connected in Switzerland, for the large

The "Porsche Sportwagen" meets the world for the first time at the Geneva Auto Show in 1949. Ferry Porsche, Bernhard Blank, and Louise Piëch (center) pose with a Beutler-built cabriolet and the only 356/2 sunroof coupe.

sums required to finance further production, he was like a sleeveless ball gown: no visible means of support. By late 1948 von Senger's commitments were transferred to another Zurich businessman, Bernhard Blank. Blank owned a hotel as well as an auto showroom where the new cars could be displayed prominently. He arranged for two 356/2 models, a coupe and a cabriolet, to be displayed at the Geneva Auto Show on March 17, 1949. It was the Porsche 356's first appearance on the world stage, albeit in a quiet corner of the hall. The Geneva show famously displayed dream cars and prototypes, like the Isotta Fraschini Tipo 8C Monterosa also at the 1949 event. Fewer than six of those IFs were ever built, a fate that might have befallen the 356 had it not been for hard decisions made over the next two years.

AN AUTOMOBILE FACTORY IN MICROCOSM

In the latter half of 1948, at the Karnerau compound of wooden barracks, more chassis were constructed and serial production of the Porsche sports car began. There were high hopes for scores of 356s being built by the end of the year. This Gmünd factory did not roll out every finished car, however.

Fabrication of the steel boxed-section chassis required accuracy in cutting panel sections, jigging, and welding, but not the level of skill needed for panel shaping and aluminum welding. For that, a wooden buck was constructed and 1.2mm aluminum panels were shaped to fit the contours of each section, most likely by panel beating on a separate sandbag or wooden form, then checking for correct contours against the buck. Each of the dozens of outer skin sections was welded into a larger assembly along with the supporting interior panels, then mated to the steel chassis by folding flanged edges over each other and riveting with an oil-soaked fabric layer to prevent galvanic corrosion between the dissimilar metals. Steel door skins were used; these were relatively flat and required less working with a hammer. Welded aluminum seams then required planishing and filing—time- and labor-intensive steps for the three-man body crew. Lead filler in the seams could not be used as it was on the later steel cars.

In this area a bottleneck existed in the form of Friederich Weber and his fondness for the bottle. With only two other craftsmen to build and finish bodies, it was inevitable that the company would hire some of the work to be done by outside coachbuilders. In fact, the second and third cars were built by the Beutler brothers of Thun in central Switzerland—an arrangement in which Bernhard Blank was instrumental. The Beutlers built two soft-top cabriolets to Komenda's specifications but with a few custom touches. It was one of these cabriolets that appeared with Gmünd coupe #356/2-008 (the only one built with a sliding sunroof) at the Geneva Motor Show in March 1949.

Beutler built four more cabriolet bodies in 1949, these without the rear fender bulge. Keibl Karosserie of Vienna was contracted to produce two cabriolets for local customers, one of which remains in the Porsche Museum today. Porsche went on to contract with further body builders that year in an effort to meet its production goal of fifty cars. Tatra's Vienna branch was contracted to finish coupes shipped from Gmünd beginning in early 1950. Another Vienna firm, Kastenhofer, built cars as well. Tatra and Kastenhofer cars were for the most part overseen and finished by the Porsche Salzburg group.

Porsche's record keeping at the time was as basic as the facility where the cars were constructed. Herbert Kaes had moved to a position with Porsche Salzburg, and a list he compiled noted each car's serial number and engine number, some internal references, and the buyer's name. Listed chassis and body numbers do not correspond numerically, as chassis assemblies were probably stockpiled, and as a body was finished, workmen grabbed the closest chassis to mate to it. Engines were similarly semirandom. Twelve cars were built before a standardized Porsche engine number (356-0000XX) was used, and even these were unrelated to the cars' build sequence. In total, forty-nine Porsche automobiles were finished as "customer cars" through #356/2-050, with one serial number never built. An additional eleven were constructed—through number #356/2-063, with two more gaps in the sequence—and these vehicles were some of Porsche's first competition cars.

Panel by panel, a coupe body takes shape at Gmund. The wooden buck was used for checking the fit of body panels before they were positioned and welded in place.

ABOVE: Built on a Gmünd chassis by brothers Fritz and Ernst Beutler in Switzerland, 356/2-003 follows Komenda's design but with a bit of flair, like the rear fender bulges not found in later cabriolets. BELOW: Porsche sent chassis and body panels for 356/2-025 and 026, selling the raw materials directly to the customers, who paid Keibl separately for the finished cars. These featured unique stylistic touches, including a chrome center dash section with instruments, built to order to a customer's specifications and their own take on interior appointments.

LOOKING FORWARD

In 1949 building cars by hand was somewhat secondary in Ferry Porsche's mind. With the VW contract in hand, the company needed space beyond the crude sheds at Karnerau—somewhere its engineers could meet the challenges of a new German economy and perhaps even continue building cars. Engineering was still the company's bread and butter, and patent applications were made regularly: various cylinder heads, "frames" or chassis, a manual flywheel starter, fuel-injection pump controls, tractor implements, and even an electric single-wheel drive for trolleys. "With the signature of this contract . . . our thoughts about moving back to Stuttgart crystalized into a definite decision," Ferry wrote. A transfer to their offices in Zuffenhausen was obvious, but the U.S. Army still occupied the buildings, using them as a motor pool and repair facility. Reports from Stuttgart, however, gave Ferry hope that the Americans might vacate by mid-1950. On that belief, a small contingent was sent to Stuttgart, the vanguard of what would be a complete move of the company back to Germany. The question was, when? With a return to engineering consultancy work for VW, Ferry Porsche was questioning whether his company should even make cars. The answer was complicated.

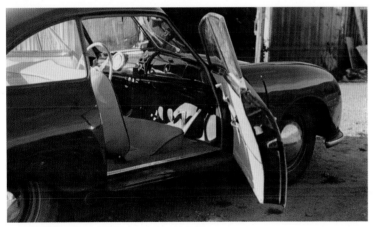

ABOVE: The only remaining Gmünd coupe still having all its original equipment, #040. Owner Jerry Seinfeld says, "I love it because to me, it looks like a little alien flying saucer." It retains its originality in part because previous owner Otto Mathé was not concerned about appearances and never restored it. Used by Porsche as a test car for several years, its hand-hammered aluminum shell has been rough since day one. "The body came out so badly they never sold it," Jerry observed.

LEFT: The Gmünd-built Porsche Limousin was a well-appointed grand touring car in spite of its humble roots. It would soon be replaced by a new model, built in Germany.

BOTTOM LEFT: Porsche 356/2-045 was one of fifteen cars sold to Swedish truck maker Scania Vabis. Restored by Road Scholars, it is shown here in raw metal the way it would have looked before paint in Gmünd. Steel doors and trafficator slots are evident, and rivets in the front wheel well show where the body and chassis meet. This joint between dissimilar metals was filled with an oil-impregnated cloth strip. It won a class award at the Pebble Beach Concours in 2011 for its owner, Hans-Peter Porsche.

ENGINOLOGY: CREATING A 356 ENGINE

Engine design for the original Typ 60 Volkswagen was problematic and anything but linear. In January 1936 young Austrian Porsche engineer Franz Xaver Reimspiess produced a table comparing his "E-motor" to other VW engine options. He proved the worth of his engine design analytically to Professor Porsche, and from that point forward an air-cooled flat-four was the baseline for the KdF-Wagen. Key to the engine's acceptance, and later long life, was that all components were stronger than needed for the power produced.

For the postwar Beetle, engine specs were standardized at 1,131cc, with a 75mm × 64mm bore and stroke, producing 25 horsepower. Through wartime experiments with supercharging, overhead cams, hemispherical heads, fuel injection, and more, Ferry Porsche knew the engine possessed more performance potential. His personal car had been a supercharged VW. For the 356 being built in Gmünd he and his engineers considered ways to increase power without exotic or expensive changes. Three ideas came to the fore.

Typ 366 was essentially a standard VW engine featuring dual Solex carburetors with 22mm venturis. The compression ratio increased to 7.0:1, producing 34 horsepower—a 36 percent improvement from the original 25. A second idea was to use the experimental Typ 367 cylinder heads, which were individual for each cylinder with angled valves. One example engine was built, but the unit was deemed too complicated and expensive. The team settled on the third option, Typ 369, using a dual cylinder head like the KdF but redesigned to allow larger valves operating in a V angle. Exhaust rockers were modified as well. This new engine design used domed pistons with a 73.5mm bore and a compression ratio of 7:1. The result was a higher-redline 1,086cc engine that comfortably produced 40 horsepower at 4,000 rpm and allowed the 356 to race in the 1.1-liter class.

Dual carburetors gave a published figure of 40 h.p., up from 25 in the VW.

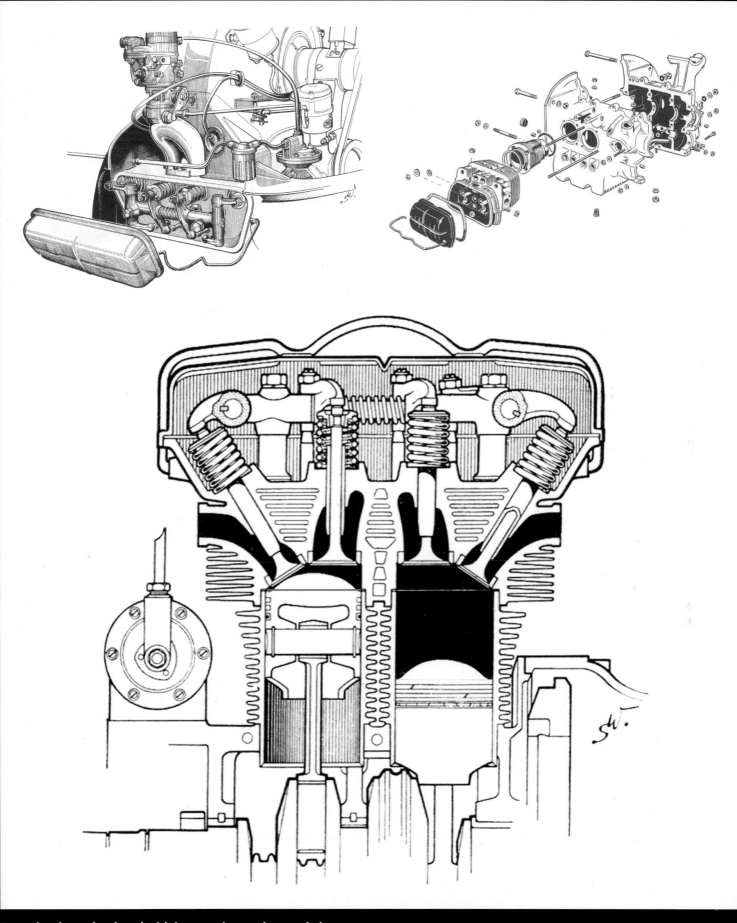

A new head was developed with larger valves and an angled
exhaust port, for much better flow. Exhaust valves were opened
by bell crank rockers. Pistons were higher compression, and bore
was reduced to 73.5.

Production of steel-bodied cars began slowly in Stuttgart and Zuffenhausen during May and June of 1950. Chassis 5012 was initially used by Porsche and sold as a used car in March 1951. Fortunately retaining much of its originality over the years, with a new owner in 2008, a meticulous restoration had begun. Painted in its original color of maroon (503) with beige leather (358), it debuted at the 37th International 356 Meeting in Merano, Italy, in 2012.

HOME TO ZUFFENHAUSEN

Albert Prinzing came out of Allied detention just in time to play a key role in the rebirth of the Porsche company in its home of Zuffenhausen. A schoolmate of Ferry Porsche, Prinzing studied political science and economics in Germany and Rome, receiving an undergraduate degree and then a doctorate in 1934. By twenty-seven he was a lecturer at the University of Berlin, and at thirty-one he became a full professor there. He was appointed a German Foreign Office diplomat to Mussolini's government and starting in May 1945 was interned by the Allies for three years in Ludwigsburg, at which point it was determined he was a "lesser offender" and he was released.

Ferry Porsche's autobiography relates, "Sometime late in the war, around 1944, he visited me at Zell am See and during a walk around our farm we talked about the future. We agreed there and then that after the war we would embark on a joint venture of some kind. I would contribute my technical experience and know-how, while Prinzing would specialize in economics." True to that informal agreement, after his release Professor Prinzing worked with Stuttgart mayor Arnulf Klett to reclaim the Porsche buildings in Zuffenhausen from the U.S. Army. He also became a minority partner in the new German company,

Porsche KG. As a trusted advisor—and also now a stakeholder in the firm—his counsel to Ferdinand and Ferry Porsche was to continue the automobile-building enterprise, even if it was not immediately profitable. Ongoing income from the VW contract and rental payments from the Americans were creating a tax liability that had to be offset. The expenses of manufacturing automobiles would nicely fit into this equation.

Building cars was not the first choice among Porsche family members; both Ferry and Louise were hesitant to commit to the idea. The firm's role originally, and now again with VW, was as design and engineering consultant. Production in Gmünd had been fraught with obstacles, and chassis for the 356/2 were still stacked up as bodies were slowly created. The ledger sheet did not lie: little if any money had been made from building automobiles. Prinzing was as much a diplomat as an economist, however, and his arguments persuaded Ferry and the others to continue making cars in Germany. But exactly how and where was another question.

The U.S. Army was put on high alert during the Korean War, delaying the return of the property to Porsche.

Albert Prinzing came to Porsche as finance chief and a minority partner.

Aside from design and mechanical development, the Porsche team acknowledged that building bodies should be left to specialists and solicited bids in May 1949. A committee of the two Ferdinand Porsches, Anton Piëch, Karl Kirn, and Komenda considered the results. Karosserie Drauz in Heilbronn and Binz in Lorch made proposals, as did Reutter, Porsche's neighbor in Stuttgart and Zuffenhausen. The Binz price for chassis and body was DM 7,768, Reutter's DM 8,783, and Drauz's DM 9,203. Although Reutter's number was some 13 percent higher than the Binz bid, Ferdinand Porsche spoke convincingly of the firm's experienced and skilled workmen. Ferry negotiated a lower price with Reutter, and in order to keep men employed and work flowing, the company acquiesced. In the end it was not Reutter's proximity but Ferdinand's recommendation that sold the group

on Reutter. After many more discussions, in November 1949, the parties signed a contract to produce five hundred bodies. That figure was based on an estimate of several years' worth of sales.

Reutter itself was faced with a number of difficulties as the plans began to take shape. Postwar appropriations by the French had diminished the machine stock in Zuffenhausen, but its largest press had proved too heavy to move. To build the new Porsches, additional machinery was ordered for Augustenstrasse, and fortunately the company's credit rating allowed it to be delivered without delay. By early 1950 Reutter was ready.

FINANCING THE OPERATION

Porsche's credit was not as solid, however. Banks were under restrictions, and loans to Porsche to finance the considerable startup costs were not available. Some relief came through a contract with Georg Allgaier Presswerke, a manufacturer located some 40 kilometers east of Zuffenhausen in Uhingen. The company, which produced tractors, steel stampings, wind turbines, and other farm products, had introduced its model R22 tractor in 1946, a machine uncharitably described in the press as a "stationary engine on wheels." Company head Erwin Allgaier had worked with the Porsche firm for years, and meetings in Gmünd in late 1949 led to a contract in December. Porsche's Typ 313 tractor design would be the basis for a small twin-cylinder, air-cooled diesel tractor, to be called the AP 17. Development was fast, and by June 1950 a prototype was presented to the public. Production began the next month, and so began a tractor line that went from strength to strength for several years, the culmination of something Ferdinand Porsche had envisioned for over a decade. The contract and the clear success of the new tractor allowed Porsche to obtain credit for its carmaking venture, but would it be enough?

The Algaier tractor design was an immediate success and gave Porsche the fees and royalties that would pave the way for credit to start building cars.

Before any cars were built in Germany, Ferry Porsche and finance officer Prinzing knew they had to promote the product. To that end, in early 1950 the latter led a caravan of two cars— Gmünd coupe #356-010, which was in service as the company car and demonstrator, and a Beutler cabriolet—on a tour of German VW dealers. Showing the existing cars and describing those to come, Prinzing's sales pitch was effective. Ferdinand Porsche's name still carried weight, and customers booked scores of orders for scores of cars. An innovative down-payment plan asked each dealer to pay for the last car they would receive, netting Porsche some DM 200,000 up front.

A contingent of Porsche engineers had moved back to Stuttgart in the fall of 1949 to revamp the 356 design, but the only space for them was at the Porsche villa on Feuerbacher Weg. It became a hive of activity once again, just as it had been during the early KdF testing days when prototypes were built in the garage there. Working in cramped quarters, the team completed drawings by November.

RIGHT: Ferry Porsche (left) and his father with a Gmünd-built coupe at the temporary Zuffenhausen offices at Feuerbacher Weg in 1950. BELOW: Taking the show on the road, a Gmünd coupe is shown to staff at the Max Moritz VW dealership.

The "new" 356 would be built in steel, and a frame similar to the box-section unit underpinning the Gmünd cars would be made from stamped parts. Erwin Komenda gave it enough strength to be used in an open car, although it was not as beefy as the Gmünd original.

At Reutter's Augustenstrasse shops in Stuttgart a wooden buck was assembled. Large shaped parts were made in Zuffenhausen, and many other steel panels were hand formed, fitted, and welded to create a prototype of the new coupe. It was ready in late March 1950, on wheels, but unpainted and unglazed. Ferdinand, Ferry, and Komenda inspected it in a courtyard of Reutter's Stuttgart shops. Sitting in a chair, scrutinizing the car head-on, the elder Porsche took several minutes to consider the shape, then declared that the fenders were not symmetrical.

A later inspection revealed his eye had not erred; a difference of 20mm from the centerline was measured. Within a few days the first car was assembled, painted, trimmed, and adorned with its seven letters on the nose and a Reutter badge on the rocker just behind the left front wheel. The first production Porsche 356 was trucked 11 miles (9 km) to Zuffenhausen, where it awaited its powertrain and a final inspection at the Reutter works there. The light gray coupe, #5002, was named *Windhund* (*Grayhound*) and immediately became the focus of much photography for promotion and advertising.

The planned production of 270 coupes and 20 convertibles for calendar year 1950 got underway in earnest, with 6 coupes in May, 13 in June, and 22 in July—along with the first cabriolet, a prototype. An output of 60 cars per month was slated for

Building a 356 in steel meant starting from scratch. New plans were drawn and modified with Komenda subtly changing the car's shape.

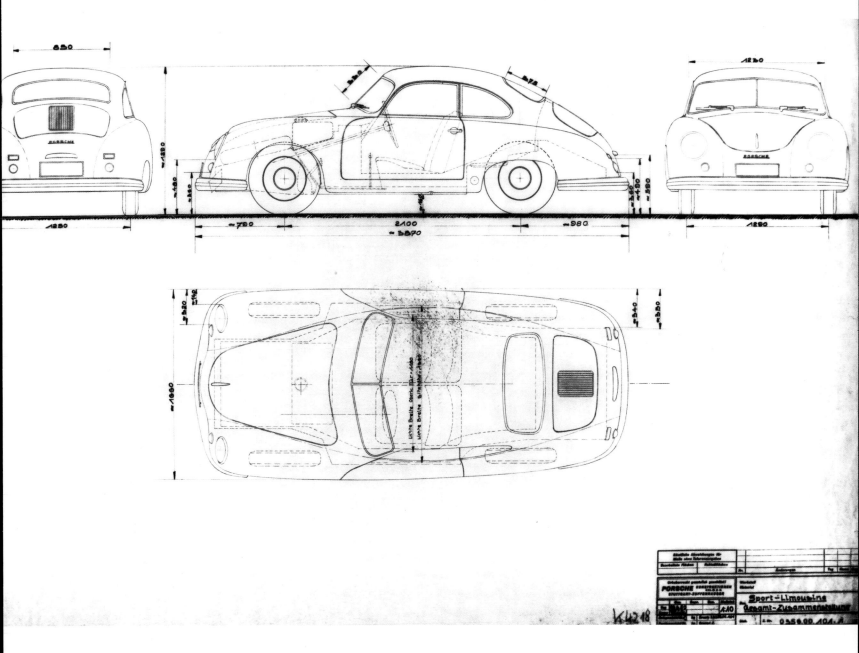

A wooden buck was built to create the shaped metal for the first car.

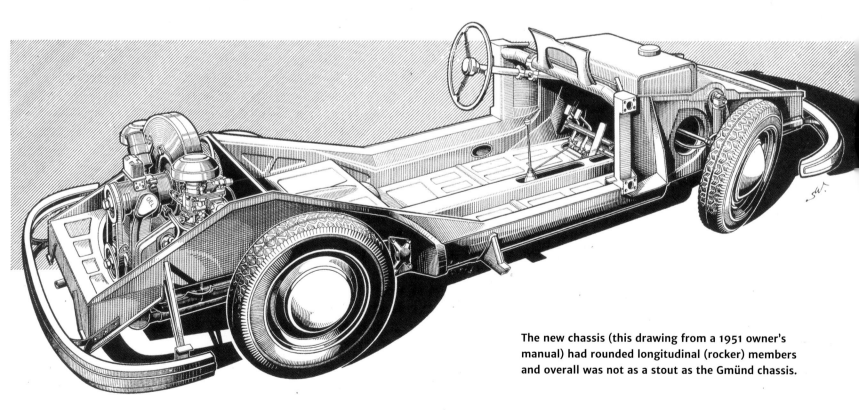

The new chassis (this drawing from a 1951 owner's manual) had rounded longitudinal (rocker) members and overall was not as a stout as the Gmünd chassis.

TOP: Ferry (gray hat) and Ferdinand Porsche (black hat) inspect the prototype 356 bodyshell in the yard of the Reutter shops at Augustenstrasse 82 in Stuttgart-West. In the light hat is body designer Erwin Komenda and at left in a light-colored coat is Reutter's general manager, Walter Beierbach.
BOTTOM: 500 Porsches were built by March of 1951. Foreman Hans Klauser is behind the wheel.

Ferdinand Porsche gets an up-close look at the "assembly line" in the rented Reutter space. Transmission installation required one man to lie on a dolly to muscle it into place.

The Windhund was Porsche's demonstrator and advertising model.

The Reutter assembly line in 1950.

October. Serial production of cabriolets began in November. At that time the two companies returned to negotiating, in this case for a further run of 500 coupes, 350 cabriolets, 180 chassis, and a similar number of "pressed parts." A contract was signed, and men at both Porsche and Reutter expressed amazement at the wildly successful launch of the new car. Just over a year after the first one left Reutter's shop, the 500th 356 was completed on March 21, 1951.

CROWDED CONDITIONS

Most of the Porsche contingent were moving back to Zuffenhausen, although their headquarters there were still under control of the U.S. Army, and it was unknown for how much longer. To accommodate the group, a deal was made in October 1949 to rent a portion of Reutter's Zuffenhausen property. The 6,000 square feet for workshops, office space, and drafting studios meant crowded conditions for the men who would install engines, transmissions, and mechanical components in the trimmed bodies. Other space was needed for management and engineers with their drafting boards. Some sixty employees were now on staff, considerably fewer than the two hundred–plus at Gmünd. There were two production lines with three cars each. Alongside were offices,

Coupe 5012 was built for the American market with a 1500 Typ 527 engine. The bumpers were reinforced for the United States with slotted wheels, Telefunken radio and antenna, a passenger reclining seat, a tachometer, and a speedometer in miles.

A worker poses with a Gläser-built cabriolet.

the engine/transmission assembly room, the dyno room, and the racing and development area. (This last was not an actual room like the others—it just had a curtain along one side.) By fall 1950 Porsche leased more space.

Hedging its bets and working under the belief that open cars would be popular, the company needed to construct cabriolets. Beutler in Switzerland declined the work, so Porsche looked elsewhere. Karosserie Gläser was an old and respected firm that had built custom carriages in Dresden for decades but was destroyed in the firebombing of 1945, after which owner Erich Heuer moved the remnants of the firm to Weiden in Bavaria. Porsche placed an order with Gläser for 250 units, with chassis assemblies and pressed parts shipped from Reutter. The contract was an attempt by Heuer to restart his family's body-building enterprise, but he may have been overzealous in that pursuit. It soon became clear he was losing money on every car, and Porsche was not willing to renegotiate the price. According to 356 authority Dr. Brett Johnson, Gläser produced 247 cabriolets from 1950 to 1953 before it went into bankruptcy. The last of those cars were finished by Reutter, which then took over cabriolet production.

Gläser cabriolet 5142 shows a subtle difference in shape and trim and a higher-mounted hood handle.

MAX AND THE U.S. MARKET

Ferry Porsche continually strove to expand the market for his namesake automobile outside of Germany, and he had allies in that pursuit. Max Troesch, the Swiss engineer and journalist whose glowing report about the first Porsche appeared in the *Motor* in 1948, visited New York in 1950 and stopped to see importer Max Hoffman. When Troesch showed him photos of the new 356, his reaction was very positive. In an interview with Betty Jo Turner in 1980, Hoffman recalled his response: "I told him I liked it very much, as much as I could see, and that I was very interested. He went back and talked to Mr. Porsche, Mr. Porsche wrote me a letter and so the whole thing started."

Born in Vienna in 1904, Maximilian Edwin Hoffman was a former bicycle and motorcycle racer, a true auto enthusiast, and a consummate salesman. He knew Anton Piëch, who had done legal work for him in Austria. At age thirty Hoffman was selling American vehicles there, but with that country's annexation to Germany, he moved to Paris, then New York by 1941 as war raged in Europe. In the United States he reinvented himself as a maker of costume jewelry, did well, and after the war returned to selling automobiles with a showroom in Manhattan. Signing on with Porsche as the marque's representative in 1950, his plans were much more ambitious than Ferry Porsche's

Max Hoffman had a showroom on "Auto Row" in Manhattan, on Broadway at 82nd Street.

A Hoffman ad distributed at the 1952 Bridgehampton races.

goal for America, which was to sell in the single digits annually. "If I can't sell five cars a week, I'm not interested," Hoffman said. He would make good on that boast, and then some.

Two cars were sent to America, a blue coupe and a red cabriolet. Hoffman promoted them at the Watkins Glen, New York, races in September 1950. A home movie of the event shows the two Porsches on the track (public roads closed for the event) with race participants during practice. Hoffman also displayed them trackside at a Concours d'Elegance, where their smooth, modern lines stood out. Sportsman and racer Briggs Cunningham was there, and Hoffman sold him the coupe, although it is said he traded it back because the 1,100cc engine was underpowered. Briggs would soon add a racing Porsche to his stable.

The following month Hoffman was in Paris, where he met Professor Porsche at the Grand Palais for the auto show. "He was a very lovely nice person. A strong man," he opined in the 1980 interview.

Hoffman exerted other influences that were directly related to the future of Porsche cars, including suggesting that an emblem would be an image builder in the American market. The story goes that Ferry Porsche sketched out a heraldic design on a luncheon napkin during a meeting with Hoffman, but the actual creation process was considerably more involved, getting underway in early 1951.

Already on May 12, 1950, Porsche coupe #5006 was on display at the Reutter booth at a trade fair in Reutlingen. A customer car belonging to Dr. Domnick was displayed at the Berlin Auto Show a few weeks later. A more important exhibit took place in October at the Paris Motor Show, where two Porsches could be found in a small corner of the Grand Palais. A sign above the coupe and cabriolet read "1900 PORSCHE 1950," celebrating a half century of designs from the celebrated engineer. It was at this event that Max Hoffman met Ferdinand Porsche, and other connections were made as well. A French auto dealer and racer named Auguste Veuillet met with Porsche

THE PORSCHE CREST

Two enthusiasts urged Porsche leadership to create a badge to identify their product. Max Hoffman knew Americans would be impressed by something along the lines of Enzo Ferrari's Cavallino Rampante, used since 1947. Stuttgart doctor Ottomar Domnick was a Porsche owner and über enthusiast who concurred with Max and Ferry about the need for a crest. Dr. Domnick went so far as to organize a contest among art-school students across Germany, with a smart brochure and cash prizes offered. Entries were displayed at a Stuttgart gallery in April 1951 and prizes were awarded, but none of the submissions were actually used. Instead, an in-house effort was undertaken, with engineer Franz X. Reimspiess—who had designed the original KdF "VW" logo—taking the lead.

Reimspiess began with the crest of the state of Württemberg with stag horns and horizontal stripes, adding the coat of arms of the city of Stuttgart with its prancing horse and the name Porsche displayed prominently above. Care had to be taken in retaining the state and city elements without modification. The drawing was finalized by the design department with help from Erich Strenger, who had begun producing sales brochures for Porsche in 1951 and would create much of the literature and many famous posters in the years to come. The new crest first appeared on the steering-wheel center button at the end of 1952.

Reimspiess's close-to-final drawing of the new Porsche crest.

to discuss motorsports in general and two things in particular: he was interested in becoming the French agent for Porsche sales, and toward that end he recommended that the company enter a team of cars in the upcoming 24 Hours of Le Mans. Veuillet had raced there in 1949 in a Delage and knew the promotional value of the huge crowds. Porsche asked about the speed necessary to be competitive and to finish in the 1,100cc class. To Veuillet's response he applied some calculations on his slide rule and noted that it could be done—not easily, but it was possible.

Le Mans race director Charles Faroux also visited the elder Porsche, who was a friend, that month. "The fame of the Porsche car is already reaching out beyond Germany and I have heard nothing but praise for it," Faroux told him, according to Ferry Porsche. "Why don't you enter at least one car for the Vingt-Quatre Heures next year? We'd be glad to have you and you would stand a very good chance to win the 1100 cc class." The decision to enter the race was made. Ferry wrote, "As far as I was concerned it seemed like a great idea, though our limited facilities would be heavily taxed in making the right preparations. Still, we had about eight months to get ready."

The first presentation of the 356 at the May trade fair in Reutlingen featured 5006, one of the first coupes, at the Max Moritz booth, promoting Reutter's skills. A small sign also touts Lechler paint, maker of the special strawberry-red metallic finish. Porsche 5006 was found in 2013 in a German backyard, where it had languished for decades. Restored by the Automuseum Prototyp in Hamburg, it is now on display there, one of the oldest surviving steel 356s.

At the Paris Auto Show in 1950 Ferdinand Porsche and his new automobile were the center of attention for journalists. From left: M. Jullien (France Union Automobile), André Reichel (editor *L'Action Automobile*), L. V. Reustel (director, *L'Action Automobile*), and at right, Professor Porsche's nephew and secretary Ghislaine Kaes.

Ferdinand Porsche in 1950.

Gmünd coupes were expendable
and light, perfect for racing.

SUNSET FOR THE PROFESSOR

Ferdinand Porsche reached a milestone on September 3, 1950, when he celebrated his seventy-fifth birthday. Several 356 owners, in addition to race driver Rudolf Caracciola and other luminaries, attended a gathering in his honor at Schloss Solitude, a château on a hill above Stuttgart. "It was a satisfying occasion as well as a moving one," Ferry wrote, "for the turnout showed that we were already earning ourselves a place among the world's manufacturers of fine sports cars."

A 356 coupe built in Stuttgart and named after Ferdinand was presented to him as a gift. The black car carried its namesake, along with his driver and secretary Ghislaine Kaes, to Paris the following month.

In November Porsche father and son visited Wolfsburg, where the incredible success of the Volkswagen works made an impression on the man who had created it all. He was only able to savor the moment briefly, however. "On November 19, the night after our return to Stuttgart," Ferry related, "he suffered a stroke that was to prove fatal. From that time on he was paralyzed on one side and in poor health." Nursed at home over the holidays, he was taken to a hospital in Stuttgart late in January and died on January 30, 1951. A memorial service was held the following week, and he was temporarily interred in a local cemetery before being laid to rest in a chapel at the family home at Zell am See in 1952.

The family mourned, but there was much work to be done. Some of the professor's dreams had yet to be realized.

RACING TAKES CENTER STAGE

By late 1950, preparations were already being made for Le Mans. It was an opportunity for considerable exposure, but the cost and logistical problems were significant, and anti-German sentiment still ran high in France. For a 24-hour race, Ferry Porsche was stretching the company's capabilities, but his father had believed it could be done, and this first factory racing effort laid the groundwork for a developing Porsche philosophy. He wrote, "Journalists' reports of races are far more effective and convincing than most forms of advertising, and they cost little or nothing. Money thus freed from unnecessary advertising can be used to gain valuable racing experience, and the lessons so learned mean that next year's model can be a better car."

Chosen for battle were four "leftover" aluminum Gmünd coupes, lighter and more aerodynamic than their steel Stuttgart siblings. With 46 horsepower and higher gears they could just top 100 miles per hour. The additional power came from a new camshaft designed by a young engineer named Ernst Fuhrmann. Officially, the cars were 1,400-pound prototypes with numerous body modifications and larger fuel tanks with external fillers. The factory published a brochure offering these options on what it called the 356 SL, but such a car existed only on paper, solely to homologate its entry in the race.

Early in 1951 the last aluminum Gmünd cars that had been assembled by Tatra were in Zuffenhausen. An order was written to adapt four of these to "SL" specification in preparation for

the 24-hour race, which was now a few months away. Two were sent to Dannenhauer & Stauss, a Stuttgart firm that was making custom cabriolets on VW chassis; two more were to be adapted by Reutter. This adaptation was no simple process. Historian Frank Jung notes in his book *Porsche 356: Made by Reutter*, "For the sake of comparison, at this time Reutter offered Porsche a completely new body for DM 4085. The price for finishing the aluminum bodies was only DM 800 below that—evidence of the considerable effort needed for this essential work."

Paul von Guilleaume, a seasoned racer, was chosen to lead the organizing effort. A small garage in the French village of Teloché would be race headquarters. Early on, one of the cars was damaged during practice. Another was written off after an autobahn crash. The salvageable parts of these two cars were combined, and another Gmünd coupe was quickly drafted into service as a racer. This, too, was badly damaged when driver Rudolph Sauerwein went off the road at the end of night practice. With Sauerwein in the hospital, the hopes of the team were invested in a single car driven by Auguste Veuillet, who had

originally suggested Porsche's effort, and another seasoned French driver, Edmond Mouche; they had driven before as a team.

The June 23, 1951, start saw the fast cars out front in the rain. In the 1,100cc class, Porsche was joined by a French Simca and a Panhard. At the finish the following day after a steady and uneventful run, the 356 SL—the only German car in the race—had bested them and the 1,500cc cars, finishing in twentieth place overall with an average speed of 73.5 miles per hour. Ferry Porsche spent much of the race in the pits with his crew and celebrated with them at the checkered flag.

The Le Mans race was followed by a mid-August entry in the Liège–Rome–Liège Rally. An aluminum Gmünd coupe covered more than 3,000 miles of roads of all description, pummeling narrow mountain passes where both climbing ability and braking power were important. The power output now pushed to 51 horsepower on gasoline, the fuel mandated for the rally. Driving was shared by Petermax Müller and Huschke von Hanstein, who the next year would be hired by Porsche and later become racing director. They brought the

Gentleman racers Paul von Guilleaume and Heinrich von der Mühle drove 356/2-055 in 1951. The car today is restored and in the Revs Institute museum in Florida.

1,100cc car to the finish line second in class. Another aluminum Porsche was entered in the 1.500cc class, finishing third overall and first in class despite transmission problems.

RUNNING FOR RECORDS

Petermax Miiller was an avid racer who returned to the tracks after the war in his own streamlined aluminum open racer on a VW floorpan. He constructed several *Eigenbau* (homebuilt) racers over the next few years, and along with Helmut Polensky and Huschke von Hanstein he took an Eigenbau to Montlhéry, near Paris, where banking up to 52 degrees allowed them to capture several national time and distance records. In 1950 they ran again for 48 hours and achieved eight new world records for 1,100cc.

By 1951 Müller had developed a relationship with Porsche (he would become a dealer in 1952) and urged the company to make some speed record attempts with its cars. In preparation for a Porsche attempt, the factory "racing department" readied two cars, 1.1- and 1.5-liter aluminum Gmünd coupes fitted

Metzeler was an early sponsor of Porsche's record program and displayed a Gmünd SL wearing the the Le Mans class winner number at their trade show stand, noting the Montlhéry records rather than the class win.

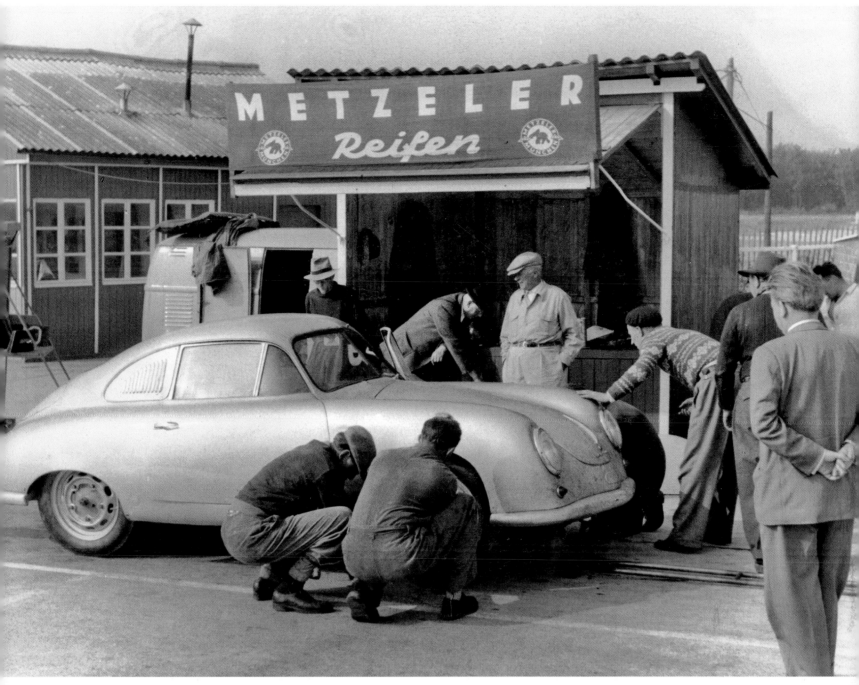

Porsche set records at Montlhéry, once again using "leftover" Gmünd coupes.

with flush skirts over the wheels. Along with Müller, the drivers were to be von Hanstein, Richard von Frankenberg, Hermann Ramelow, and Walter Glöckler, who also brought a roadster of his own. In the last week of September 1951 the Porsche contingent went to Montlhéry. The 1,100cc car set new records for 500 miles, 1,000 kilometers, and 6 hours, each at just more than 100 miles per hour. Glöckler's roadster also set three short-distance records.

On September 30, Porsche #356/2-055 with a 1,500cc engine began a three-day enduro intended to supersede the existing European mark for 72 hours. After two days, the car was averaging about 99 miles per hour and had secured a number of class records. In spite of a refueling snafu and the transmission

getting stuck in third gear, the car survived and at the end of its run had amassed seven new class records, including the class 72-hour speed mark at 152.32 kilometers per hour.

Some new records would last only a year, but for that time it was a promotional opportunity on which Porsche was quick to capitalize. Taken directly to Paris for the opening of the 1951 auto show, the 1.500cc car still wore a coating of dirt and oil. It joined a Stuttgart-built car on the Porsche stand, where it attracted curious crowds and the attention of automotive writers who were quick to accomplish what Porsche had set out to do—boost the image of the company and the sale of cars. Sponsor Metzeler tires was also happy to make promotional hay with the car, featuring it at its show booths as well.

THE AMERICA ROADSTER

A young machine tool company owner in Stuttgart, Heinrich Sauter, had an idea. He owned a 1300 coupe, which he felt was too heavy for rallying. Purchasing a new chassis from the factory, he had a low, light version of the cabriolet body built at Hans Klenk's shop just outside Stuttgart. The doors would open toward the front to speed in-and-out movement at rally checkpoints. Klenk was well connected in the automotive city and was regularly in touch with Porsche during construction. The finished car, ready in the spring of 1951, was almost surely the product of suggestions from Max Hoffman, interpreted by Porsche and built by Klenk with input from Sauter.

Sauter entered a Nürburgring race in the spring and the Liège–Rome–Liège Rally in August but completed neither and sold the roadster to the Porsche factory. The car was then resold to François Picard, who raced it with more success in 1952. Back at the factory again, it gathered dust while the Glöckler roadsters took the competition limelight. In early 1953 it reached California, where Stan Mullin, its new owner, ran a season of races. Following a familiar course of neglectful owners, the Sauter car was advertised in the *Road & Track* classifieds as "the odd door Porsche" in 1982. Ray Knight of Indiana purchased it and undertook a restoration project of immense proportions, and today

The Sauter roadster at Reutter, showing a clear pattern for the America Roadster.

The steel roadster was painted black and raced by Hubert Brundage in spite of its weight, and many years and owners later it has returned to the track in its original Rosedegrun color.

the car is close to its original condition. The roadster may have been a one-off, but the Zuffenhausen men didn't waste much time making their own version.

Max Hoffman had seen the Sauter car and expressed approval. By early 1952, Komenda drawings showed a very similar "*Zweisitzer*" (two-seater) Typ 540 roadster. Ferry Porsche placed an order with the Gläser firm, which was already producing cabriolets, for the new model's aluminum bodies. It was understood that these car were "for export only," and Hoffman would sell them in the United States. It would be known as the America Roadster.

Introduction of the car coincided with a new 1500 engine, and the first one was equipped with a Typ 502. Most subsequent cars carried the 1500S Typ 527 engine. Four were sent across the Atlantic to the United States in 1952 and about a dozen more the next year. The cabriolet chassis were trucked to Erich Heuer at Gläser, who welded and finished the aluminum bodies and sent the assemblies back to Zuffenhausen for mechanicals.

At its first race at Brynfan Tyddyn, Phil Walters took an overall win.

AMERICA ROADSTER

Wealthy car enthusiast Briggs Cunningham ran his own sports racers beginning in 1950. After Le Mans in 1952, where his C-4R racer finished fourth overall, he and his driver Phil Walters were invited to Stuttgart by Ferry Porsche. Long-time owner of the ex-Cunningham America Roadster #10465, Rev. Ron Roland recalled correspondence with Walters in 1991: They were shown an America Roadster, because Porsche wanted Cunningham to race the car for them in the Brynfan Tyddyn race [in Pennsylvania]. Porsche no doubt knew that the race had been restricted to two-liter cars and thought their chances were good. Walters thought Cunningham probably paid for the car and had a 'gentleman's agreement' to race it through 1952."

The car Cunningham later received had already been shipped to Max Hoffman in early May. That radium green car was the second America Roadster, #10465, with a thinner aluminum body, a Typ 528 1500 Super engine, bigger brakes, and a tiny racing windscreen, among other tweaks. It was on the grid at Brynfan Tyddyn on July 26, 1952, with Phil Walters behind the wheel, arguably America's best sports car pilot at the time. It took first place in the 10-lap main event, a milestone as Porsche's first overall racing victory. Gordon ine and John Bentley also competed in 356s.

Cunningham and his son raced the car a few more times, including at Thompson, Connecticut, in August where America Roadsters took the first three places in SCCA's 1.5-liter race. The car was returned to Hoffman at season's end. Roland wrote "The owner of importance, though, is not Cunningham, as much as the car's second owner, John Bentley. Already an avid Porsche owner/racer, he couldn't wait to get this car from Cunningham.

Ron Roland's restoration honors the car's heyday with Bentley

As a magazine publisher and writer, he then publicized this car's attributes and victories well past its prime giving Porsche invaluable advertising exposure."

Bentley got his hands on #10465 in the spring of 1953. After a repaint to bright yellow with green fender accents, he raced it that year and once more in January 1954 at McDill Air Force base near Tampa, Florida. As editor of *Auto Age* magazine, he featured it on the cover in December 1953 and made sure the car (and Porsche) got plenty of press.

It went through ten owners over the next twenty years, the last of those being Vic Skirmants of Detroit, Michigan, who sold it to Roland a year later where it joined a group of other old Porsches in his garage. An accomplished Porsche restorer, he wrote a column for *Porsche 356 Registry* magazine for years with detailing methods for tackling steel bodywork and sheet metal repair. When it came time to restore the roadster's thin aluminum body, however, he farmed out the work. He took it to a local body fabricator to weld some cracks in the aluminum. 'I told him I didn't want any panels cut off or a new body built," Roland recalled. But the fabricator cut off the rocker panels to make new ones. "I rescued the car and learned to weld aluminum by welding the 'unweldable' rocker panels back together."

Aside from some aluminum skin, the steel longitudinal members and central floorpan were replaced. "The car now

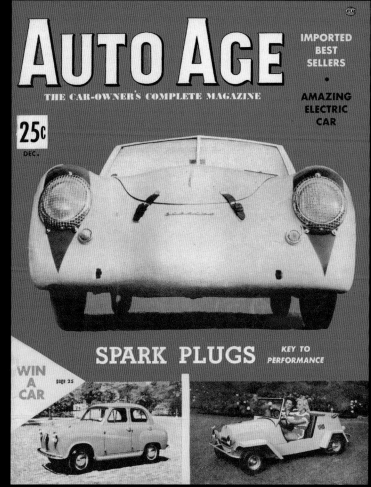

John Bentley painted the car yellow and put it on the cover of the magazine he edited.

retains about 95 percent of the original aluminum body panels and about 75 percent of the steel," Roland notes. Its original non-synchromesh transmission is in place, as is the original 1500 Super engine, after an unknown number of rebuilds. The seats are original and plush, as race cars go. He softened the vinyl with lacquer and re-stained them in the original green color. Restoration on the America Roadster was finished in 2010, and Roland displayed it at a Porsche 356 Registry Holiday in Michigan. It has since appeared at many Porsche gatherings and other car shows, along with a fascinating display of race results and promotional material from John Bentley. Wearing number 78 (its Brynfan Tyddyn number) on the hood, plus number 18 (Brigg's son) and 77 (Bentley) on its doors, it proudly recalls its racing heritage. Not only was #10465 a significant part of Porsche racing history, but it served as a key media promotional tool for the fledgling carmaker.

Briggs S. Cunningham and Briggs III in the Porsche America roadster at Greens Farms, Connecticut, 1953.

The last America Roadster was built in steel by Gläser, whose primitive working conditions show why the company folded.

This cumbersome arrangement partly explains why only seventeen roadsters were built—but having lost around DM 1,600 per car, Gläser was already on the verge of insolvency and the new Typ 550 was on the way by 1953.

In May 1952 a meeting took place with Max Hoffman and Porsche management to address the issue of the roadster's price: about $4,600. Erwin Komenda later produced a drawing (540.000.020) for a revised Typ 540 to be built in steel with a fixed windshield. Gläser was to build two hundred copies but only began work on one before all production ceased there. Three unfinished cars were then completed at Reutter: two aluminum and one steel. It was the end of the America Roadster line, but the concept of a simple, light sporting roadster was not dead. Max Hoffman had more ideas.

RIGHT-HAND DRIVE

Ferry Porsche hoped the English market might be fertile ground for growth in the future. In May 1951 he set in motion a plan to produce right-hand-drive 356s for England, and perhaps for British colonies in the future. A cost analysis was done to determine feasibility, and several necessary changes were noted, from battery placement to speedometer cable length—totaling up to an unacceptably high manufacturing premium of some DM 1,000. Costs came down by half as Reutter was able to make adjustments in the build process, and the first right-hand-drive car was finished in June 1951.

At about this time Australian businessman Norman Hamilton, who was in Switzerland for his pump business, was

Norman Hamilton with his right-hand-drive cars on the way to
Genoa for the trip to Australia.

driving over a mountain pass in a rented Oldsmobile when
a sleek silver sports car passed him. Meeting the driver at an
inn further along the route, he discovered it was Richard von
Frankenberg, who showed him the car and arranged for him
to visit the factory, where Hamilton met Ferry Porsche. After
a tour of the assembly area, he secured the rights to sell
Porsches in Australia and New Zealand on a handshake. It is
said that part of the agreement called for him to contribute
to tooling costs for the right-hand-drive changeover.

Hamilton ordered two of the first right-hand cars, a maroon
coupe and a metallic silver-blue cabriolet, which were built
in July. Returning to Germany in August, he and a friend drove
them to Genoa, where they were shipped to Australia. He
introduced these first two 356s at a special event for celebrities
and motorsports personalities in Melbourne on November 1,
1951. Hamilton and the coupe later distinguished themselves in
the September 1953 Round Australia Trial, a two-week, 10,460-
kilometer rally. Sales grew slowly, with single cars in 1952
and 1953, five in 1954, and fifteen in 1955. Norman's son Alan
Hamilton, who also raced for years, ran the successful company
until Porsche took over control in 1992.

Porsche's entry into England began in October 1951, at
the Earl's Court Motor Exhibition in London. Charles Meisl,

a transplanted Czech who worked for Connaught Engineering
and who built and raced Formula 2 cars, had seen the 356 at
the 1950 Geneva show and was able to have parent company
Continental Autos get permits to import two Porsches for Earl's
Court and a third for demonstration purposes. Meisl had also
arranged a positive magazine review in the *Autocar* in April, but
when Continental's conservative business attitude led to few
cars being sold, he moved down the road to John Colborne-
Baber's VW garage and found a more receptive attitude. It was
slow going, however; Brits were not flocking to buy Porsches,
which were more expensive than the sleek Jaguar XK120 that
boasted almost four times the horsepower.

Another member of the English car trade, Bill Aldington,
had also taken note of the 1950 Geneva display and Porsche's
favorable press. He and his brothers were the proprietors of
AFN Ltd. and had imported BMWs before the war under the
name Frazer-Nash-BMW. In 1950 the brothers were struggling
to reestablish themselves.

After the Porsches were shown at Earl's Court, Bill's brother
Aldy went to Stuttgart and approached Porsche with plans to
take the moribund English sales program to the next level. He
met with an old friend from the BMW racing days, Huschke von
Hanstein, who was now Porsche's racing and public relations

manager, and was introduced to Albert Prinzing. The finance chief explained that Meisl held the English agency rights. To make an import license work, Aldy suggested that Meisl come to his company as sales manager. Porsche and Meisl were both amenable, and late in 1953 the first cabriolet, #60277, arrived at AFN. The first sale was January 1954, beginning a slow uptick in volume that took some years to accelerate.

POWERING UP

At the Frankfurt Auto Show in April 1951, along with upgrades, a new engine was announced: the Porsche 1300, Typ 506. The engine was well received by buyers, who by midyear were resigned to waiting a month or two for the cars they ordered through the VW network.

Another engine was in development at the same time, designed to fill what was a popular market displacement of 1.5 liters. In July work began on reaching that displacement goal with the existing VW crankcase—which posed a large problem. Bore was already at its 80mm maximum, so expanding

displacement meant a longer stroke. Camshaft lobes, however, would interfere with connecting rods swinging any lower into the cam space just below the crankshaft. The separate protruding bolts that held the rod cap on were the culprits, but these bolts and nuts and their bosses needed to be beefy.

A means of eliminating the rod cap protrusion was achieved with the help of a Stuttgart specialist supplier, Albert Hirth AG. Hirth had invented (among the 350 patents he owned) a special form of toothed coupling that would allow a crankshaft to be assembled in parts. This meant Porsche could fit smooth one-piece connecting rods, eliminating the "bolt bump" of two-piece rods. Enough room was saved between the rod and cam lobe that 5mm could be added to the crank's orbit at bottom dead center. With 5mm more also at top dead center, an additional 10mm of stroke total gave the engine a displacement of 1,488cc. The Porsche engine had grown in size from the original by 36 percent in just a few months.

FULL SPEED AHEAD

A Swiss gateway for parts and material had allowed the first Porsches to be built. The Geneva Auto Show had been a launching point for the 356 in March 1949. During the

Hirth advertisement for their modular roller-bearing crankshaft. The phantom view at upper left shows the special threaded fastener that holds the toothed sections together.

Ferry Porsche presents a sales award to Hans Stanek for the thousandth 356 to Switzerland.

On the 1300 (Typ 506), which still used the VW case and the forged VW crankshaft with a 64mm stroke, the bore was increased from 73.5 to 80mm for a 17 percent increase in displacement. In a concession to the poor fuel available, compression ratio dropped to 6.5:1, but a 10-horsepower bump still resulted. (The 1950 owner's manuals recommended a mixture of 60 percent gasoline and 40 percent benzol.) New alloy cylinders from Mahle were the big news, with chrome bores and unusual new pistons with offset domes.

On the 1500, the space between the crankshaft rod journal and rod interior was filled with thin cylindrical rollers rather than the common two-piece shell bearing. Porsche engineers were familiar with it; the roller-bearing arrangement had been used in both the Auto Union and Cisitalia Grand Prix racers, as it reduced friction losses and allowed higher engine speeds. A serious downside was that the rollers needed a constant supply of clean oil; poor maintenance would drastically shorten their life. In addition, if the engine was "lugged," where high stress was applied at low rpms, the pressure on those rollers under compression would tend to make them out of round over time. This was not an engine for a casual owner. Hirth assembled the crankshafts with rods and took care of repairs and any warranty work. This arrangement would last for several years, and although the street engines later reverted to shell bearings, a new four-cam racing powerplant would use the Hirth system into the 1960s.

The first 1500 engine was Typ 502, which had 7:1 compression, Solex 32 carbs, and 55 horsepower and was offered in early autumn 1951. By October a more potent version was available with larger carbs and a new camshaft designed by young Ernst Fuhrmann, who had just received a doctorate of mechanical engineering. Typ 527 with Solex 40 PBIC carbs and a 7:1 compression ratio for 60 horsepower came online after only sixty-odd Typ 502s had been built. Shortly thereafter a compression ratio bump to 8.2:1 was made, resulting in 70 horsepower in the Typ 528 Super engine. Displacement-wise, Porsche was now squarely in the middle of the European sports-car scene.

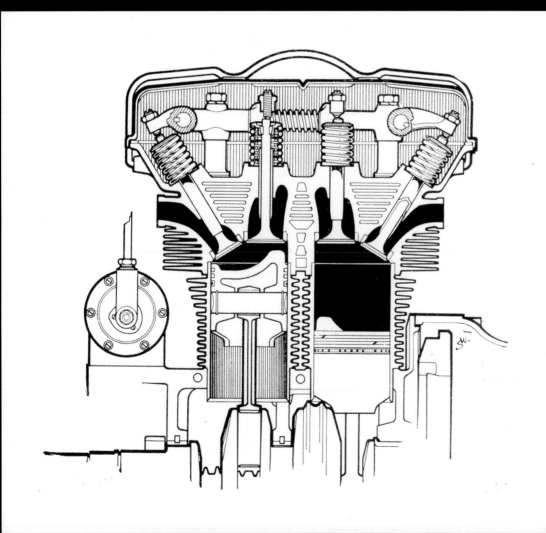

The 1300 employed unusual domes on the exhaust side of the piston top. Issues later developed with the pistons "rocking" and causing excessive oil consumption. Chrome-plated cylinder bores were a first for Porsche.

following year, 356 production began in Germany with a new product and expanded manufacturing capacity. Bernhard Blank, who had been granted distribution rights for Switzerland, was finding it difficult to scale up a sales organization beyond his own showroom. Whether that was from lack of ability or interest, Porsche management saw a need to replace him. Conveniently, the new company was now registered in Germany as Porsche KG, and legally it had no obligation under the old contract with Blank. But who would step in for Swiss sales?

On April 29, 1948, Automobil- und Motoren AG (AMAG) signed an agreement with the British military authorities, who ran the VW plant at the time, to import Volkswagens into Switzerland. The Zurich-based auto company had been founded by Walter Häfner in 1945 and by the end of 1948 had already brought over 1,600 VWs into the country. Häfner set up dealerships around Switzerland, along with repair centers, and made sure his customers (relatively well off compared to other countries) were happy with their cars. His sales manager was Hans Stanek, an enthusiastic Swiss racer who admired the new Porsche. His boss, however, was not interested in sports cars, although he had been instrumental in placing large orders for the VW Type 14A, a convertible to be built by Hebmüller in 1949. It is certain that Stanek's ongoing prodding led to AMAG having a conclave with Ferry Porsche and Albert Prinzing at the 1951 Geneva show. It's very likely that Heinz Nordhoff, now the VW boss, encouraged the marriage as well. A few weeks later, on April 5, a document was finalized making AMAG the official Porsche importer. Porsche had high hopes for the new arrangement, planning for fifty cars to be sold in Switzerland in 1951. By the end of the year, seventy-eight cars would find new homes there, and sales would steadily increase over the years that followed.

SUPPORT IN SWEDEN

In Sweden, Scania-Vabis was one of the first companies to handle Porsche outside Germany. The truck and industrial engine firm became the Swedish general agent for Volkswagen in 1948 and, following that, handled the sale of several Gmünd models. Reflecting the number of auto enthusiasts in the country, a June 1950 rally was initiated to span three days and some 1,400 miles, starting in the south near the sea at three locations. The Swedish Royal Automobile Club offered cash prizes in several classes, and two new steel 356s were entered, along with one Gmünd-built coupe.

Enthusiasm for the new marque brought German enthusiasts to Sweden, with an opportunity to put their new Porsches to the test there in competition. Completing speed stages, hillclimbing, and long distances over gravel roads, all three Porsches made it to the finish line at Kiruna, well beyond the arctic circle. Count Konstantin "Tin" Berckheim's coupe took third overall, the cabriolet was eleventh, and the Gmünd car ninth. More important, in their 1,100cc class, the two Stuttgart cars finished first and fourth. The women's class was taken by Countess Cecilia Koskull in her aluminum Gmünd coupe. These were the very first wins for Porsche in international competition—a modest beginning to decades of dominance in motorsport.

NO TURNING BACK

After five hundred units had been built by Reutter by March 21, 1951, a second order was placed with the firm and a new numbering system was put in place. Coupes built from early April began with chassis #10531. Cabriolets had a separate series beginning with #10001. Gläser/Heuer cars were numbered from #10351. Also in April, four of these new Porsches, two coupes and two cabriolets, were sent to the International Automobile Exhibition, for the first time held in Frankfurt. The exposure was so successful that by June, orders were backlogged at the factory. On September 20, 1951, Reutter celebrated a milestone: its one thousandth Porsche built. Of these, 40 percent were sold outside Germany.

As 1951 came to a close, extensive testing had been done on problem areas, but solving the issues was like playing whack-

Two new 356s took part in the Swedish Midnight Sun Rally: a coupe driven by Count Konstantin von Berckheim and a cabriolet by Count Günther von Hardenberg. Accompanying them were Prince Joachim Fürstenberg and his brother Fritzi.

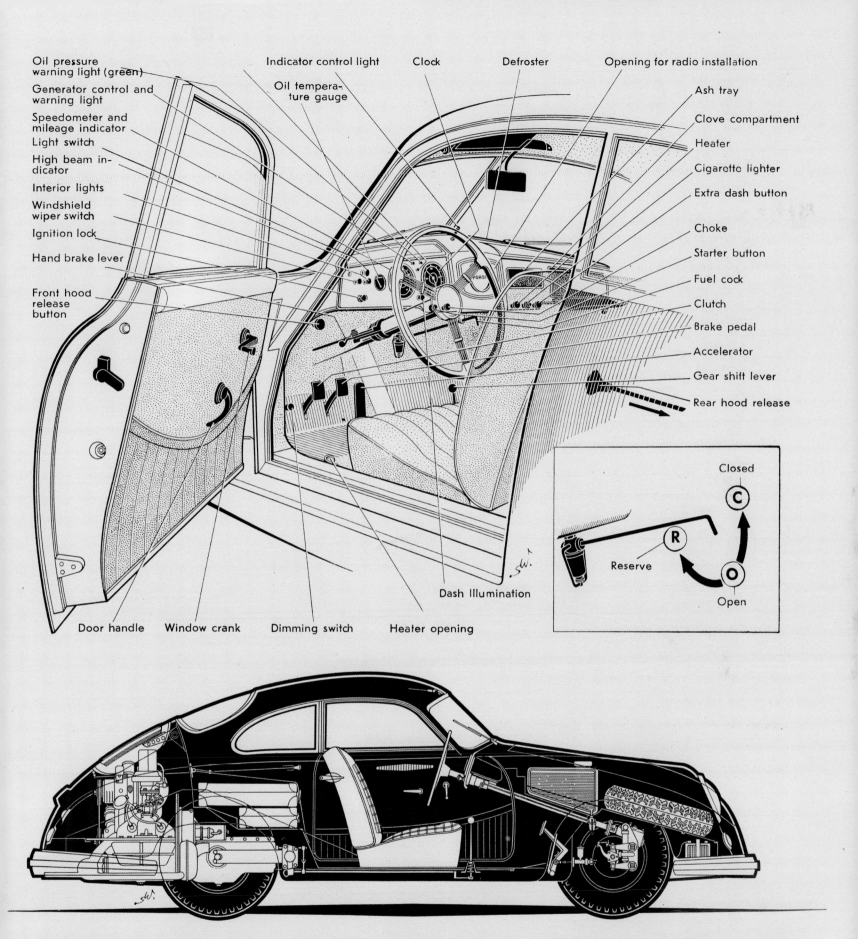

Oil pressure warning light (green)

Generator control and warning light

Speedometer and mileage indicator

Light switch

High beam indicator

Interior lights

Windshield wiper switch

Ignition lock

Hand brake lever

Front hood release button

Indicator control light

Oil temperature gauge

Clock

Defroster

Opening for radio installation

Ash tray

Clove compartment

Heater

Cigarette lighter

Extra dash button

Choke

Starter button

Fuel cock

Clutch

Brake pedal

Accelerator

Gear shift lever

Rear hood release

Dash Illumination

Door handle

Window crank

Dimming switch

Heater opening

Closed

C

R

Reserve

O

Open

TOP: From a 1951 owner's manual, an illustration of the controls. Conspicuous in its absence is a tachometer. The fuel cock would be used throughout the 356, with one position opening a "reserve" from the bottom of the tank—convenient since the early cars had no fuel gauge, either. Another position would turn the supply off, especially handy if the car was parked nose up on a hill, where gravity could allow gas to flood the carburetors.
BOTTOM: A Siegfried Werner phantom view of the car from the side shows the spare tire was mounted in a way that precluded using the trunk for bags; thus a system of straps and specially shaped luggage was employed in the rear seat.

The first International Automobile Exhibition (IAA) in Frankfurt/Main from April 19 to 29, 1951. From left: Ferry Porsche in conversation with Dr. Theodor Heuss (president of West Germany, center); Walter Kolb (mayor of Frankfurt am Main); and Heinrich Nordhoff (general director of the Volkswagen plant).

a-mole. Noise was one concern, and solutions included foam, rubber, tar paper, jute pad and carpet, and a Teroson spray coating. Climate control was another; over the years drivers have described the heat in a Porsche as like having a cocker spaniel breathe on your ankle. The ducts carrying warm air were revised in diameter to promote better flow, and dash defroster vent slits were lengthened. Real heat was still several years away, when German law would mandate enclosed heat exchangers.

In the chassis, new rear telescoping shock absorbers were planned but had to wait until hub carrier supplies from VW were available. A tachometer, driven by gears and a cable from the engine oil pump, was offered to replace the dashboard clock. In the rear interior, the luggage floor was lowered, and later, seat backs were provided that folded down to a luggage shelf. Several smaller changes were made, such as hooded instruments, and other options became available, such as a steering-wheel extension. Additional problems were recognized, but the engineers and the accountants had to wait to implement them. As would be the case for years to come, improvements came in an evolutionary manner, although there were big annual announcements as well, and 1952 would see some significant changes as Porsche moved away from its VW roots.

The 356 was evolving incrementally as can be seen by comparing this black 1951 Reutter-built cabriolet with its 1952 counterpart, built by Heuer/Glaser. Many changes took place under the skin, and not necessarily at a new model year—a process that would continue throughout the 356 series.

4

BUILDING CARS, BUILDING A NAME

At the beginning of 1951 Porsche KG was contractually obligated to Stuttgarter Karosserie Reutter & Co. for the building of a fixed number of cars and parts. By the summer the companies had reached their production goals, and negotiations were underway for a further run of bodies, pressed parts, and superstructures to be shipped to Heuer for convertibles. Reutter was very interested in keeping its workers on the job without slowdowns and suggested several ways to meet the price concessions that Porsche finance men were requesting. An agreement was finally reached in October 1951 with an order for one thousand more cars; after the first two hundred, a new model would be introduced. That model would be ready in March 1952 and encompass several significant changes and many smaller ones, implemented over a period of months.

FOUR SEATS IN A 356: TYP 530

In November 1951 Porsche requested bids from Reutter—under strict secrecy—to construct prototypes of an extended-wheelbase coupe and, later, a cabriolet, intended to seat four people. The wheelbase was up from the 356's 2,100mm to 2,400mm.

Both cars, equipped with a Typ 527 1500 engine and 280mm brakes, were thoroughly tested and, we can assume, found roadworthy. Being market-worthy was another matter, however. By the middle of 1952 the "new" Porsche 356s were selling well, and it was decided that complicating assembly matters at Reutter with another model would not be worth the projected sales. The four-seater idea was quietly dropped, although the concept would reappear regularly for decades.

A NEW MODEL YEAR

Visual changes on the "new" 356, introduced in early 1952, included a single-piece windshield, bent in the middle and curved at its outside edges, to replace the two-piece glass with a center divider. A bright surround gave the windshield a dressy touch, and the same was added to the rear window. Rear side windows were now hinged to open slightly at the back. The hood handle was enlarged and given a hollow center for easier gripping. Bumpers were extended outward slightly and given new, stronger mounting points and trim. The spare tire was now stored at an angle in the nose rather than almost flat, allowing some luggage space. The 3.25-inch-wide, 16-inch-diameter wheels were now slotted, their first use being on the 1500-equipped cars. "Baby moon" hubcaps continued in use, and most wheels were painted body color. Slotted aluminum "turbo" trim rings were an option.

Inside, a rear seat back could fold forward to increase luggage area there. Door caps were now metal instead of

TOP: The 530 coupe's body on the extended chassis had longer doors, with the rear edge of the door window slightly swept back. The entire roof, rear deck, and fenders were modified to create smoothly flowing lines, and the rear side windows were elongated to match the contours. Current-style underbody bumpers were used with small overriders. Inside, the rear seat area had better bottom cushions and more space, with seat backs that could fold down for luggage.
ABOVE: The cabriolet version of the four-seater had significant changes from the coupe. Bumpers were raised and now were extended beyond the lower edge of the body, with larger overriders. The door windows were frameless, and the rear side windows could be lowered like on the American convertibles. A new dashboard featured a hood over the instruments. The windshield was a single curved expanse with no bend in the middle, although to disguise the fact, a rib was placed over the glass in the center.

wood—painted to complement the interior colors—and chrome hinged door pulls were added. Door panels and window winders were slightly changed. Many other changes, not all visible to the eye, were put in place to address heating, weather sealing, interior trim, hood hinging, noise, and mechanical issues. The Porsche was seen as a premium automobile, and its price reflected that, but after building a thousand cars there were still problem areas to be addressed.

By late summer 1952 the steel drum brakes of the VW were dropped in favor of cast-aluminum drums that were lighter and larger—by 30mm in diameter, to 280, and 10mm in width, to 40—with integral wheel studs. On the outer perimeter two ribs helped dissipate heat, while inside a steel liner was shrunk into place for brake-shoe friction. The center was machined for steel ball-bearing races.

Anticipating all of those changes, Reutter took a week of holiday in April to adjust, then production slowly ramped back up. In October one of the new changes required a further pause, as Porsche was having trouble bringing its new synchromesh gearbox online.

Built in April 1952, #10267 is one of the last split-window cabriolets. Demonstrating that changes were made on the fly, this interim car went to Max Hoffman in New York. In mode (fashion) gray with blue leather, it had new bumpers that were not finalized in production for a few more months. The two large dash gauges were not yet recessed or hooded. The 1500 engine size is not noted on the rear script; Hoffman took the large engine only.

The VW cast-iron brake drum was replaced by a larger aluminum drum with cooling ribs and pressed-in wheel studs. This factory poster shows an antiroll bar, which came later.

PORSCHE *Suspension*

PORSCHE's famous torsion bar suspension is unequalled in automotive history. Forget costly maintenance and complicated adjustments. Fast acting, positive, torsion bars give 100% wheel contact with the road at all times. The results to you are — a smooth ride, unsurpassed handling ease, and greatly increased safety qualities. The torsion suspension is one reason why PORSCHE is years ahead!

PERFECT-YET SIMPLE

SYNCHRONIZING GEARS

A long-awaited switch from the VW "crash box" to a transmission synchronized in all gears was made in early 1952, solving several problems. The 1500 Super engine was putting out torque and horsepower that stressed the VW box beyond its original design. Gear ratios available were limited; racers were constrained in choosing combinations. Most importantly, although the ability to double-clutch and smoothly shift the unsynchronized gears was a badge of honor among Porsche drivers, the crude VW sliding-gear transmission was becoming unacceptable for a premium automobile. The answer came from an in-house designer.

Porsche engineer Leopold Schmid joined Porsche in 1941. He had worked on transmission projects from the Kübelwagen to the Maus tank, and beginning in Gmünd in 1948 he had created a synchromesh system for the Cisitalia racer. For the 356, he adapted it to fit within the existing VW magnesium

With new synchros in forward gears taking more space, reverse was moved to the nosepiece (left) of the VW split case.

So einfach im Aufbau ist das vollsynchronisierte Viergang-Getriebe, das von der GETRAG für die verschiedenen PORSCHE-Typen serienmäßig gefertigt wird.

GETRAG

GETRIEBE- UND ZAHNRADFABRIK GMBH · LUDWIGSBURG/WÜRTT.

Getrag refined its manufacturing capabilities and became a key supplier to Porsche for many years. Shown are the double rubber mounts used in 1955. *Christophorus* magazine carried many supplier ads like this one.

Leopold Schmid (left), Erwin Komenda, and Karl Rabe.

housing. His creation was a compact circular clutch unit with internal chamfered gears and split balk rings that would, through friction, match revolutions between the input and output. With new constant mesh internals and modified machining, these clutch assemblies would all fit—except the reverse gears, which had to be moved to a new nosepiece. The new transmission, Typ 519, was complete on paper in late 1951, and a convenient supplier a few kilometers north in Ludwigsburg was commissioned to build the gearboxes and provide completed units to Porsche.

Getriebe und Zahnradfabrik Hermann Hagenmeyer AG (Getrag) in Ludwigsburg was founded when a twenty-one-year-old accountant bought the Pfeiffer gear company in 1935. Young Hermann Hagenmeyer had no technical experience, but he knew enough to let the engineers of his sixty-person company make product decisions. Known as a maker of motorcycle transmissions, the company flourished through the war, but afterward it was restricted by the Allies to making small consumer goods such as meat grinders. A chance to return to large-scale manufacturing (and profits) came with Porsche's order in 1951. Unfortunately, Getrag's ability to produce consistent-quality gearboxes was lacking at the time. With few alternatives available Porsche decided to bring assembly, along with testing, in-house.

One of the mechanics who drove tens of thousands of test miles in 519-equipped 1500 Porsches was twenty-four-year-old Rolf Wütherich, the second employee of the new racing department. He and several other drivers proved the new system could work. Getrag may have succeeded had the company been given more time, but that was something Porsche did not have. Ironically, Getrag in the following years became one of the largest producers of automobile transmissions in the world, including for Porsche. The patented Porsche/Schmid synchro system would also conquer the automotive world for decades. In the next few years alone, Getrag would design gearboxes for several European automakers to be used in street cars, race cars, and trucks, from three to eight speeds. Eventually license fees on the over two hundred patents granted would bring in millions for the company, and the system was used by Porsche in its own transmissions until 1987.

In the August 1952 Liège–Rome–Liège enduro Polensky's #81 Porsche took an overall win on Dunlop tires. The iconic photo was used in this poster, with versions in different languages, hastily produced by Richard von Frankenberg and Erich Strenger.

ON THE TRACK AND ON THE ROAD

By 1952 automobile racing in Europe was back in a big way. Public attention was on the Mille Miglia, Le Mans, and Marathon de la Route, the Liège–Rome–Liège Rally. A February rally at Sestriere in the snowy Italian Alps saw two 356s finish second and third. At the Nürburgring Eifelrennen in April Porsches had a class of their own, with twenty-five entrants. There was no shortage of enthusiastic Porsche owners there. In the main sports race, two Glöckler Porsches took the 1.5 and 1.1 class wins.

At the Porsche "Factory" three more aluminum 356 SL cars were prepared for the 24-hour race in 1952.

In May there was a single works entry for the Mille Miglia Grand Touring class: an aluminum Gmünd coupe, now producing about 70 horsepower. Driving was shared by two titled gentlemen, Counts Giovanni Lurani and Tin Berckheim, who managed a class win despite having to finish the race in third gear. Privateer entries included a 1500 and two 1,100cc steel cars, one of the latter driven by Prince Paul von Metternich and Count Wittigo von Einsiedel, also taking class honors. Another 1.5-liter car with Helmut Polensky rolled but

valiantly returned to the fray after some impromptu bodywork, though a transmission failure kept it from finishing.

The 1952 June classic at Le Mans saw Gmünd coupes used once more. No. 51 with an 1,100cc engine didn't last, and No. 47, a "private" 1500, was disqualified at a pit stop. A third car was the No. 50 1100 coupe, with a reprise of the Veuillet/ Mouche team from the previous year. They finished eleventh overall and first, once again, in the 1,100cc class, covering ten more laps than in 1951. Porsche was now two for two at Le Mans.

OTTO MATHÉ

Born two years before Ferry Porsche, Austrian Otto Mathé trained as a mechanical engineer and began racing motorcycles at sixteen. Ten years later his right arm was paralyzed in a fall. Undeterred, he returned to racing; he would go on to develop lubrication products that improved engine life and open an automotive machine shop postwar. He also invented a single-hand ski binding. He purchased the Typ 64 that Ferry Porsche had sent to Italy for a cosmetic refresh as well as a 356/2 coupe that had been used for testing at Gmünd. It was his occasional rally car but was often used to tow his Fetzenflieger, a mongrel racer he built in 1952 from Porsche and VW bits. First with a 1,500cc Porsche engine and later a four-cam, the single-place car could switch from open wheel to fenders in minutes. Mathé campaigned it in hillclimbs, in dirt road races, and on frozen lakes—almost always winning. Like so many others, his connection with Porsche was mutually beneficial, bringing excellent publicity to the company.

At the Monterey Historic Races in 1982 Otto showed and drove his Typ 64 to the delight of the crowd.

In 1947 Ferry Porsche had the remaining Typ 64 restored in Italy, with the letters Porsche on its nose. It was sold to Mathé in 1949, who owned and raced it for decades.

At the 1953 International Austrian Alpenfahrt, Otto Mathé flogs his Gmünd coupe through the mountains.

On a frozen Alpine lake Mathé (center, tassel cap) readies his four-cam-powered Fetzenflieger in open-wheel configuration. A quick change to fenders could be made with the pieces he carried on a trailer behind the tow car, his Gmünd coupe.

In the 1952 Marathon de la Route, over four days and some 3,500 kilometers, the factory entered a 1,500cc aluminum coupe that won outright at the hands of Helmut Polensky and Walter Schlüter. Private entrants swelled the ranks of Porsches in the first ten places: third, fourth, ninth, and tenth overall. The company was quick to make promotional fodder from a photo at the event.

PORSCHES BEYOND GERMANY

Auto shows on the continent continued to be important places to show off new cars. In January 1952 Ferry Porsche and Albert Prinzing visited the Brussels show and met with their Belgian importer, Pierre D'Ieteren. D'Ieteren Frères began as a coach-building firm in 1805 and by the turn of the century was making auto bodies. In the 1930s it began importing Pierce-Arrow, Auburn, and Studebaker, then assembling the latter from supplied parts. In 1948 the company contracted to be the Belgian Volkswagen distributor, and soon thereafter for Porsche as well. The connection with Porsche would prove important in the future, for building as well as selling cars.

MAX SELLS THE SIZZLE

Despite Max Hoffman's enthusiasm, the road to success in the United States was full of obstacles, not the least of which was the price. A small four-cylinder, air-cooled, rear-engined car with a strange shape was not an easy sell to people who were used to Fords and Plymouths—and for the $4,000 it took to buy the car from Stuttgart, they could have both of those sedans and change. But servicemen returning from Europe were bringing back cars unlike any Chevy they had driven at home. MGs and Jaguars from England paved the way, and 1950 was just the beginning of a wave of foreign cars that would swell over the United States in years to come. Maxie, as Hoffman was known in the trade, recognized that the Porsche automobile—with its "jewel-like finish," as his advertising copy put it—had a feel of quality that could justify the price to those who appreciated a well-designed and well-executed piece of machinery. Although the early cars seem crude and fragile by today's standards, they consistently outperformed larger, more powerful machines on the racetracks, often with Hoffman himself at the wheel.

Ever the matchmaker, he made a suggestion to his friend Richard Hutchinson, a vice president of Studebaker. Hoffman could see that the postwar feeding frenzy would soon end in the U.S. car market, and tiny Studebaker would be unable to compete with the Big Three. He also sensed an almost unlimited demand for a small, efficient VW-type car. His idea was to have Studebaker market something the Big Three didn't have—an "American Volkswagen"—and who better to design such a vehicle than Porsche?

Max Hoffman was an early distributor for VW in the United States, but his efforts were half-hearted in spite of upbeat advertising.

Max Hoffman and Ferry Porsche in South Bend, Indiana, with the Typ 530 brought for demonstration.

BUSINESS IN AMERICA

Ferry Porsche came to the United States in December 1951, his first trip across the ocean since 1937. He was able to visit the Hoffman Motors showroom, where he was suitably impressed by Hoffman's style and marketing savvy. The trip was necessitated by a short-notice appointment with the Mid-American Research Corporation (MARCO) in Kansas City, which was interested in developing a lightweight truck for "vertical envelopment operations," i.e., deployment by helicopter. A similar idea came from the West Coast.

The next spring Porsche was contacted by Wendell Fletcher, whose California-based aviation company had plans to produce an amphibious jeep for the U.S. Army. Using a number of Porsche components, it would be a large enough project to justify another trip to the United States, which would include a visit to the Studebaker plant in South Bend, Indiana.

The May visit with Fletcher Aviation was only mildly successful. Fletcher's idea was to provide the U.S. Army with the small utility vehicle it wanted, one that could ford streams and was light enough to be carried by an airplane. In the end, the army declined to pursue the project, but Fletcher's sponsorship of Porsche's 1954 Carrera Panamericana effort was a side benefit, typical of Porsche management, who always looked for financial help in their racing.

On the most important part of the trip, Hoffman drove with the group in his Cadillac from New York to Indiana, where the plans for a new Porsche-designed small car were shown to Studebaker management. There were meetings at South Bend and a show-and-tell with a Typ 530 sedan the group had brought from Germany. According to Hoffman, the demonstration rides were not impressive, but Max the salesman helped create a contract between Studebaker and Porsche that would consume three years of time but add some half million dollars to Porsche's coffers.

There's an irony that Hoffman recognized a gap in the marketplace for a simple and inexpensive small car. He had

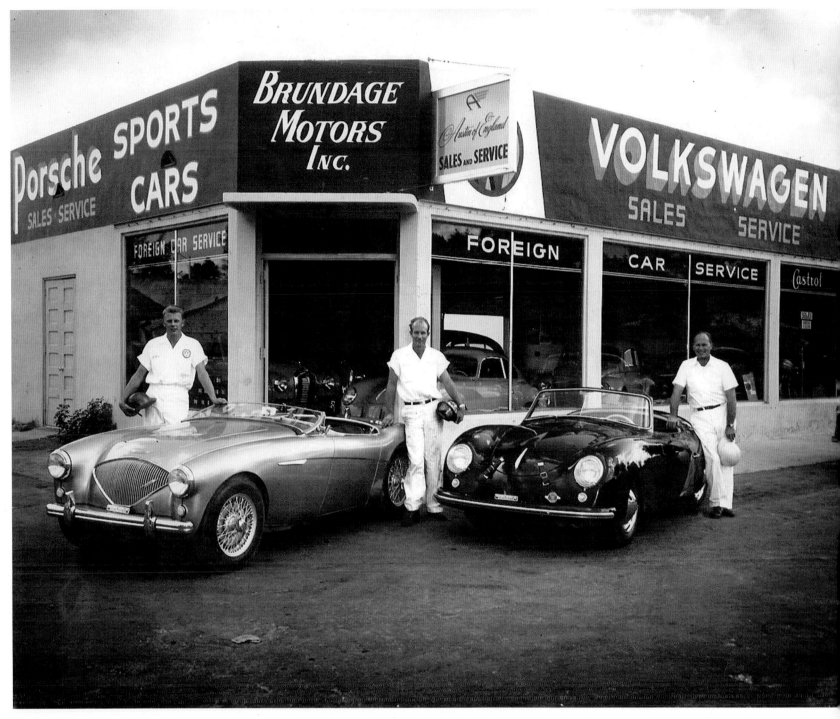

Brumos began as Brundage Motors, an outgrowth of the family hardware store in Florida. The America Roadster in steel is shown here at the dealership in Miami. The company became a VW distributor and, later, Porsche distributor for the Southeast United States in Jacksonville.

become the VW importer for the eastern states in 1950 after VW itself had been able to sell only two cars in the United States. But VW chief Heinz Nordhoff became disappointed in Hoffman's attitude; Max considered the VW cheap and hardly worth the effort, and not many cars were selling. "His strategy for moving VWs through his warehouse was more akin to extortion than a marketing plan," historian Sean Cridland notes. "If [dealers] wanted more Porsches, Jaguars or whatever else, they had to take more VWs." In 1954 VW set up its

own entity, Volkswagen of America, and approached Hubert Brundage, an enthusiastic VW dealer in Florida, to take Hoffman's place in the Southeast. Already a Porsche dealer with a racing team, Brundage Motors successfully took on the Beetle, expanded its Porsche business, and moved to Jacksonville. In September 1959 the company, now called Brumos, became the Porsche distributor for Florida, Georgia, and the Carolinas in America. In the meantime its racing efforts with Porsches and connections with the factory were increasing.

STUDEBAKER BY PORSCHE

Richard Hutchinson was vice president of Studebaker and through Max Hoffman was the key player in creating a contract for Porsche to design a small car for his company, a "VW for America." In another ironic twist to the VW saga, Hutchinson had secured import rights for the Beetle just after the war, but his bosses at Studebaker emphatically said no. In 1952, by the time the engineers in Zuffenhausen began work on the project, designated Typ 542, their brief had changed to a larger, front-engine, conventional design. Porsche proposed a V-6 with a 120-degree angle, compact and with a mixed cooling system: finned cylinder heads were cooled by a round front fan, and liquid-cooled cylinders with a separate radiator in the ducting and a heater core in the car. By August 1952 drawings and a model of the body were ready to show Studebaker. Ferry was accompanied on a trip to America by chief engineer Karl Rabe. While at sea, news came of Anton Piëch's death from a heart attack. Unable to return for his brother-in-law's funeral, Ferry and the group sailed on toward America and the opportunities that lay ahead.

With approval of the plans from Studebaker, work continued, including the design of a water-cooled engine. Both

Typ 542L (*Luft*) had air-cooled heads.

Typ 542L (air cooled) and 542W (water cooled) used aluminum pistons in an iron crankcase and heads. The 90mm bore and 80mm stroke gave 3,054cc, or 186 cubic inches. Overhead valves opened via pushrods from a cam in the engine's V, below a manifold with a single Stromberg carb. Electrical and ignition systems were also of American origin. Horsepower ranged from 96 to 106 in the mid–3,000 rpm range. A three-on-the-tree transmission was sent from Indiana, but Porsche gave the car all-independent suspension—way ahead of the curve in design for an American car.

In 1953 Reutter built a prototype "unibody" that was two pieces connected at the firewall. Studebaker's production process involved moving unfinished automobiles via railroad cars, standing on end, and the front section was only added at the final assembly. Erwin Komenda's four-door shape was mildly interesting, but nothing like the Raymond Loewy designs for the newest Studebakers. It was painted and trimmed with mechanicals installed by early 1954, and testing took place over the summer. One of the Studebaker engineers who came to Europe for assessment was Klaus von Rücker, a former BMW man who had risen at Studebaker to assistant head of R&D. He would later join the Porsche team.

In November 1954 the finished prototype auto, engines, and associated parts were shipped to South Bend. Studebaker, however, was in dire financial straits after declining sales the previous two years. There was no money to bring the new model to production, and the company was shortly thereafter absorbed into the Packard Motor Car Company. Though the project was a dead end for Studebaker, it was an expressway to success for Porsche.

Ferry Porsche and his designers had put on paper what they believed the American market could truly use: a small car with a rear-mounted, air-cooled 2.0-liter engine. Sketches and drawings were made available to Studebaker, but it was too late. This concept, Typ 633, never got past paper drawings

The air-cooled engine installed.

Erwin Komenda's design for a two-part unibody was built by Reutter

The finished prototype at Schloss Solitude outside Stuttgart.

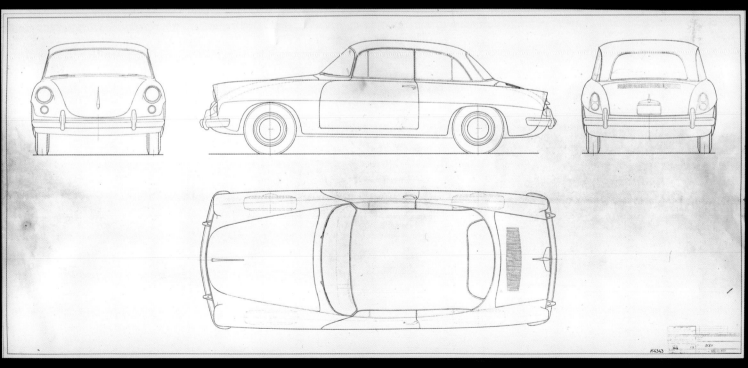

Porsche's idea for a real "American VW" was too late for struggling
Studebaker.

Werk II nears completion in the fall of 1952. The cars in Reutter's repair area include an America Roadster.

A SPACE RACE

Porsche's use of space in the Reutter compound in Zuffenhausen had always been considered temporary. In 1951, as the Korean War dragged on, the Americans were making no moves to vacate the original Porsche buildings (Werk I), so the company began plans for a second factory building. Unimproved land was available adjacent to the Reutter shops, but development would require cooperation with the city of Stuttgart. Discussions took place, and a purchase agreement was eventually made. A local architect, Rolf Gutbrod, was hired to design the building. As 1951 ended, all was in place except the money to go forward. That all changed when Studebaker's first payments began to arrive after a contract was signed in the summer of 1952. With much of the building material already on site, work began in earnest. It was a simple and efficient design, attractive in a modern way and, most important, well suited to the company's needs. By late fall 1952 the building

was almost complete, and by December 1 the 356 bodies from the Reutter Augustenstrasse plant were being finished in the new space. Engineering, sales, and management were in new offices by early 1953.

Just meters away was the Reutter Werk II main complex, and as Porsche people vacated their makeshift quarters there and in adjacent outbuildings, space opened up for more body-building capacity. Four days after Porsche officially moved to its new building, Reutter management discussed moving all 356 body production to Zuffenhausen from Augustenstrasse in Stuttgart, some 10 kilometers away. Cabriolets were already being finished at the Zuffenhausen Reutter shops, and with Porsche final assembly now comfortably streamlined in a new building, it was clear that demand for bodies would increase. A decision was made to build a new paint shop and relocate the repair shop and some other departments, effectively expanding the Zuffenhausen factory. Construction began in late 1952, and by September the following year all 356 body production was moved there.

CREATING COUPES AND CABS

A large measure of efficiency had now been brought to the manufacturing process, with body construction carried out directly adjacent to Porsche's final assembly area. Reutter workers pressed scores of raw sheet-metal pieces into shapes that were then welded into a chassis assembly with a combination of gas and resistance electric spot welding, all in dedicated jigs for alignment. A heavy tube for the rear torsion bars and a twin tube assembly for the front suspension became part of the unit. Body panel sections were added in more alignment jigs; panel gaps and body seams were finished by adding lead, then filing and sanding. Hand planishing with a

LEFT: Reutter upgraded its Zuffenhausen works, including the paint shop, for 1953.
BELOW: The Porsche/Reutter complex in 1956. At left center is Porsche Werk I, built in 1938. The dark-roofed building with the smokestack is the main Reutter assembly area, with Porsche Werk II at right center. Its angled roof sections let in natural light.

hammer to smooth surfaces was common. Removable parts (doors, hood, deck lid, and bumpers) were carefully fitted to the body, then each stamped with the last two or three digits of the serial number and removed to be painted separately.

Priming, undercoating, and painting took place in the new paint shop, then each body—with bumpers, doors, and lids now reinstalled—was wheeled on a dolly to receive its glass, interior and exterior trim, instruments, wipers, and lights. Upholstery was created on site in the Sattler department. The nitrocellulose lacquer was polished twice; any imperfections could be resprayed and blended by polishing. Door and lid alignment were checked, along with paint finish and a careful inspection of the interior. One small complication was in building cars for the U.S. market: sealed beam headlights for these were left out, to be installed at the dealer in America.

At that point the bodies were moved across an alley to Porsche's new building, where they were lifted onto special three-wheeled dollies. Each dolly held two large angled trays of smaller parts, from torsion bars to shift rods. Larger components were strategically placed near the line, mostly preassembled, including transmissions containing the mounting hoop, brake drums, cables, and lines. With an assembly line of six to eight cars, each was pushed along by hand as it received its steering components, suspension, brakes, engine, and transmission. With the latter, three men would muscle the unit into place, one of them directly under the car. Engines were installed with a floor jack. The wiring harness was connected, fluids added, seats installed, and adjustments made, and a new Porsche rolled out into the sunlight. Its next stop was not a transport truck to a dealer, however. Each shiny new car was taken for a test drive, a heavy cloth "*Steinschlagschutzshulle*" protecting its nose. Only after several inspectors had checked all systems and the car had been given a final polish was it ready for delivery. The same process would carry on though the years of the 356 and well into the 911 era.

ABOVE: Suspension parts accompanied each car on trays under the three-wheeled dolly. Transmission, engine, and tires were stored near the line. Seats were installed near the end.
BELOW: The Reutter Sattler department built seats, door panels, and other interior appointments.

Space was a continual problem at Reutter, and in good weather working outside in an alley was not a bad idea. Here the extensive use of lead to fill seams is shown.

LEFT: Shortly after moving into the new Werk 2, there seemed to be plenty of space.

ABOVE: By later in 1953, however, assembly areas for all the components were in place. Cylinder heads were machined, assembled and measured before mounting in an engine. Brake assemblies were put together, and steering boxes were broken in on a machine that turned the shafts back and forth for hours. These and other sub-assemblies were readied for the line of seven or eight cars at a time.

THE 1953 LINEUP

By the time the new plants for both Reutter and Porsche were in operation, a new model year was in place and several significant changes had been made to the cars, officially available from October 1952. Immediately obvious to an observer were bumpers that extended out from the body. A decorative strip with rubber insert, along with bumper guards, was now standardized for both Europe and American exports. The "bent" windshield carried over, but the outer curved edges of the glass were a regular source of customer complaints about distortion. Cabriolet rear glass remained glass until later in 1953, when a larger plastic window was introduced. Front turn signals were moved outward, just under the headlights. In the rear, two round "beehive" taillights were placed above a reflector on each side. Slotted steel wheels were standard, with round chromed hubcaps and optional aluminum vented trim rings.

Inside, a new two-spoke steering wheel from VDM carried a horn button with the Porsche crest. A stalk on the left of the

Shift linkage was anything but direct. A sensitive touch was necessary with the "monkey motion" linkage. In this author's long-ago first encounter with a Porsche transmission, it was described to him as, "like stirring a spoon in a bowl full of snot."

Reutter coupe 50685 was an American-market car with a 1500S engine and deluxe appointments.

AN ALUMINUM ANOMALY

column now controlled the turn signals. A tachometer was optional to the right of the steering column, and a few other controls were moved. The synchromesh transmission's new nose made necessary a new shift lever and rod, with changes to the tunnel and "hump" covering the linkage below the rear seat. Being out of alignment vertically by some 80mm, the tunnel rod and trans shift rod required a complicated system of rods, joints, and hinges to connect. This and the later 356A connectors would earn the name "monkey motion" shifters for their complexity.

Reutter built a mysterious one-off 356 cabriolet in 1953 with a body of aluminum. The question of why and for whom seems to have been lost over the years, and the car's history is spotty, with only a record of a for-sale ad from England in the 1970s. Next seen in Germany years later, it was sold to an enthusiast who coordinated with the Porsche factory to restore the car, a six-year undertaking. A sensitive restoration was done, supervised by engineer Rolf Sprenger, and the car is back on the road today, looking good and probably going just a little faster than a comparable steel-bodied 356.

ENGINOLOGY: THREE FOR 1953

Engine choices in 1953 included 1100, 1300, and 1500, the latter now designated Typ 546. The "new" 1500 used a plain-bearing Alfing crankshaft and a VW cam but produced a respectable 55 horsepower at 4,400 rpm, just 5 less than the Hirth-crank Typ 527 it replaced. A hotter 1500S topped the line. An October 1952 Porsche bulletin to its European dealers noted, "We will deliver, on special request, a 1.5 liter Typ 528 Super engine with an output of 70 hp with Hirth crankshaft and Fuhrmann camshaft, for race drivers who take part in organized competition." Leaving no doubt, the bulletin listed a price of DM 1,100 for the S and stated, "We stress once again that, except for special cases, sale of this engine should be restricted to race drivers."

In September 1953 another new engine was added to the lineup, addressing the desire of owners to compete in 1,300cc racing classes. With the long-stroke roller crank already in stock, it was used with 74.5mm barrels and the "Fuhrmann" cam with an 8.2:1 compression ratio to produce 60 horsepower, 14 more than the existing 1300 Typ 506. This Typ 589 1300 would be the last iteration of a Porsche engine based on the VW two-piece case.

In this re-creation of a factory photo, the Typ 528 1500S is shown sans fan shrouding. A compensating "balance" tube connected the manifolds in front of the fan shroud. The 1500S engine numbers began with a 4.

MOVING FORWARD CAREFULLY

With a new factory and more overhead, the Porsche managers were now carefully counting their beans, and lengthy discussions took place both in-house and with Reutter to determine where costs could be shaved. Initial ideas involved using cheaper materials, deletion of window bright trim, painted side window frames, acrylic lacquer paint instead of high-quality nitrocellulose lacquer, and fixed rear side windows. Much of the impetus for cost cutting came from Max Hoffman, who was acutely aware that the Porsches he sold competed in the marketplace with larger sports cars of much higher horsepower and began to take only 1500-engined cars for the United States. While European buyers could mix and match equipment when ordering a car, that process was entirely too cumbersome for Hoffman, who offered either a "standard" or a "deluxe" model. The deluxe had leather and cloth seats (or all leather in cabriolet) and equipment such as a Hirschmann antenna, Telefunken radio, oil-temp gauge, windshield washer, passenger reclining seat, right sun visor, and jump seat back. Much of this was missing in the price-leader standard version, where the seats were vinyl and cloth, the upholstery was simpler, and in the door panels the backing was hardboard instead of aluminum. Both models wore the new bumpers with guards that Hoffman insisted on in order to deal with American traffic and parking habits. Mechanically, both were the same except in the engine bay. The standard Typ 546 1500 engine was described by the factory as "smoother at lower rpms and provides better acceleration

This 1500S "racing" engine came with instructions for changing the 40 PICB carb venturis and jets from "city" to "competition."

Reutter recliners were a new and welcome product.

than the previously delivered Typ 527." For the deluxe model, the Typ 528 with roller crank, Fuhrmann cam, 8.2:1 compression, and 70 horsepower was used. Remarkably, this was the same engine Porsche supposedly reserved only for racers in Europe.

Changes to the cars during 1953 were incremental, and many were not readily visible. Rubber transmission mounts and more sound-deadening material helped quiet the interior. Door pockets and coat hooks were added, and reclining seats (a Reutter patent from June 1952) gave driver and passenger more comfort. Color choices for 1953 were more limited than before; six for coupes and six for cabriolets. Interior choices were textured vinyl for coupes and leather with corduroy inserts. Cabs had leather with a choice of five top colors. Exterior, interior, and top color combinations were now standardized to a great extent, but a customer could have what they wanted, for a price.

MOVING INTO 1954

In April 1954 small chrome grilles were added just inboard from the front turn signals. A Porsche announcement read, "2 standard Bosch horns emit such a loud sound through the horn grilles that they are clearly audible to every truck about to be passed, despite even the loudest engine noise." On the steering wheel, a lower crescent ring "permits horn operation without requiring that the driver remove his hands from the steering wheel in a critical situation." The pedal assembly, which had been bolted to the floor from the earliest cars, was changed so that the angled arm for clutch and brake was now two pieces, "adjustable for every physique and leg length," according to Porsche. New for 1954 was a welcome addition for passengers: a dashboard grab handle. A windshield washer and fuel gauge were standard for the new cars.

Steel sunroofs appeared as a regular option from June 1954, although custom installations had been done earlier. Customers had expressed concerns that the coupe was too hot in summer, and Porsche did extensive measurement of temperatures on light- and dark-painted cars at different points with the sunroof closed and open. With confidence that it would be a popular option, a new brochure proclaimed, "Fresh air in no time" and "You don't just drive through nature, you are in nature and have caught the sun in the car." Golde Schiebedächer in Frankfurt supplied roof hardware that could slide the panel by hand, by cranked cables, or, later, by an electric motor. The first production steel sunroofs on Porsches were "bent" on their front edge to match the roof shape above the windshield.

In 1954 prices for a Porsche in Germany ranged from DM 11,400 ($2,715) for an 1,100cc coupe—with a DM 2,400 ($3,286) premium for the 1500S—to DM 15,800 ($3,761) for

In 1954 the 356 underwent a last incremental update before a big makeover the following year. The only obvious change was small horn grilles in front.

Competition Motors started out in a cinderblock garage but
expanded to these larger quarters by 1955. It was here that
James Dean prepped his 550 Spyder for a fateful drive to the
Salinas races in September, 1955.

the 1500S cabriolet. In New York, Hoffman Motors' list price was $4,284 for the 1500S coupe and $300 more for the cabriolet. A Jaguar XK120 with 160 horsepower could be had from Hoffman for $3,975. The Chevrolet Corvette's price dropped from $3,498 to $2,774 in 1954. Porsches were expensive.

THE BENEVOLENT TYRANT

Max Hoffman was racing Porsches himself, adding that depth of experience to his sales pitch for the cars he sold. He was a keen supporter of all the Porsche racers, and of course he had a lock on supplying them all with parts. Porsche dealers were required to buy all replacement parts from him; warranty work reimbursement would not be honored unless the parts came from New York, even bolts or washers. Racers would often improvise, but any OEM parts or factory special tools came from Hoffman Motors.

For the owner who wanted to do his own work, metric tools were hard to find, but Porsche provided a tool kit with each new car, and the owner's manual gave clear instructions for many normal procedures. Repair manuals were rare, although Porsche published comprehensive parts books and shop manuals beginning in about 1952, with updates and supplements as needed. They were all available, of course, through Hoffman.

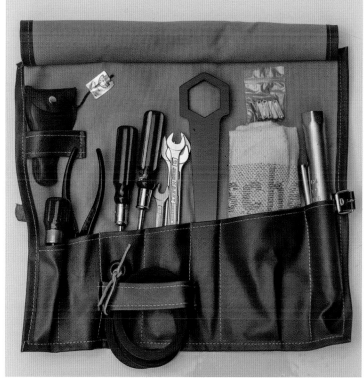

Tool kits came with all Porsches, allowing owners to do simple repairs. A tire gauge, a fan belt, and sometimes spark plugs were included. The specific tools and bag style changed over the years, but along with a detailed owner's manual, an owner could deal with most common problems.

THE WEST COAST MARKET

John von Neumann was of the Hoffman mold, the son of a well-to-do family that had fled Austria to America after the 1938 Anschluss. Arriving in New York in his late teens, he whetted his automobile appetite by visiting Hoffman's dealership in the city. He enrolled at New York University, then transferred to the University of Southern California, bringing his new wife, Eleanor, a Ziegfeld Follies dancer, with him. During wartime service in the army, he used his language skills in intelligence, and in 1945 he was back in Austria to aid in de-Nazification. He would have noticed the adaptable Kübelwagen at the time, as well as other VWs from the slowly rebuilding Wolfsburg works.

In postwar Los Angeles, "Johnny"—as he was to be known in his adopted country—drove a Jaguar SS100, got involved with amateur racing, and, along with friends, founded the California Sports Car Club. He sold imported sports cars with one of those friends, Roger Barlow, but after a year was persuaded in 1948 to open a car store in North Hollywood. Competition Motors was financed by another friend, Secondo Guasti Jr., whose father at one time owned the largest vineyard in California. It was a modest garage, selling MGs and Simcas and servicing them with the few manuals available at the time. Soon, however, Guasti's lawyers became concerned about liability issues, and von Neumann bought out his partner for a modest amount, becoming sole owner.

The MG TD was introduced in 1950, and von Neumann decided to promote the new car he was selling by racing it. In 1951 he visited Max Hoffman's dealership, where a ride in an 1,100cc 356 (and Max's consummate salesmanship) convinced

him to buy the car. Shortly after driving back to LA, he resold it (the first Porsche sale west of the Rockies) and began regular trips to New York for more cars, bringing Eleanor so they could take two cars back. As the volume of his sales grew, he discussed with Hoffman the idea of becoming a West Coast distributor of Porsche cars. By 1952 he was an official Porsche dealer, and the following year a VW distributor.

Porsche #356/2-063, one of the Gmünd "SL" racers Max Hoffman imported, went to von Neumann in early 1952. After conversion to an open car he made it a real competitor—and it would remain so for decades in many different hands. By this time von Neumann had a personal relationship with the factory and Ferry Porsche. He bought another racer directly from Zuffenhausen, the last aluminum America Roadster. When it got to California it was prepped for racing at Competition Motors and a young driver named Jack McAfee was tapped to drive for von Neumann's team. The first time out at Moffett Airfield in August 1953 McAfee won, swapping the lead with MG driver Ken Miles several times until Miles went out with clutch problems. Both drivers would go on to notable careers: Miles would drive Porsches and Ferraris and later famously bring the Shelby Cobra to prominence.

McAfee spent four years as a navy aviation mechanic and opened his own repair shop in Manhattan Beach. He was involved in dry-lake, drag, and sprint racing and was behind the wheel of a Ferrari at the 1952 Carrera Panamericana. He was a well-seasoned racer by the time he started driving Porsches, and during the 1950s he drove Spyders for John Edgar and Stan Sugarman along with Ferraris and other exotics.

Experienced racer Jack McAfee drove von Neumann's America Roadster at Moffett Airfield.

McAfee opened his own VW/Porsche dealership at 13323 Ventura Boulevard in Sherman Oaks. By the late 1950s he had a larger shop in Burbank.

In addition to racing, in 1952 at age twenty-nine he became the youngest-ever Porsche and VW dealer. Starting with a modest block garage in Sherman Oaks he expanded with a new building in Burbank, then a larger store 2 miles away near the Golden State Freeway, which operated until 1974.

John von Neumann didn't slow down, on the track or in his business. Replacing his red Gmünd roadster was one of the first Porsche Spyders. Car #550-03 made its way from the 1953 Carrera in Mexico back to America and to von Neumann, who painted it red and took it to the April 1954 Pebble Beach races, where he finished second in the 1.5-liter class behind an OSCA. Over the next two years he would expand his company's race activities but step back from driving Porsches himself, hiring Ken Miles and Richie Ginther to do so. Meanwhile, his distribution empire—which by 1955 included Southern California, Nevada, and Arizona—would be selling a sixth of Porsche's production by the late 1960s. Aided by his wife in running the business, and with behind-the-scenes financing and management by Sam Weill, the Porsche and VW business did very well.

In 1956 von Neumann purchased his first Ferrari and followed up by buying several more that he raced. He became a Ferrari distributor in 1957 and opened a dealership in Hollywood with Eleanor ostensibly in charge and Ginther as

manager. His adopted daughter Josie regularly raced some of the cars, and he switched from driving Porsches to mostly prancing horses in 1956. Max Hoffman, meanwhile, frowned upon the Ferrari business; it was one of the few European makes he didn't handle. Max was also muscling in on Johnny's West Coast turf, surreptitiously building a Porsche car and parts center in California. Disagreements led to a letter in July 1956 wherein Hoffman wrote to von Neumann, canceling his sub-distributorship. The latter quickly boarded a plane and was in Stuttgart to present his case to Ferry Porsche, pointing out his sales figures, racing results, publicity, and other efforts for the marque. The pipeline of Porsches and parts to California resumed in a week.

Trouble between John and Eleanor, who was seventeen years older, had been brewing for some time and resulted in a divorce in 1959. Eleanor got most of the Ferrari business, and Porsche mechanics who worked out of the Competition Motors shop in support of West Coast racers were moved to another dealership owned by Otto Zipper. Sam Weill took over management of the von Neumann Porsche and VW business. John was called in to take over the Brumos Porsche business after the death of Hubert Brundage in November 1964; he briefly owned the dealership and the distributorship for the Southeast, selling to

PORSCHE'S PRINTED MEDIUM

Richard von Frankenberg was not yet thirty when he became involved with Porsche in 1950. Born in Darmstadt in 1922, he went with his family during World War II to England, where he was introduced to journalism. On returning to Germany postwar, he combined a lifelong interest in cars with his technical studies and writing skills to become a press agent of sorts for the young Stuttgart carmaker. He developed sales material and, in 1951, a book about Porsche (written under the pen name Herbert W. Quint); he then went further in 1952 by creating a quarterly "Magazine for friends of the house of Porsche." *Christophorus* was named after the patron saint of travelers and provided customers and "friends" with news about the company, racing results, travel stories, technical information, and other pieces of interest to discerning readers. He worked closely with Erich Strenger, a young graphic artist he had met in 1950. The first issues were in German only, but beginning with #18 in 1955, English was added.

Strenger designed sales catalogues, driver's manuals, advertisements, and a great many posters that celebrated Porsche's racing victories. With a modern style that often incorporated colors or elements of the race's location, Strenger would prepare as much of a design as possible in advance, then add type and images after the event, producing posters sometimes in a day or two to be quickly distributed to dealers, workshops, and the public. In the 1950s it was Porsche's most important advertising scheme, and Strenger's skill ensured that it was effective.

Porsche's suppliers were also the company's sponsors for racing. Tire makers and oil companies promoted their successes along with Porsche on posters, and almost every vendor was expected to advertise in *Christo*, as the magazine was known.

Von Frankenberg was also an important and successful member of Porsche's racing teams, both in competition and in record runs in the early years. He retired from racing in 1960, and along with independent writing and even television work, he continued as editor of *Christo* until his untimely death in 1973. Strenger's excellent work for Porsche continued until his retirement in 1987.

ABOVE: Richard von Frankenberg.
TOP RIGHT: Erich Strenger in the 1960s.
RIGHT: Strenger was a talented painter as well as a graphic artist. This 1956 poster was printed in 4-color offset, then various text was applied with letterpress. As a showroom poster it carried just the word "Porsche." Over a few years it also touted victories at LeMans, the Mille Miglia, Rheims, and Senegal, in several languages.
FAR RIGHT: The first issue of *Christophorus* magazine.

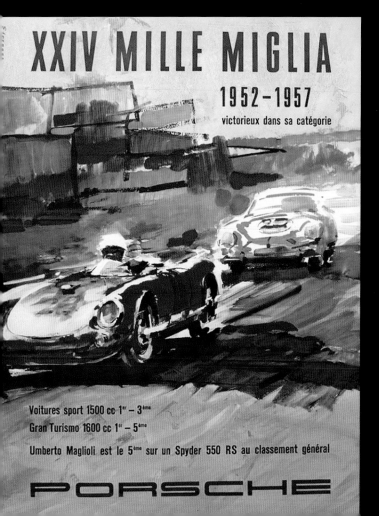

XXIV MILLE MIGLIA
1952 – 1957
victorieux dans sa catégorie

Voitures sport 1500 cc 1er – 3ème
Gran Turismo 1600 cc 1er – 5ème

Umberto Maglioli est le 5ème sur un Spyder 550 RS au classement général

PORSCHE

Christophorus
ZEITSCHRIFT FÜR DIE FREUNDE
DES HAUSES PORSCHE

Nr. 1 / 1952

Peter Gregg in 1965. He moved to Europe in 1965 and began other businesses in Ferraris, yachts, and charter jets. His auto business was eventually sold to Porsche and Volkswagen in 1971. He died in 2003 and is remembered as one of the most colorful and influential Porsche personalities in America.

PRIVATEER RACING

Porsche owners were nothing if not enthusiastic and took to competition at all levels. The company sponsored rallies for owners, including a 1953 event in Wiesbaden that included a hillclimb where, according to a participant, "Two cars got all messed, requiring a lot of body work." Overall, it was a genteel affair, however, with champagne and a handshake from Ferry Porsche at the end. Later, the factory hosted *Treffen* (meetings) in Europe, often welcoming Americans who were taking delivery of their cars in Stuttgart. The tradition carries on to this day with the Porsche Club of America.

A bit more serious were races at the Nürburgring, which often featured enough 356s to fill a one-make event. These were meant as a means to get to know the capabilities of your car rather than as fender-to-fender competition and were popular with American servicemen. The concept would continue for decades as clubs organized their own "driver's education" events. Owners also took part in serious competition, supported by the factory.

In November 1952 Mexico held the third Carrera Panamericana, a 2,000-mile multistage rally from Tuxtla Gutiérrez in the south to the U.S. border at Ciudad Juárez. For this third edition of the grueling, dangerous contest, Mercedes and Ferrari sent factory teams and their ace drivers. Porsche's presence was less dramatic, with a private coupe and cabriolet. Prince Alfonso von Hohenlohe-Langenburg, the importer for VW in Mexico, had just acquired rights to sell Porsches there as well. He imported the two cars for the race and oversaw the operation, riding as navigator as Tin Berckheim drove, but their coupe was out on the second day after an accident. Mechanic Herbert Linge, sent by the Porsche factory to prepare and maintain the cars, traveled with the Mercedes support group; in addition to many tire changes, he spent most of one night repairing a stuck valve in the cabriolet's engine. Linge then finished the race's last leg as Paul von Metternich's co-driver in a sprint that saw speeds of up to 112 miles per hour. It was a modest investment and a less-than-auspicious result, but in the next few years Porsche would take from the event not only class honors but a name synonymous with high-performance racing: Carrera.

Rallies like this gathering at Wiesbaden in 1953 were opportunities for owners to enjoy their cars in like company, and for Porsche to promote the brand and show off the newest models. Ferry Porsche himself greeted finishers.

ABOVE: Prince Paul von Metternich's cabriolet at the 1952 Carrera. Herbert Linge is in the back seat.

LEFT: Racing at the Nürburgring (and other tracks) was open to any 356 owner, and many took part in these sprints, often with enough entrants to have a one-make race.

Shown at the Porsche factory, the Speedsters were built with as much care as the coupes or cabriolets, and received slight modifications as the A series was introduced. Here a clear difference can be seen between the tall padded top of the cab and the simple Speedster top with no roll-up windows, which required plastic protection in transit to the dealer.

THE SPEEDSTER EXPANDS THE LINE

Growth for the fledgling Porsche car company was steady, with 1,303 cars built in 1952 by 158 employees and 1,978 cars in 1953 by 229 workers, including 50 in engineering, according to historian Dirk-Michael Conradt. He notes that 1954 production was down to 1,934 cars, although employment was up to 277. The American market was absorbing 40 percent of those cars at the time, mainly through the efforts of Max Hoffman. Given that he was the company's largest customer, Ferry Porsche and business manager Albert Prinzing were inclined to pay attention to Hoffman's suggestions, and something he felt was badly needed was a Porsche with a lower price tag. The new Austin-Healey 100 (so named for its ability to reach 100 miles per hour) was priced at $2,985. The MG TD was $2,250 and the Chevrolet Corvette was $2,774. The least expensive Porsche, a coupe, was about $3,500, and an open car had a $300 premium. Hoffman wanted something less expensive to sell, and his price point was $3,000. Another item on his wish list was a competition model for the everyman—something light and simple along the lines of the short-lived Typ 540 America Roadster. He was adamant about getting both things in a single car, and he even had a name for it: Speedster.

In the offices at Werk II in Zuffenhausen, there was skepticism about these ideas. The Porsche "*Limousin*," as the coupe was called, bore that name for a reason, with a hand-built finish and attention to detail throughout. The cabriolet included most options as standard, with a well-padded weatherproof top. Those two cars constituted the complete lineup, and although Porsche was experimenting with other models, signs pointed upmarket. Simpler and cheaper was just not in the Porsche playbook. However, bowing to marketing realities, Ferry Porsche reluctantly agreed to Hoffman's demands, with assurances from John von Neumann that a simple top or lack of a heater would not be a hindrance to buyers on the West Coast, the car's target market. Von Neumann had chopped the top off his Gmünd coupe, and it was seen as a template of sorts for what he and Hoffman wanted. The next move was to make it all work financially.

Mechanical components already existed, but a new body would be an expensive undertaking. Drawings were made, reusing the project number 540 from the America Roadster. In May 1954 discussions between Reutter and Porsche began, with the latter setting out parameters and a production drawing. A letter from Erwin Komenda to Reutter stated, "For the execution, it is intended that a majority of pressed parts of the outer and inner skin of the convertible will be retained, only transition parts on the side wall will require reworking." In reality, much more than that was changed, with the doors sloping downward to the rear and blending to a new rear cowl shape. A short, curved windshield would be removable; a simple folding top would retract into the body as deeply as possible; no rear seat would be provided; side windows would be plexiglass panels inserted by pegs; and interior appointments would be minimal, such as flat door panels. Archivist Frank Jung notes that Reutter gave a quote with a minimum purchase of two hundred units in twelve months, and an order was placed in July. Construction of a first prototype began, and three more were scheduled before the August holidays. Max Hoffman inspected the first one in late July and expressed his desire for two hundred more roadsters by year's end.

The actual number of cars that could be sold was still an unknown, however. While Ferry Porsche had expressed belief that one thousand would be needed, a formal order for this quantity was not issued until October, after several concessions by Reutter, which had already expended a great deal of money in tooling costs. Over the summer many details were changed, including one significant new element: a larger hood handle that would carry the Porsche crest for the first time. By fall, when series production began, the new model had evolved with unique attributes. A simple flat dashboard had two large dials—speedometer and tachometer—under a padded "eyebrow," flanking a small temperature gauge. Three warning lights indicated oil pressure, generator, and turn signal. The dash was padded on top, and a double gold spear across the right side framed the Porsche name. The key slot and separate starter

In 1954 Ferry Porsche had built the family company into a successful auto maker, but there were still challenges to come.

No heat ducts or defroster vest were built into the prototype or the first cars. Warning lights were separate, and a start button joined the keyed ignition. Speedometer and tach flanked a central oil gauge.

The Speedster prototype encompasses the shape and equipment of the production car, but trim is missing from the dash, sides, and rocker panels. At this stage Porsche may have been considering no door handles, à la Austin-Healey Sprite, for which it was necessary to reach into the car to open the door.

Speedster bucket seats were one piece but pivoted from the front on wooden frames above sliding rails.

Max Hoffman held a reception to announce his "brainchild" at his New York showroom.

button were on the right of the two-spoke steering wheel, with a grab bar at the far right. There was no gas gauge, windshield washer, air or defroster vents, sun visors, cigarette lighter, or place for a radio in the dash. On early cars, a crude fastener for the top required a leather strap to be wedged between slotted brackets at the windshield. After November a hook and toggle latch was used.

The bucket seats were light and simple, with thin upholstery over aluminum frames, hinged at the front on a wooden base with sliders. Carpet and vinyl covered the rear area, which was smaller than in a cabriolet. Rather than a fitted trunk as provided for cabriolet buyers, a snap-on flat tonneau covered the entire area behind the seats. Door panels were plain vinyl, with mounting screws showing and a single latch handle. Door caps had two receptacles for side curtain pins. Outside, an aluminum side spear ran along the fenders and doors at handle height. On the rocker panels, an aluminum trim strip carried a rubber center. On the front fender flanks, a stylized "Speedster" script was placed, and a new Reutter badge graced the lower right. To keep the weight down, as well as the price, some sound-deadening material was left off. Limiting the choices and combinations of exterior and interior colors was also important for price control, so the original cars were painted in synthetic enamel, which was less expensive than the traditional nitrocellulose lacquer. Three colors were available, reflecting the new car's spiritual home: red, white, and blue. Hoffman had met his goal of a $2,995 "stripper," but he had used some typical American car salesman techniques to do so. Extra-cost equipment such as a heater and tachometer were already built in but were noted as separate line items on the sticker. In effect, there were no "$2,995" Speedsters, but the public was still enthusiastic in receiving the new model.

Weighing in at more than 100 pounds less than a coupe, the car's performance—especially with the $500 optional 1500S roller-crank engine—was lively, aided by new gears for

Speedster tops had no padding, and little effort was made to seal the edges from rain at the cowl or the windshield. No back seat was provided, although a bottom cushion was available.

Pre-A Speedsters had the tuck-under rocker panels and wide deco strip with rubber center. The door handle was nicely integrated into the aluminum belt line trim. Original tops were low and secured with two small leather straps at the windshield frame.

It was all true, sort of—everything except the $2,995 part. John von Neumann was noted as West Coast distributor in this Hoffman ad.

A tool kit included a measured wooden stick to determine fuel level. Side curtains could be packed in their storage bag. Small concessions were made to save money, such as a canvas tire strap instead of leather.

The side curtains were certainly not "as modern as tomorrow," but they helped keep the price down. Most owners rarely used them.

third and fourth. "BBAB" gear sets allowed the engine to pull harder with shorter top gears but limited the top speed. It was a moot point, however, since at high speeds the car was an aerodynamic brick compared to the coupe, whether the top was up or down. But even at low speeds, and especially on the twisty roads, there was much open-air fun to be had behind the wheel. With top up and side curtains in place, however, claustrophobia set in, and if it rained hard, you were going to get wet. Leaks could come from above and below the windshield, at the side curtain edges, and around the rear cowl. But otherwise, the Reutter craftsmanship shows through—the body was as well built as any other Porsche, and there had been no mechanical shortcuts. Even though it was an entry-level car, it gave much driving satisfaction, and many owners later moved up to more comfortable coupes and cabriolets. A Porsche brochure of the day read, "The Speedster takes us back to the carefree days of roadster driving, but does so with features as modern as tomorrow."

In the used market, there were always buyers waiting to experience the visceral joys of Speedster driving, and the car introduced several generations of enthusiasts to the marque.

Both Hoffman and Porsche admitted later that there was little money to be made selling Speedsters, but as an iconic emblem of the marque, it was a roaring success.

While it wasn't necessary to go fast to enjoy a Speedster, legions of racers chose the Typ 540 as their Sports Car Club of America (SCCA) weapon of choice. At Torrey Pines in November 1954, von Neumann co-drove a red Speedster to eighth in the 6-hour race, and stepdaughter Josie drove the car to a win in a combined F and G Production race. An old movie of the event shows the red Speedster sliding sideways, spinning off the road in a cloud of dirt, and returning to the melee, typical of racing in those days. It was appropriate that the car's maiden race was in California, its spiritual home. There would be many more races and many more wins to follow.

MISADVENTURES IN STYLING

The notion that a Porsche should seat four people somehow kept rearing its head. The Typ 530 project from 1952 had produced a legitimate contender, but after those two prototypes were built, the perceived fear of losing market share slowly faded as the 356 continued to sell. Still, in July 1954 plans for another extended-wheelbase four-seater were begun. A clay model was made of the Typ 656, using the VW's 2,400mm wheelbase. The rear had pronounced haunches with single round taillights and a long grille. The greenhouse was lengthened, of course, but otherwise it resembled the planned 955 356 coupe. There were discussions of making the body from reinforced plastic, but any further development would have consumed time and money that was not available, as other ideas were also being worked up.

By November 1954 a new project number, Typ 644, was given for a successor to the existing 356. Komenda experimented with a slightly longer wheelbase of 2,250mm and American-style "hardtop" styling. These ideas never made it past the paper stage, but another 1954 concept rolled out of Reutter's shop fully formed, a styling exercise straight out of Max Hoffman's dreams. A standard 356 sunroof coupe was given high, attached chrome bumpers with two exaggerated upright

TOP: A bizarre attempt to Americanize the existing car, this 1954 styling exercise was less than successful.
BELOW: Typ 656 was yet another idea to produce a Porsche four-seater Porsche, something surveys had indicated customers wanted.

horns. A matching-height side spear ran along each side. The areas below that bright belt were painted silver, contrasting with the dark paint above. A large chrome ornament graced (if that's the word) the hood. It was a one-and-done sample, thankfully never seen again.

ENGINE REVOLUTION

At the same time the Speedster was coming online, big changes were taking place with the Porsche engines. In 1954 Karl Rabe and his engineering staff were charged with solving several problems inherent in the VW-based magnesium engine case. It had reached its limit in bore size, so a completely new engine case was designed. Oil capacity would be needed with any increase in power, so the lower part of the new engine casting, now made of silicon aluminum, was made significantly wider, allowing more oil in the sump. Ribs on the lower case would support the new heater boxes, and the sides sloped outward to direct hot air away and down. The strainer and sump plate were enlarged and made rectangular, and the diameter of the oil pickup tube was increased, all these changes improving both lubrication and cooling.

While the new split crankcase carried three main bearings, a separate front cover carried the fourth journal and bearing. This cover became oil central, with drilled passages taking oil from the sump to the machined-in (now larger) oil pump, then to a bypass valve, a pressure-relief valve, and on to the engine. Oil warning and pressure senders were now very accessible. The

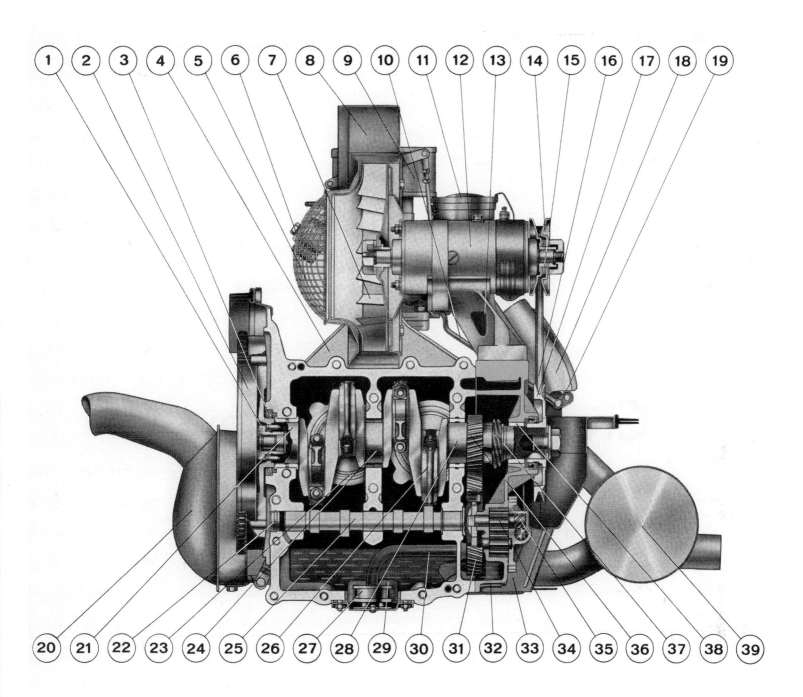

① ② ③ ④ ⑤ ⑥ ⑦ ⑧ ⑨ ⑩ ⑪ ⑫ ⑬ ⑭ ⑮ ⑯ ⑰ ⑱ ⑲

⑳ ㉑ ㉒ ㉓ ㉔ ㉕ ㉖ ㉗ ㉘ ㉙ ㉚ ㉛ ㉜ ㉝ ㉞ ㉟ ㊱ ㊲ ㊳ ㊴

LEFT: The last year of what would become known as the pre-A cars was 1955, with big changes on the way for 1956. Owing to the limited space, fitted luggage was offered for the trunk and the rear seat area. It's doubtful that all these pieces actually fit in the car, however. **ABOVE:** The third piece (in yellow) of the new Typ 616 engine allowed access to the oil pump gears (34), distributor drive and gear (37), and cam gear (31) without splitting the case. The distributor drive (35) ran off the oil pump. New were horns (18) that carried hot air to the carbs, controlled by a thermostat (6) and rod (10, 19). The generator rode on a separate stand (13), which doubled as an oil filler/breather (11). A larger oil pickup tube (30) scavenged from a bigger, rectangular sump with a screen and magnet (27, 29). **RIGHT:** A new cast-iron rocker stand debuted, and the angled exhaust rockers—one short, one long—were simplified.

distributor drive and fuel pump drive rode in the cover, which, when removed, gave access to the cam gear. Deflector ribs inside would regulate oil blowby at high rpm. A new separate generator stand with attached oil filler and cap made adding oil easier, and the generator and fan could be more easily serviced. The crankshaft pulley was resized for a thinner belt, and a modern oil seal was used. Inside the case, the steel cam followers got a thinner shaft and now rode horizontally, with cam lobes pushing just off center so each follower would rotate, minimizing wear. At the other end of the pushrod, rocker-arm supports were new, made of high-strength iron, and exhaust valve rockers were angled, greatly simplifying installation. The engines kept their Typ numbers, but with new designations: 506/2 (1300); 589/2 (1300S); 546/2 (1500); and 528/2 (1500S). The 1,100cc engine was quietly dropped.

Aside from the engine, the 1955 cars didn't appear much different from their predecessors, but there was a stabilizer bar in the front with new torsion bar leaves, giving a slightly softer ride. The clutch release lever and disc were modified, and a heat control between the seats allowed fine adjustment by turning a knob. Bungee cords now held the rear seat backs upright (perhaps the easiest fix ever to a persistent problem). The crested hood handle from the Speedster was now used across the line. The new engines came out in mid-November 1954, but their arrival was not trumpeted to the heavens. Such a significant change might disappoint any customer who had just bought a previous model, so Porsche had undertaken the project in relative secrecy. If there were any hard feelings, however, they quickly dissipated, and 1955 proved to be a banner year for sales. By year's end 2,952 cars would be produced with an increase to 337 employees. The Speedster was a success, and coupes and cabs were selling well, but another, even bigger change was on the horizon.

TECHNICAL PROGRAM 1: 356A

While ongoing ideas to stretch and stylize the future Porsche were all dropped by April 1955, work under the project name Typ 644 continued, with the focus now on improving the existing car both outside and deep under the skin. At the beginning of 1955 it became clear that the existing contract to produce 150 bodies a month from Reutter was not going to meet demand. In March 258 bodies were produced, but Hoffman was soon requesting 300 cars per month just for the United States. Although 608 had been sold there in 1954 and it was unlikely that number would increase by a factor of six, the pressure was on to ramp up production nonetheless.

The new 356A, available in coupe and cabriolet. For the 15-inch wheels, chrome was an increasingly popular option.

The paint department was a bottleneck, and Reutter suggested using the less expensive (and faster) synthetic enamel paint on the entire line, not just Speedsters. Initially against the idea, Porsche later agreed, and production was anticipated to increase as painting costs fell. Also helping was a decision to offer only seven colors plus the three Speedster hues for the new Typ 644. Porsche at this time anticipated that it would purchase two thousand bodies for the coming model year and placed an order with Reutter in March for delivery of cabriolets beginning in September and coupes following in December. Reutter, once again, had to spend large amounts for new tooling, some of which would not arrive until late fall. Therefore, the initial run of preproduction cars for September would require a large amount of hand work.

The roof dies, it was discovered, were nearing the end of their useful life, so replacements were ordered from Allgaier with a new windshield curve and a slightly larger rear window area, allowing use of Sekurit tempered glass there that was less expensive. Sigla laminated glass (whose edges could be ground for fitting) was retained for the windshield, but the new curved

design was also cheaper to buy. The roof, cowl, and dashboard would need new tooling, as would the rocker panels and a few other areas. In addition to changing many pressed parts for the new model, the fixtures used to hold parts and sections together during welding had to be modified. While assembly of the current model continued unabated, Reutter scrambled to ready the plant for the new cars and a planned introduction at the Frankfurt International Automobile Exhibition in September 1955. It was the "big show," and it only happened every two years. As the deadline approached, the Typ 644, developed under the internal descriptor "Technical Program 1" (T-1), was given an official name in order to avoid confusion and promote continuity. The 1956 models were to be called the Porsche 356A.

The 356A had a lower floor inside, owing to removing the wooden boards used previously; control cables were now routed through the central tunnel. The dash was flat, no longer removable, and painted the body color, and it featured a padded vinyl cover that gave some protection from the sun for the three large gauges in front of the driver. Warning lights were incorporated into these gauge faces. A central tachometer

The "A" Speedster instruments changed to three large VDO dials with a reshaped hood. Defroster vents were added in late 1955.

ABOVE: The new padded "A" dash put the VDO oil and temperature gauges together on the right dial, with oil-pressure (green) and generator (red) warning lights. A central tachometer carried green stripes for the power band of each engine. The headlight switch was accessed by reaching through or around the steering wheel, which here has a deluxe full horn ring. At left under the dash are the handbrake, windshield-washer pedal, and high-beam switch. Radios, especially on U.S. cars, were often aftermarket.

LEFT: Max Hoffman's idea for a name was shot down by Ford after 1,200-odd cars were imported to the United States with this script.

carried green stripes to indicate the power band and red stripes for rev limit, as before. Each engine type had different markings. At left was the speedometer and on the right the oil temp (with numbers) and fuel gauge. In the Speedster, three large round gauges were now used under a widened padded "brow." The VDM steering wheel in beige or gray could be had with a deluxe full-circle horn ring. Upholstery colors were limited, as the saddlery department at Reutter was also under production pressure and there was a need to keep things simple.

Distinctive outside were the rocker panels that no longer rolled under, with aluminum trim and rubber strip inserts, as on the Speedster. Also influenced by the Speedster (and Max Hoffman) was a fender script with a name. Porsche's 1955 models bound for the United States (and a few other exports) had carried the designation "Continental" for a short time, until Ford Motor Company cried foul and threatened to sue. For late 1955 and early 1956 another name was used: "European" in a similar, although less elegant, script. It was applied to only about 150 cars, proof that Hoffman's ideas were not always winners. In spring 1956, U.S.-bound 356As were given an enhanced bumper treatment with taller guards, made of bright anodized aluminum. They supported a chromed steel overrider bar that looped from near one end of the bumper to the other. It was another effort by Hoffman to adapt the little car to American driving (and parking) habits.

DISPLACEMENT INCREASE

Not only the body was changed in this new model; the 1500 engine got a size bump to 1,600cc. Cylinder bore was increased to 82.5mm, an easy expansion that had already been planned with the new three-piece case. Both the Normal—or "Damen," the lady—and the Super increased their compression by a half point and horsepower by 5, to 60 and 75, respectively. The new engines came online in September 1955 with the Typ 616. The Normal used plain shell bearings and a slightly modified carburetor, the Solex 32 PBIC, while the Super carried on with a roller crank and the Solex 40 PICB setup. To address cold engine warm-up, two short vertical tubes through the rear engine plate directed warm air from the muffler area toward the carbs, thermostatically closing as the temp rose.

Not seen, but significant as well, was a new transmission nose that was supported by two rubber mounts. Rear torsion bars were now longer and 1mm thinner, with shocks mounted more vertically and a rubber buffer controlling long suspension travel. In the front, a new antiroll bar worked with softened torsion-bar leaf packs, roller-bearing trailing-arm pivots, and heavier shocks. A small steering damper was mounted horizontally between the top torsion tube and the right steering rod, and suspension geometry was subtly changed. Adding one more item to the suspension package, Porsche changed the wheel size to 15 inches and width to 4.5, specifying lower tire pressures. The result was overall softer springing, but firmer damping and better handling.

Front suspension included a new stabilizer bar and mountings, a steering damper, and revised torsion bar springs and shocks. Unlike a VW assembly which was bolted to the floorpan, the Porsche assembly was welded to the chassis along the vertical sheetmetal flanges.

Assembly of the bodies at Reutter was under scrutiny by inspectors at every stage.

FOUR CAMS FOR STREET AND TRACK

In February 1955 Porsche expressed a desire to install the recently developed four-cam engine in production cars. Expecting that 10 percent or more of customers would opt for the special engine, it was reasoned that all bodies should be built with some of the brackets, specific holes, and other items to accommodate the four-cam's ancillary needs. It was wise to consider all this as the new model was being planned, but it added to the complication during a very hectic period at Reutter. By September that year, planners at Porsche were requesting an increase from fewer than 300 cars to 450 per

month for the following year. It was an unrealistic number, but Reutter responded by building a new workshop addition, investing in machinery, and expanding its apprentice program to train new workers. It was a point of pride that quality came first, and quantity followed.

At the September 1955 Frankfurt Internationale Automobil-Ausstellung, Porsche's display included the new Speedster and a Typ 550 racer, plus a 356 coupe outfitted with a four-cam engine. The racing engine was already in use in the 550, but its availability in a street car caused something of a sensation.

Four-cam engines await their T-1 bodies at the Werk II factory. Special front mufflers doubled as heat exchangers, connected to ducts in the car. These early engines had distributors driven from the rear of the intake cams.

The exotic powerplant was the brainchild of Vienna native Ernst Fuhrmann, who had come to work for Porsche at Gmünd in 1947 at age twenty-nine. In 1950 he received a doctorate in mechanical engineering, and two years later he was given the task of designing a new racing engine for the company. It had begun life on Fuhrmann's drawing board in the summer of 1952 as Typ 547. Components were produced and three examples were built for testing by the spring of 1953; installed in a 550 in August, it was tested at the Nürburgring and in a hillclimb. On display at the Paris salon in October, the Spyder had yet to open its engine lid to the public. Auto show attendees saw a placard with specifications, but not the engine itself: "1498 cc, 4 overhead cams, air cooled, 4 cylinders, 110 hp at 7000 rpm with pump gas, top speed 225 kph." Dealers were told, "To draw attention, we are exhibiting a race car, not intended for sale . . . as it is our experience that this also heightens customer interest for the regular production cars." There was no price yet, but it would be sold "in limited numbers to individual interested parties for racing purposes." By early 1954 the four-cam engine was poised to take on all comers in the 1.5-liter racing classes, but Fuhrmann and Ferry Porsche both thought it could be the ultimate for street cars as well. They both had one installed in their personal 356s.

Going forward to the 1955 Frankfurt show, the 356 coupe on display looked like any other 356, with only a few subtle clues inside and out. The interior was well appointed with leather, but the dash carried two extra switches, and the tachometer maxed at a serious 8,000 rpm, although the redline started at 6,000. The speedometer as well seemed to mean business, with markings to 250 kilometers per hour. Just visible in the left rear wheel well was an oil tank, part of a new dry-sump oiling system. Aside from slightly larger exhaust pipes, the only other sign that this car was special was gold script on the fenders, with a smaller version on the tail. "Carrera," they read, and any Porsche fan would recognize the name of the Mexican contest in which Porsche had taken class wins. And anyone who wasn't yet familiar would be soon enough, as Carrera would come to mean "race" in the language of Porsche.

The engine had been designed to be compact, from flywheel to pulley and also from side to side. Its output end needed to mate with existing Porsche transmission mounting points and main shaft. Having met these parameters, Fuhrmann's engine could fit in a 356, and it was offered as an option on coupes, cabriolets, and Speedsters. Ancillaries such as extra coils, fuel filters, oil tank, coolers, and lines were stuffed into the car, and distributors were mounted toward the rear of the engine. Some glaring problems remained, however. Changing eight spark plugs was time-consuming and difficult, as was valve adjustment. In a Spyder, the entire rear bodywork could be opened or removed for access; not so in a 356. What service could be done in situ was slow and methodical, by necessity, and even with the engine removed it required a specialist with training to even perform a tune-up. Mechanics, at least the ones who were willing to take on the challenge, understood what was required to keep the engine in top shape. Owners, on the other hand, were sometimes poorly informed or outright negligent.

The roller bearings at the heart of the engine lived a happy life in the middle of the rev range. Properly warmed up, anything between 2,500 and 6,000 rpm would keep them spinning without undue stress, and even an occasional run up the tach to 7,500 was acceptable. But near the idle speed of 1,000, or even double that, heavy throttle action might not cause a stumble but would quickly foul the plugs and eventually ruin the bearings. Even well-intentioned Carrera drivers sometimes had to grit their teeth when following a truck up a hill, revving the motor and hoping for a clear chance to pass. Dawdling was not something a Carrera did well.

What the four-cam motor excelled at in a 356 was excitement. A lower-restriction muffler gave a distinct throaty sound that crescendoed as the revs rose much higher than a pushrod engine. For the driver, third gear meant 90 miles per hour, and for a passenger, the dashboard grab handle was not

Outside the original Werk I offices, a 356A shows off its optional Rudge center-lock wheels. These "racing" wheels were in fact heavier than the standard open-center five-bolt units.

4-cam engines were installed in all three 1956 models: coupe, cabriolet and Speedster. Blue and red is a typical German color scheme, as seen here at a California Porsche event in 2012.

just decoration. As an everyday car, the Carrera was exciting rapid transit but only practical to a point. Where it really shone was on a racetrack, especially in its lightest iteration, the Speedster Carrera. From its introduction in 1955, the Carrera would be a star in sports-car racing for decades. A sales brochure crowed, "With the Carrera engine, the Porsche production car takes advantage of the FIA Grand Turismo class, and becomes the first production sports car in the 1500 class to reach 125 MPH limit, and at the same time remain a comfortable and easy handling touring car."

Ferry Porsche called the Carrera "an excellent dual-purpose car for the enthusiast." Toward that end, the company offered a kit for weekend racing that included larger carburetor venturis and different jets, with bolt-on velocity stacks. In

Ferry's words, "They would serve all week as quite docile go-to-work transportation, then on the weekend could be driven to a racing event and 'converted' on the spot." This bit of cheerleading oversimplified the ownership experience, but a four-cam in a street body, for most owners, was well worth any downside, and Porsche would continue to enlarge, develop, and refine the motor in the coming years.

New 356As were gassed up in the back lot between Reutter and Porsche, tested on the road with a front "bra," and, after any final adjustments, prepped for delivery to the dealer. Speedster tops were wrapped to prevent water damage during transit.

GOING HOME AGAIN

As the Reutter plant was bulging with new work, Porsche suddenly was in the opposite position. December 1, 1955, was a significant date for the company, now in its fifth year back in Zuffenhausen. On the twentieth anniversary of its founding in Stuttgart as a consulting engineering firm, the original Werk I, built in 1938, was returned to it. Ferry Porsche wrote, "A small cholera outbreak occurred in Stuttgart. The mayor was at once faced with the need to find an isolation hospital." An American barracks in the Bad Cannstatt section of Stuttgart would be suitable, but the army was opposed. "They would not allow those cholera cases anywhere near Bad Cannstatt. . . . As a result, our factory was converted into the needed hospital but the outbreak subsided as quickly as it had started and the mayor eventually gave us back our premises."

It had been ten years, and suddenly the company had space to spare, but not for long. After some work to return the building to proper condition for use, management, including the engineering staff under Karl Rabe and financial department headed by Hans Kern, moved across Schwieberdinger Strasse to a new office in Porsche's old home. Racing and development returned to the lower-level shops and workshops across the parking lot where so many wartime projects had taken shape. Historian Karl Ludvigsen notes that employment was at an all-time high with 616 people working for Porsche at the time.

ENGINOLOGY: TYP 547 CARRERA

Complicated engines meant to produce high power output were not a new thing at Porsche. The Auto Union Grand Prix cars; Porsche's concept for its own sports car, the Typ 114 from 1938; and the Cisitalia Typ 360 from 1947 all contributed ideas for the design of a new Porsche competition engine. With his 1950 doctoral thesis, "Valve Trains for High-Speed Combustion Engines," Ernst Fuhrmann was well positioned to lead the effort. Working in the rented Reutter space, beginning in 1952, he explored a gear system to drive overhead cams. This was the biggest challenge, although there were many innovations in the engine, which he designed from scratch.

Engine size was a given: 1.5 liters was a standard displacement for racing classes and—as was probably in the back of Fuhrmann's mind all along—a popular and practical size for a road car as well. Displacement being determined by stroke and bore, he opted for a larger bore and shorter stroke, radically oversquare at 85mm×66mm, giving 1,498cc. A two-piece aluminum alloy crankcase had three main webs for bearings. A lower part of the central web was cast and machined for an intermediate shaft. The ten-piece, heavily counterweighted roller-bearing crankshafts were made by Albert Hirth and came to Porsche completely assembled with rods.

A gear on the flywheel end of the crankshaft drove a layshaft directly under the crank at half speed. The layshaft's other end was at the central web near the crankcase center, where back-to-back spiral bevel gears turned two smaller bevel gears on thinner, hollow vertical shafts (now at crank speed) that extended out to the cylinder head exhaust cam boxes. From here a shaft rose vertically to the intake cam box. The entire system, including the layshaft and cam arbors, consisted of nineteen pieces. Doubling the speed of these shafts meant they could carry the same amount of power with half the torque, allowing them to be made lighter, placing less stress on the system, and requiring less power to turn. Two distributors were driven off either end of the intake cams. The cam drive system is a so-called hunting-tooth gear set, in which any tooth on either gear will contact every tooth on the other gear before meshing with the same tooth again, spreading the wear evenly over all the gear teeth and increasing life. At the very tip of the layshaft, a gear drove the high-capacity oil pump, which both scavenged from the sump and supplied pressurized oil. Oiling to the heads was achieved through the hollow gear driveshafts.

Cylinders were the now-familiar Mahle aluminum with chrome bores, with machined bases that extended well into the crankcase openings. Pistons were distinctly crowned, with cutouts for valves and three compression rings plus an oil ring below the wrist pin. The deeply finned head was designed for efficient cooling, and a high-volume, double-sided fan forced air through a smoothly ducted shroud, running at engine speed

The roller-bearing crank was built separately and installed in the special 547 case as a unit. At the flywheel end it drove a large layshaft gear at half speed to a set of bevel gears for the cam drives.

More bevel gears at each head; this 550 engine's distributor is driven from the flywheel side of the camshaft. At the other end is the tachometer drive.

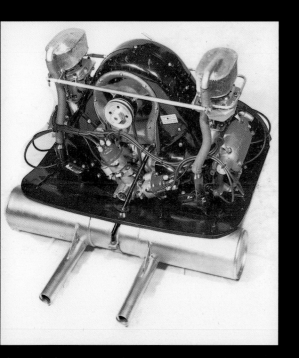

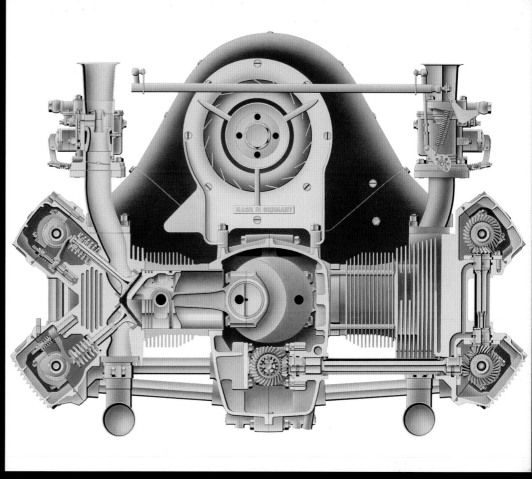

The typical Carrera engine package was a tight fit in the 356. The distributors were moved to the end of the crankshaft in mid-1958, with an increase to 1,600cc.

An illustration by Wolfgang Franke (a later plain-bearing Carrera 2.0-liter engine) shows the gear and shaft arrangement, with the finger followers and adjusters used to set valve lash. Large valves fed direct-flow intake and exhaust ports, and domed pistons could be varied for different compression ratios.

At the very end of the valvetrain were finger followers between the cam and valve tip, mounted on ball-topped studs that could be screwed in or out to adjust clearance. Those cams were separate pieces, interchangeable on the shaft for various needs. The valves were large, 48mm for intake and 41mm for exhaust, sodium filled. Ports were fairly straight and wide, with exhaust exiting downward. Front mufflers for each bank received two pipes from the heads, with a small crossover pipe between, and in turn fed a larger silencer behind the engine. Dual exhaust pipes were larger diameter than pushrod cars.

The near-hemispherical head chambers held two plugs, each fired by a separate distributor driven by the intake cam shaft. Feeding the intakes were Solex 40 PII carburetors, usually with velocity stacks, whose length and shape influenced the flow of intake air. Trunk-mounted dual electric pumps provided fuel through a filter on the engine firewall. Also mounted there were dual Bosch coils, one for each distributor. At left in the engine compartment were the neck and filler of the dry-sump oil tank.

Assembly of the engine required close tolerances and adjustments, matching bevel gear sets and perfect timing of all valvetrain components. And in spite of perfect preparation, the early four-cam engines suffered from camshaft harmonics. The problems were such that the early cam-driven distributor's

advance mechanism would wear quickly, resulting in uneven timing that could lead to engine failure. Problems with the tach drives—which ran from the intake camshaft—were also sometimes found. Eventually, Werner Enz of the racing department found a solution in installing small flywheels on the camshafts, but a permanent fix was only made when the distributors were relocated to run off the nose of the crankshaft. The original four-cam engine was used in the Spyder (although a Gmünd SL used one to win the 1954 Liège—Rome—Liège Rally) and was well developed by the time the Carrera coupe was introduced at Frankfurt in 1955. The version installed in street cars was detuned slightly, with a 9.0:1 compression ratio, and given the name Typ 547/1. With 100 horsepower at 6,200 rpm it was king of the street Porsches.

Some special modifications were made for Le Mans engines in 1954 and 1955, with a bore of 73mm for a displacement of 1,098cc, a testament to the flexibility designed into the engine. The 547 and its successors brought Porsche into the victory circle many times in their dozen years of competition. Initial questions about the ability of an air-cooled engine to generate high power output had long since been laid to rest by the time the final 2.0-liter version of the four-cam produced almost 200 horsepower.

GLÖCKLERS TO GRANDMOTHER: THE COMPETITION PORSCHES

Racing in Germany and on the continent had disappeared during World War II, but the competitive spirit of racers was quick to resurface afterward. New to the field at the Nürburgring and other tracks were entrants the racers described as *Eigenbau*, or self-built, which proliferated in the 1.1-liter group; many were based on the VW.

Petermax Müller created one of these using special VW wartime experimental heads sourced from Porsche at Gmünd. He set speed records with his cars, reflecting well on Porsche, which had a good relationship with him. But the Zuffenhausen men were even closer to another independent builder.

Entering the realm of dedicated race cars, the first 550s built were essentially prototypes and varied widely. Five of these have been restored and were shown together at the 2012 Porsche Race Car Classic at the Quail in Carmel, California. From front, 1953 Porsche 550-03, 1953 Porsche 550-04, 1953 Porsche 550-01, 1954 Porsche 550-06, and 1954 Porsche 550-09.

ABOVE: Müller's *Eigenbau* used heads from a war-surplus stock of VW performance parts at Porsche in Gmünd.
BELOW: Max Hoffman's Glöckler at Bridgehampton, 1952.

Walter Glöckler had an advantage, with two decades of experience racing cars and motorbikes. An early VW dealer in Frankfurt, in 1950 he hired vehicle engineer Hermann Ramelow, who used VW suspension parts and Porsche's Typ 369 engine in a tube frame with a smooth, lozenge-like aluminum body by Frankfurt's Karosserie Weidenhausen. The engine and VW transmission were turned à la #356-001 for a midengine layout with leading suspension arms. The engine was tweaked to 48 horsepower, and the short-wheelbase, 1,000-pound car won at the June 1950 Nürburgring race and a German sports car–class championship that year, something that was very satisfying to Ferry Porsche. Glöckler had become the Porsche dealer in Frankfurt in March 1950, and the following year they joined forces. Glöckler would receive advanced parts and assistance from Zuffenhausen, just 2 hours away, and his race cars would carry the Porsche name on their hoods.

With a new Glöckler-Porsche—this time with headlights, to better relate to production car appearance, and a midmounted early Porsche 1500 Typ 502 engine with 10.5:1 compression

Petermax Müller's streamlined "Rekordwagen" at the Automuseum Prototyp in Hamburg.

Glöckler's first car initially carried the script "Eigenbau" later replaced with "Porsche" as his cooperation with the fledgling car maker increased.

and 85 horsepower at 6,200 rpm—Glöckler took the 1.5 class win at the August 1951 Schauinsland hillclimb. The next month he joined Porsche to set records with four new 1.5-liter distance marks at Montlhéry in France.

The car then went to New York, where Max Hoffman raced it in Florida in late 1951 and March 1952. At Bridgehampton in May he took second place after a spin, bashing some hay bales; the problems with a leading-arm rear suspension were becoming evident. It went on to be raced by Ed Trego's dealership in Hoopeston, Illinois, still wearing "Porsche" on its nose.

Glöckler's third racer, on a shortened 356 chassis, would also be driven to success in Europe and by Hoffman in America. Two more were built, showing the world what racing Porsches could do—even though they weren't really Porsches—and also showed the carmaker itself what a racing Porsche could be. There

TOP: A new frame reverted to the trailing-arm rear suspension with torsion bars closer to the car's center. BELOW: Porsche 550-02 in the rain at the 'Ring in August 1953.

was now a clearly delineated path to building the company's first dedicated sports competition car. Working in the rented Reutter buildings, Porsche engineers began drawing in late 1952 under the designation Porsche Typ 550.

CREATING TYP 550

As a base, Porsche chose a ladder frame, similar to the Glöckler design, as well as the Maserati brothers' OSCA MT4. Karl Rabe oversaw a team led by Wilhelm Hild in designing the car's underpinnings. The longitudinal members were tubular steel, running beneath the engine and transmission, with six lateral members. A standard VW double torsion-tube setup was in front and a rear torsion bar crossmember placed far back, with radius arms reaching forward, as in the early Glöckler specials and Porsche #356-001. The new synchro transmission included a limited-slip differential from ZF, and most of the running gear was straight from the production cars. Unique were the hydraulic clutch and front-mounted oil cooler. The car used a 1500 Super engine with Solex 40 PII dual-throat carbs, now tuned for a power output of 98 horsepower on alcohol at an outrageous 12.5:1 compression ratio.

At Le Mans in 1953 the 550s kept Porsche's class win streak alive.

At Le Mans in 1953 the 550s kept Porsche's class win streak alive.

As with the Glöcklers, the aluminum bodies for the first two cars were built by Weidenhausen, with removable hardtops. At the end of May 1953, racer Helm Glöckler, a cousin of Walter's, drove Porsche #550-01 to victory in the rain in the six-lap Eifelrennen race at the Nürburgring.

In June Glöckler drove the car at Le Mans with twenty-five-year-old Hans Herrmann, recently hired by Porsche as a driver. Richard von Frankenberg and Paul Frère, a Belgian automotive writer, shared #550-02. Engines for the cars were detuned to run on pump fuel, as required by Le Mans rules, and at 9.0:1 compression they returned about 77 horsepower. The tops were installed in order to enhance top speed, shown in practice to be around 124 miles per hour on the Mulsanne Straight. In spite of driver discomfort and high engine oil temperatures, both cars outsped and outlasted their competition,

The first 550 shows little attention to design in the rear, but the leading arm torsion-bar pivot can be seen behind the rear wheel. A hardtop was considered necessary for long-distance racing.

In testing before the 1953 Carrera, Karl Kling (with cigarette), Hans Hermann (rear), and Herbert Linge confer with Fletcher Aviation support members. In spite of this talent, both factory 550s were DNF.

with von Frankenberg and Frère taking a 1,500cc win and a new class record. The other 550 was right behind. Porsche was now three for three in its class at Le Mans.

Herrmann won the 1,500cc class at a Nürburgring race on August 2, 1953, and at the Freiburg hillclimb a week later. These first two prototype 550s were getting a thorough workout, but their replacements were already being built.

TYPE 550/1500 RS

A further refinement of the 550, drawing on experience gained in racing the first two cars, was already under construction by early summer 1953. The design was still based on the midengine configuration, but a revised ladder frame now placed the rear torsion bars ahead of the engine, similar to the switch made after #356-001, and the trailing arms were longer. The frame was arched over the rear axles, and a bow-shaped engine-mounting crossmember, extending downward, was bolted in place rather than welded, to facilitate powerplant removal. Erwin Komenda scribed a new body that had more refined curves and rear fenders that ended in chunky fins, and these next few aluminum bodies were built by Karosserie Weinsberg. The hood of car #550-03 curved down to an air inlet mouth. Four separate grilles were located on the rear deck, and louvers were built into the sides behind the doors. On the next car, chassis #550-04, a high rear deck was bolted in place for testing purposes, along with a full-width windscreen and small side windows.

The new engine designed by Ernst Fuhrmann was ready for installation in a vehicle, and when #550-03 was finished in July 1953, a new era began. At the Nürburgring on August 2, young Hans Herrmann, who was now Porsche's number-one driver, and Huschke von Hanstein both made a few practice laps. The elegant machine attracted interest among the spectators, but no one got a look under the hood. Those familiar with the 356 engine noticed a different exhaust note, though, and speculation intensified the next week when Hans Stuck drove the car at Freiburg. Stuck was an acknowledged hillclimb ace, but it wasn't his day. The engine cover remained closed.

The first two cars were meanwhile refurbished and shipped to Guatemala, where their new owner had entered them in the 1953 Carrera Panamericana. Considering the opportunity of exposure in Mexico, Porsche management also decided to send #03 and #04, albeit with pushrod Super engines. Fletcher Aviation agreed to provide sponsorship and logistical support. Added to the trip was a stop at Albany, Georgia, for the first American race sanctioned by both the SCCA and the Fédération Internationale de l'Automobile (FIA), with huge crowds expected. Hoffman had also arranged a large press reception in New York to show off the racing team. With great fanfare, Porsche entered the two 550 racers, one driven by von Hanstein, the

The third 550 with pronounced rear fenders at the Freiburg hillclimb with Hans Stuck at the wheel. Ernst Fuhrmann (center) looks on.

Max Hoffman observes at left as 550-01 is prepped for the sports-car race at Turner Air Force Base in 1953. The small rear engine lid was not used on later 550s.

At the 1953 Paris Auto Show 550-05 caused a sensation with its four-cam engine.

other by Karl Kling, who had won the Carrera Panamericana the previous year in a Mercedes-Benz 300SL.

In those races at Turner Air Force Base, Porsche 356s took the first eleven places in the F Production race on October 25, 1953. In eighth place in the modified race was a custom-built 356 racer from Lou Fageol that featured twin Porsche engines—front and rear. Another entry in that class was the steel-bodied America Roadster of Hubert Brundage, the Florida sports-car dealer who was just getting involved with Porsches and VWs, which finished eighteenth. The two new 550s, however, failed to finish. The team then left Georgia for southern Mexico to earn a name that would come to mean Porsche racing: Carrera.

CARRERA 1953

The fourth Carrera Panamericana was the first in which the factory was putting forth an effort, and von Hanstein had high hopes for his team, with sponsorship by Telefunken Radio and Fletcher Aviation. #550-01 and #550-02 were there for Jaroslav Juhan, a Czech native who operated a dealership in Guatemala City. In the race, Juhan and co-driver Antonio Asturias Hall were fast but DNFed with a breakdown in a late stage. Their other team car, driven by José Sala Herrarte Ariano and Carlos Gonzales, finished thirty-second overall but first in Sport 1600. Right behind in thirty-third was Fernando Segura, an Argentine who had bought his new 356 Super just before the race. Kling in #550-03 and Herrmann in #550-04 were both DNF with mechanical issues, as were three other Porsches.

Juhan's 550s next raced at Buenos Aires in January 1954 at the opening of that year's World Sportscar Championship. After 1,000 miles the Juhan/Hall team took a 1.5 class win. In spite of limited budgets and manpower from the factory, the Porsche name was being written indelibly into racing's annals.

The next 550, chassis #05, sported a new style of nose with a more conventional hood and, at the rear, a single grille and revised fins. Intentionally trimmed as a road car—with a real windshield and wipers, folding top, two seats, and even a glove box—it was shown at the Paris Auto Show in October 1953, accompanied by the announcement that this new sports racer, the Typ 550/1500 RS (*Rennsport*, racing) with a four-cam engine, was available for sale to customers. The new powerplant was no longer a secret, but in reality, many more changes would be made before a production 550 was released.

Back in Zuffenhausen, the removable high deck tried on chassis #04 showed promise in wind-tunnel testing, so a body was built (#550-06) to incorporate the "humpback" shape, and in that form the car was shown at the Brussels Auto Show in January 1954. A hinged rear body shell allowed easy access to almost all of the mechanical components—necessary now, since the chassis reverted back to underslung. In April 1954 these two were thoroughly tested at Hockenheim, Germany,

ABOVE: Factory mechanics' work was simplified with a new pivoting rear deck. The frame rail rear shock towers, and brake drums with drilled outer ribs can be seen. Trailing arms were also lightened by drilling.

LEFT: Ferry Porsche addresses workers after the 1954 Mille Miglia. Hans Hermann and Herbert Linge's 550 wears laurels, as does Richard von Frankenberg and Heinrich Sauter's #229 coupe for a GT 1.5-liter victory.

Four cars were prepped for Le Mans in June 1954. Posing with them at right is engine designer Ernst Fuhrmann, in front of the 1.1-liter class winner (47).

At Porsche Werk II, the racing department was greatly expanded by 1954. Here four early 550s are assembled as engineer Wilhelm Hild (blond, center left) and racing director Huschke von Hanstein look on.

Von Hanstein proudly stands with driver Hans Hermann to his left and Jaroslav Juhan to his right after #55 took a third overall and first in the Sport 1.5 class. Juhan's #56 was a minute behind.

giving the factory enough confidence to enter #550-08 in the upcoming 1954 Mille Miglia. The Typ 547 engine to be used in Italy was already a second-generation unit, using Weber carburetors and incorporating numerous detail changes.

Hans Herrmann was behind the wheel with Herbert Linge, the Porsche race department mechanic, as co-driver when they left Brescia on May 1 at 3:51 a.m. for 990 miles at speed on Italian roads. Rain caused ignition failure at one point, but the most memorable moment came when the pair rounded a sharp bend to find a railroad crossing gate lowering into their path and a locomotive bearing down on them. They had been using flash cards and hand signals to communicate, and Hermann gave his navigator a decisive signal by slapping the top of Linge's helmet; the latter ducked just as the low car roared under the crossing gate. They went on to sixth place overall and a 1,500cc class win. To many at Porsche, this "private-entry" success made the upcoming Le Mans look like a sure thing.

LONGEST-DAY TRIBULATION

Four cars were prepared for the French classic in June 1954. Three were equipped with third-series 547 engines reflecting a number of small improvements and generating 114 horsepower at 6,800 rpm on blended pump fuel. These cars carried rear fender stripes in red, blue, and green. The fourth, with yellow stripes, was an entrant in the 1,100cc class, driven by Gustave Olivier and Zora Arkus-Duntov, an engineer with General Motors, where he was busy developing the new Corvette. In Arkus-Duntov's Porsche, the small-displacement four-cam, with a bore of 72.5mm, was producing just over 72 horsepower— enough to finish the race reliably, in fourteenth place, after every other car in its class had dropped out.

The "large"-engine 550s were having a rough go of it, however. Holed pistons took out two cars; the bad cylinder was deactivated in the third, and the car plugged along on three

At Le Mans in 1955, driver Zora Arkus-Duntov discusses strategy with Ferry Porsche (right) during a pit stop. The 1.1-liter car took a class win for the second year in a row.

for the last few hours. The only other cars left in the class, two OSCAs, went off a curve in the rain during the last hour of racing, allowing Porsche to back into a class win, twelfth overall. The victories looked good on paper, but the engineers knew they had a lot more work to do.

That summer the racing department was kept busy modifying and preparing cars for competition. By August engineer Helmuth Bott had created an airfield skid pad, based on suggestions from Arkus-Duntov. In a sports-car race that preceded the German Grand Prix at the Nürburgring on August 1, Herrmann, von Frankenberg, von Hanstein, and Helmut Polensky started and finished in first through fourth places in class after 1 hour and 18 minutes of racing. By season's end the four-cam engine was sorted out and completely at home in the body for which it was designed.

Hans Herrmann capped the 1954 season by taking chassis #04, now equipped with a four-cam engine making 117 horsepower, back to Mexico for the last Carrera Panamericana. He took third overall and the 1,500cc class title, 38 seconds ahead of Jaroslav Juhan. In the final standings of that class, an OSCA wedged itself into third place between Juhan's and Segura's 550s, but the only other finishers were three other Porsches, number five being Salvador López Chávez in the veteran #550-01, sans top. Now sponsored by his shoe company, #01 raced in Mexico for a few years, then disappeared and languished for decades before being returned to the United States for restoration in 2002.

Otto Erich Filius, who had just opened Porsche's first official office in New York, with Max Hoffman and the new 550A Spyder at the New York Auto Show in 1956.

James Dean posing with his new Porsche 550 Spyder on the back lot of
Competition Motors on September 30, 1955, at approximately 12:30 p.m.

SPEED FOR SALE:
550 "CUSTOMER" SPYDERS

The first eight experimental 550s were joined by a number of
others during 1954. The factory had a habit of rebodying some
chassis to meet new applications and selling off others as
their usefulness decreased. The result was that the vehicle was
sufficiently developed for series production. In the last months
of 1954 the Wendler coachbuilding firm in Reutlingen supplied
frames and bodies for the first "customer" Spyders, as they
were called. Max Hoffman insisted that the cars to be sold in
America have a name, rather than an impersonal number, and
he christened them the Spyders. It quickly became part of the
Porsche lexicon.

The production cars differed somewhat from their
predecessors, with slightly thicker aluminum and sheet steel
added at the bracing tubes behind the rear torsion bar tubes.
The headlights at the front were standard 356 units and running
lights, and those at the rear were a larger, circular design.
The rear fins were not so prominent, without side louvers.
Civilianizing the car brought the dry weight to about 1,350
pounds, more than 10 percent heavier than the prototypes.

The factory engine spec sheets gave conservative figures
of 110 horsepower DIN at 6,200 rpm and 87.5 pounds-feet of
torque DIN at 5,000 rpm. A full 24-gallon tank gave a front-
to-rear weight balance of 48/52, and the stock 356 brakes
could slow the light car as well as the engine could accelerate
it. California racers would often get several sprint races from
a set of linings.

THE GREATER
LOS ANGELES
SAFETY COUNCIL
Presents
JAMES DEAN'S
LAST
SPORTS CAR.

HIS ACCIDENT COULD
HAVE BEEN AVOIDED...

AT APPROXIMATELY 6 P.M., FRIDAY, SEP. 30ᵗʰ, YEAR OLD JAMES DEAN WAS TRAVELING WEST ON U.S. 466. VING THIS 1955 PORSCHE 550 MODIFIED SPYDER. A 1950, 2 DOOR FORD, TRAVELING EAST ATTEMPTED LEFT TURN IN FRONT OF DEAN'S CAR AT THE INTERSECTION F STATE HIGHWAY 41.

• DEAN WAS UNABLE TO STOP HE WAS RONOUNCED DEAD ON ARRIVAL AT A NEARBY HOSPITAL. •IT WAS CLEAR DAYLIGHT WHEN THIS ACCIDENT HAPPENED. THERE WERE NO APPARENT DEFECTS ON EITHER VEHICLE. TRAFFIC WAS LIGHT. THE HIGHWAY WAS STRAIGHT AND LEVEL. THE TRAGIC ACCIDENT WAS CAUSED NESS. IT COULD HAVE BEEN ROAD HAVE

Customers, as expected, quickly took to the tracks with their 550s, and the summer of 1955 was a banner year for the marque. Americans, especially West Coast enthusiasts such as Richie Ginther and Ken Miles, were shimming their valve springs, increasing compression up to 12.0:1, and carb swapping to get up to 130 horsepower. A *Car and Driver* review by Griff Borgeson describes a drive with Ginther along the California coast in his racing 550: "The exhaust note starts as a resonant, thundering hammer and builds to that indescribable ripping-canvas scream that can come only from a barrel-chested 7500 rpm." Away from traffic Richie gives the car its head. "The savage, lunging

Customizer George Barris repaired Dean's wrecked car just enough to not offend sensitive people but still get the safety point across. Here it is on display at the Electric Building in Balboa Park, San Diego, California, in April 1957.

character of the car under full throttle is unforgettable," Borgeson writes. "Up to about 5000 rpm it feels like one of the thrustiest machines you've ever driven, but then the cams hit their stride and the power really comes on."

In Europe records were as important as racing trophies. In March 1955 Walter Ringgenberg and von Frankenberg drove a new Typ 550 at Montlhéry to six new 1,500cc-class records. Spyder drivers won the lion's share of races early in the 1955 season, including Le Mans, where 1.5-liter cars could make almost 140 miles per hour on the straights. They took the first three places in their class and won index of performance, the first time for an engine of that size. Arkus-Duntov was back, this time with Auguste Veuillet as a co-driver, and took first in the 1,100cc class followed by a privately entered Spyder. Bigger front brakes were aided by small brake cooling inlets in the nose.

By the end of the 1955 season, however, the competition was eclipsing the 550. EMWs and OSCAs were showing their tails to 550 pilots in Germany, and in America cross-bred "Poopers"—svelte Cooper bodies with Porsche engines—were winning SCCA races on both coasts.

In August 1955 the factory continued the Spyders' mechanical evolution with a five-speed transmission. In September at the AVUS in Berlin, von Frankenberg outlasted the EMWs on the high-speed track, and the car was then sent to Belgium, where it set new 1,500cc open-road speed records for that country.

By now the Spyders had made quite a splash in sports-car circles, but at $5,800 ex-factory and $6,500 in the United States, there was no chance of them ever becoming common. Some were regularly driven on the highways, often to and from races, including one of the cars sold by John von Neumann's Competition Motors. It went to a young film star named James Dean, who had been racing a 1500 Super Speedster but wanted something faster. Dean was intending to put some break-in miles on the new car, so he drove from Competition Motors in Los Angeles to a race in Salinas on September 30, 1955. Near Paso Robles he collided nearly head-on with a Ford sedan and died instantly. Riding with him was Rolf Wütherich, a factory mechanic who was in California instructing and troubleshooting for von Neumann and who survived the accident. Porsche received a great deal of dubious publicity as the wreck was paraded across the Southwest in a display sponsored by a road safety organization. Months later, it was said to have vanished from a train car somewhere in Texas and was never seen again. The car's transaxle turned up decades later and was sold at auction in 2021 for $387,000.

550A/1500 RS

The 550's ladder frame made for quirky handling at times. Privateers would continue racing some of the seventy-eight Typ 550/1500 RS Spyders sold in 1954–1956, but by the end of 1955 the factory was well into a new program that would replace the original with a new chassis and an improved engine. The flexible handling of the original car was addressed with a space frame built from thin-wall tubing, with each section stressed to produce an extremely strong unit. The weight of both chassis and body was down by almost 100 pounds.

Front suspension remained much the same, but the rear was completely revised. New outer universal joints provided true independent rear suspension, and the changes dramatically improved the earlier car's tendency to wag its tail in hard cornering. The third improvement was in the engine, where Wilhelm Hild and the development engineers found that relocating the distributors to the crankshaft nose gave much-improved ignition control, and with 9.8:1 compression and Weber carbs, both power and torque output were up. Other detail changes were 12-volt electrics, a new ZF steering box, finned tube shock absorbers, and a few body modifications. The hinged rear engine cover was now a lift-off unit with large louvered doors on either side for carburetor and oil tank access. The 550A weighed 1,166 pounds dry and would accelerate to 60 miles per hour in 7.2 seconds, but these new models would not be available to the public until late in the year.

WINNING WAYS CONTINUE

For the 1956 season, factory drivers successfully used four examples of the improved version, though at the Mille Miglia in April Hans Herrmann was a backmarker. That same car, driven by Count Wolfgang von Trips and Umberto Maglioli, and a second driven by Herrmann and von Frankenberg took first and second in class and fourth and sixth overall, respectively, at the 1,000-kilometer Nürburgring race in May.

Michael May's wing was years ahead of the times.

Porsches appealed to the rich and famous (and titled) even in the 1950s. Berlin Philharmonic conductor Herbert von Karajan was an enthusiastic driver, replacing his Speedster with a 550 Spyder. Here Richard von Frankenberg gives him a personal introduction to the new car.

Jack McAfee at Sebring in 1956 in John Edgar's 550, which finished second in class after Hermann/von Trips. Customers were fielding Spyders at tracks all around the United States.

That contest would have made motorsports history but for racing politics. Young Swiss engineer Michael May brought a well-worn 550 Spyder that sported a curious wing appendage. Mounted above the cockpit and situated at the car's center of gravity, May had designed it to increase the downforce on the tires at speed, helping grip in fast corners. The device was adjustable from the driver's seat. In a rainy practice session May was able to pass the best drivers in the fastest cars, and his fourth-fastest qualifying time was better than that of either of the factory Porsches. Von Hanstein pressured the organizers to disqualify him, using the argument that the device blocked the vision of other drivers. But it is hard to believe that afterward, neither Porsche nor any other competitors took seriously this extremely effective tool for increasing performance. Well over a decade would pass before the concept was again applied to racing cars. May went on to become an established engineer who would work for Porsche in 1961 and feature prominently in the development of the four-cam engine in its ultimate form.

Flush with confidence in the new car after the one-two class finish at the 'Ring, Maglioli and von Hanstein hatched an impulsive plan to enter the Targa Florio in Sicily. With a hastily painted white Spyder and only two mechanics, the pair decided only days before the June 10, 1956, race to try their luck on the tortuous island course.

In the race, the larger Ferraris and Maseratis were soon felled by mechanical problems, and after 8 hours of rough, twisting roads the Italian's solo drive paid off with an overall win by 13 minutes for the little white Porsche. It was only the second for a German team since Dr. Ferdinand Porsche's 2.0-liter Mercedes had won the Sicilian race in 1924. It was hailed as Porsche's greatest victory, though the factory's effort was, as historian Karl Ludvigsen describes it, "informal to the point of being ridiculous."

From the racing department in Zuffenhausen Werk I came two new cars for the June 1956 24-hour race at Le Mans. New regulations required full windshields, and again the roadsters were converted to coupes, this time by riveting a full roof to the removable rear cover panels. The enclosed shape was good for Mulsanne Straight speeds of 138 miles per hour in the rain, and though one car retired, von Frankenberg and von Trips took class honors at fifth overall, second in the index of performance. The 1956 season continued with the first three places in the Reims 12-hour race; a one-two win at Porsche's backyard track, Solitude; and a season finale with von Trips taking the class win on the long AVUS oval in Berlin. Here, Porsche's success was overshadowed by its most spectacular failure, the results of pushing aerodynamic efficiency beyond the limit.

THE MOUSE THAT FLEW

Observing the tiny "Poopers," whose frontal area and weight gave them much advantage, and in the face of competitive pressure from other small-bore racers, a new style of Spyder, Typ 645, was

Mickey Mouse was a radical departure in size and shape. After its fiery end, some of its design features were used in future Spyders.

designed in 1955. If light and small worked well, then lighter and smaller should be even better, or so it was reasoned. New calculations department head Egon Forstner led a team to design a sleek body that they tested in a wind tunnel. The vehicle had a narrower track and shorter wheelbase (by 6 inches) than the 550A. Seen from above, its rounded nose, faired-in lights, covered passenger seat, and rear-facing engine air ducts seemed seriously aerodynamic. Underneath the magnesium skin an early-style four-cam engine was tightly enclosed—as were the tires and driver, for that matter. The single-seater had a fuel tank in the passenger's spot with other innovations, such as oil cooling lines running through ribs under the hood surface and a new sophisticated rear suspension. The car's final development was delayed, but it appeared, completed, for practice at the Nürburgring in May 1956, then raced at Solitude in July.

Richard von Frankenberg was the only man to drive the car in its three public appearances, and he gave it the name "Mickey Mouse" in recognition of its tendency to dart about at speed. Other Porsche drivers had declined to race it after experiencing its handling; the old-style front trailing arms did not play well with the new rear setup. Owing to a much smaller frontal area and light weight, the car's superior top speed would be an advantage on a course like the AVUS, but handling problems remained even after transmission, braking, and overheating defects were sorted out. In the September 16 race at the Berlin track, von Frankenberg was in the lead going into the steeply banked brick wall of the north curve when his car suddenly veered to the right, up the bank and hurtling over the wall. He was thrown from the car and landed in the bushes below, where he was found, unconscious but unhurt, minutes later. Mickey Mouse landed in a parking area and burst into white-hot magnesium flames.

Von Frankenberg and Porsche management quietly left the concept behind, quite willing to move on, although certain features that were pioneered in Mickey Mouse were included in later models.

550A "CUSTOMER" SPYDERS

With the racing season over, the 550A was offered to customers, superseding the original Spyder. Thirty-seven were built in 1956 and 1957, many finding their way to the United States, where they were consistent winners in SCCA racing across the country. Bob Holbert from Pennsylvania bought one, beginning a family connection with Porsche that would last for decades. The factory's policy was becoming clear: each sports-racing model would be made available to private buyers just about the time an improved version was ready for works drivers. By early spring 1957, a new incarnation of the Spyder was well underway, but some time would elapse between its first appearance and its readiness for battle.

TYPE 718 RSK

The ongoing struggle to control changes in camber during suspension movement led to a revision of the front torsion bars. The top tubes were moved higher and their centers canted downward, the four tubes now suggesting the letter K on its side when seen from the front. Thus, the Typ 718 was commonly called RSK, though a revised frame that allowed the cowl to be lowered by almost 5 inches and an elegantly streamlined body were bigger news than the front suspension. The frame was stronger and lower than on previous cars, and the body more slippery. Seen from above, the nose was rounded. Wind-tunnel testing had shown that the tail of the car was a good place to scavenge air for cooling, so the 718 had grilles in the seat of its pants. Mickey Mouse was not completely forgotten: faired headlights in the sloping, rounded nose and an integral hood oil cooler recalled that ill-fated car. A replaceable nose panel could carry lights or ducts if necessary.

Another distinctive body feature showed up after the car's first public appearance at practice for the Nürburgring 1,000-kilometer race in May 1957. Lateral instability was noted, so when it arrived at Le Mans the next month, square fins had sprouted on each rear fender. During practice Edgar Barth, a former EMW driver from East Germany, spun several times in the car, causing some concern about the fins' effectiveness. In the race, the car proved no faster than the previous 550As and crashed out before the halfway mark. Realizing that this was no contender, Porsche entered an RSK in only a few hillclimbs the rest of that season and began to sort out the problems.

Controls were moved to the center on a 1957 RSK with new suspension. Bulges, fins, and rear wheel spats were used at a 1958 Formula 2 race in Reims, where Frenchman Jean Behra took a win, emboldening the company to pursue their F2 aspirations.

Two new engines were added to the four-cam lineup by 1957, displacing 1,587cc and 1,679cc but for convenience called the 1600 and 1700. The smaller of these, Typ 547/4, had a bore of 87.5mm while the 547/5 carried 90mm barrels. First used in 2.0-liter hillclimb classes, these "large" four-cams later proved competitive with engines half again their size.

The bodies were still hand-built at Wendler in Reutlingen, and power from the aging four-cam just kept climbing. Fuel was now fed through 46 IDM Webers. With up to 9.8:1 compression, the motors could be tuned for power or longevity, but drivers were warned to keep revs under 7,600 rpm. A new Hirth crank was online with larger main and rod journals, but its design weaknesses eventually became apparent.

RSK IMPROVEMENTS

With more work by spring of 1958, the RSK finally came into its own at the Targa Florio with a second-overall finish, Barth and Frenchman Jean Behra piloting. The suspension had again been revised at the front: the K went back to an H, and the ball joints tried in 1957 were dropped. At the back, the torsion bars were discarded for the first time in any Porsche. Watt's linkages and coil-over shocks located the rear hubs with new universal joints inboard. The split-case transmission was gone, the new Typ 690 replacement being similar to the tunnel-case unit used on the production cars. An oil cooler was added along the left rocker panel with a scoop below and an oval outlet ahead of the rear wheel opening—a distinguishing feature of the 1958 cars, along with five slits in the side access panels. The RSK's record during the 1958 season included highlights at Le Mans, where Behra and Hans Herrmann in a 1600 placed third overall (first in the 2.0-liter class) while Edgar Barth and Paul Frère took 1500 class honors and fourth, closely followed by a 550A in fifth spot.

A center-seat adaptation, built from the Barth/Frère Le Mans car to the Formula 2 specifications that had been revived in 1957, was entered at Reims with native favorite Behra driving. The car proved faster than any of the Cooper, Lotus, or Ferrari competitions in this 1.5-liter Junior series. A second for Barth at Nürburgring and a class win by Masten Gregory at the AVUS demonstrated Porsche's serious intentions in Formula 2.

When the season ended on the Continent, Behra went to sunny California and, with the assistance of ace mechanic Vasek Polak, gave many West Coast racers a view of the RSK's tail with a fourth overall in the Los Angeles Times Grand Prix. That car stayed in the United States, the first of seventeen RSKs in the country with drivers who would dominate SCCA Class F racing for the next four years—and other classes as well, when displacement was sometimes changed by private owners. For skilled racers, the Spyder was an $8,000 ticket to the trophy stand, and Porsche couldn't build enough of them.

By the beginning of the 1959 season, Zuffenhausen was ready with a new rear suspension, now incorporating double wishbones in a semitrailing configuration, with softer springing and a bit more predictability. In the first race at Sebring, Joakim Bonnier and von Trips in a Typ 718 with the new rear suspension led Americans Bob Holbert and Don Sesslar in a three-four-five Spyder finish behind the larger Ferraris, with three more Porsches in the next six spots. At that year's Targa Florio, the finishing order was Porsche one-two-three-four, with Barth and Wolfgang Seidel's 1.5-liter RSK followed by a 550 and two Carreras.

After a respectable showing at the Nürburgring, Ferry Porsche decided to wager all at Le Mans with high-lift cams in each factory car, but one after another the Spyders retired with engine and drivetrain failures. Not a single RSK finished, but at least in this race the only victims were machines.

At the AVUS five weeks later, factory 1500 RSKs were joined by private Spyder entries, including Carel Godin de Beaufort, who early in the race entered the bricks of the north banking too fast and could retain only enough control to steer over the top and bump his way down the other side through the bushes. He found himself in the paddock and, without hesitation, drove to the pit entrance and back onto the track; officials looked on in amazement while he rejoined the fray but

With a revised frame (seen here from the rear), there was no longer a cross tube for torsion bars.

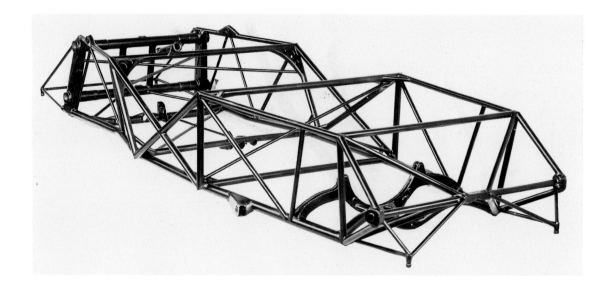

TOP: An RSK body is ready for its mechanicals at the factory. A top and luggage space were mandated by the FIA for "sports cars." A roll bar is hidden beneath the rear fairing, and louvered doors give access to the oil tank on the right. **ABOVE:** The 1958 RSK had a low scoop for oil-cooler air and an outlet just in front of the rear wheel. The stubby wings were not as effective as they looked.

FORMULA CARS

One direction Zuffenhausen took in the new decade would be toward Formula cars, first using the four-cam four, then with development of a flat eight. Formula 2 rules beginning in 1957 allowed fully fendered cars such as the 550 to compete, and tentative entries were made that year. Porsche built a center-seat RSK in 1958 and raced three times with success. In 1959 came five special RSKs, convertible from left to center steering, raced by both the factory and private owners. The first Porsche open-wheelers took to the track in 1959, using modified RSK components in a tightly packed frame and body, with a four-cam Typ 547/3 of 150 horsepower and a new six-speed gearbox. Named the 718/2, five cars campaigned in 1960 with a variety of drivers, including Stirling Moss, and season results were good enough that Porsche set its sights on Formula 1 for 1961.

The 718/2 cars were modified before and during the 1961 season, and a new chassis debuted, called Typ 787. In 1962 engineer Michael May came from Mercedes to find more power in the aging four-cam. Fuel injection and significant internal changes ended up producing over 185 horsepower, undreamed of by previous racing department engineers. It was the end of the road for both the engine and Michael May at Porsche, however. As focus shifted to the new Typ 753 eight-cylinder Formula 1 engine, May quickly was hired by Ferrari.

Developed during 1960 and 1961, the 1.5-liter flat eight had overhead cams driven by short shafts with bevel gears, as in the Typ 547. The ten crankshaft bearings were plain shells, as were the rods. Four dual-throat carbs and dry-sump lubrication were used, and valve angle and other specifications changed as the engine underwent testing. Horsepower was in the 185 range at 9,000 rpm.

A Typ 804 chassis was built of welded tubes specifically to house the new eight, with the same wheelbase as the previous 787 using Porsche disc brakes. It was first seen publicly at the Dutch Grand Prix on May 20, 1962. There, budding American star Dan Gurney wedged his tall body into the car and had to settle for a DNF after his shifter broke. For the French Grand Prix at Rouen-les-Essarts on July 8, 1962, Gurney brought his No. 30 home to win the race. It was Porsche's first and last win in Formula 1. At the Solitude track in Stuttgart later in July, Gurney and Bonnier were one-two in front of a huge home crowd, but it was a moral victory only, as the race was nonpoints.

After seven World Championship points races and two nonpoints contests in 1962, Porsche exited the Formula 1 world to concentrate again on sports-car racing, an area that was much closer to its core business of selling sports cars.

ABOVE: The Typ 804 Formula 1 car carried Porsche's 8-cylinder engine with a flat fan.
RIGHT: Porsche's open wheel 718/2 Formula 2 car was a tight fit for the 4-cam motor. On-site race repairs were done al fresco.
FAR RIGHT: The Porsche-Behra special was based on the RSK. Initially, this Italian-built adaptation was more successful than the first of Porsche's F2 entries.

soon black-flagged him. Later in the race, Jean Behra was straining for the lead when his Spyder also slid up the brick banking, at a point where a concrete pylon was located. His race and his life ended there, a great loss to both Porsche and Ferrari, with whom he had been under contract earlier that season. Von Trips won that tragic 1,500cc race, adding laurels to a season that would bring Porsche to a close third place in the sports-car manufacturer's championship points.

With the end of the 1959 season, the Spyder had proven itself in six years of development as the machine to beat in everything from SCCA racing in the United States to hillclimbs in Europe. Now it set its sights on a bigger prize—the Formula 2 rules seemed to have been written with Porsche in mind. And from there, it wasn't that far a leap to the top, Formula 1.

RS 60 AND RS 61

For 1960, the RSK ran head-on into new regulations that mandated a close resemblance to "real" cars, including a higher windshield and even luggage space. Porsche's response was called the RS 60 and featured a wider body and a 4-inch-longer wheelbase, which, drivers agreed, improved handling. Fourteen were built, and customers didn't have to wait this year; for $9,000 a select few got the same cars as factory drivers. At Sebring in March 1960 Hans Hermann and Olivier Gendebien won the 12-hour race by nine laps; a Brumos-sponsored car was in second, ahead of six Ferraris. Graham Hill came over from Lotus, and the factory team had a fairly successful season, highlighted by another victory in the Targa

The W-RS (Welt-Rennsport) 718 traveled the globe for four years as a potent road-race and hillclimb weapon.

The 718 GTR coupe had the eight-cylinder engine and disc brakes. Jo Bonnier and Carlo Maria Abate used it to win the 1963 Targa Florio.

Florio with Bonnier and Hermann. A dismal placing at Le Mans left Porsche tied with Ferrari for manufacturer's championship points. The title went to the Italians, who had one more third-place finish.

Another fourteen Typ 718 cars were built for the 1961 season and called, predictably, RS 61. It was another year of variations on a theme, including a stretched wheelbase on one open car, designed for an upcoming eight-cylinder motor, the Formula 1 Typ 753. Chassis #718-047, called the W-RS, had a built-up full-width panel above the engine, louvered on its sides and open at the back, an adaptation of an appendage tried the year before. Its career began at the 1961 Targa Florio and Nürburgring before being used as a hillclimb car for Edgar Barth's 1963 championship, with fiberglass lids and doors. Over four years and thirty races,

it was nicknamed "Grandmother" for its long and well-traveled career. Two other long chassis were used to build coupes, all three cars featuring a sharply raked nose and windshield, a new design by Ferry's oldest son, Ferdinand Alexander Porsche.

Like the RS 60, the 1961 cars had built-in round lights or horns at the front, but they also had a large front-hinged hood that extended below the nose. At Sebring, Florida, two factory cars dropped out; Bob Holbert and Roger Penske brought home their customer RS 61 in sixth for the best Porsche finish.

A racing version of the 1,966cc four-cam "Carrera 2" production engine appeared in mid-1961, with plain bearings, a bore and stroke at 92mm×74mm, and 9.8:1 compression, producing 165 horsepower and better torque. It was used in the April Targa Florio by Jo Bonnier and Dan Gurney in the W-RS,

Bob Holbert, a Porsche dealer and racer from Pennsylvania at the wheel of the Brumos RS-60 at Sebring in 1960, co-driven by Roy Schecter and Howard Fowler. They took a second to the overall winner, Hermann and Gendebien in a similar car.

ABOVE: A group of restored 718s at the Porsche Race Car Classic in 2012. Variations on the theme include a center-seater (front) and the W-RS "Grandmother" (center). RIGHT: The first "Abarth" Carrera GTL at the Italian factory. It started with ten louvers and ended up with forty-eight.

the long-wheelbase roadster. Hired English drivers Stirling Moss and Graham Hill in a factory RS 61 led until the last lap, dashing hopes for a third straight Targa win. Porsche took second and third with a 2.0 class win as consolation. At Le Mans, the 718 RS 61s managed a 2.0 class win under Masten Gregory and Bob Holbert, with a Ben Pon and Herbert Linge Carrera GTL taking the 1.6-liter class win.

At the end of the season, Porsche was a distant third in FIA manufacturer's points. Development of the Typ 753 flat-eight 1.5-liter Grand Prix engine, first begun in 1959, was maddeningly slow. The four-cam four was getting long in the tooth and was beginning to be outclassed in endurance racing when Michael May came to Porsche from Mercedes in July 1961. By spring 1962, he was able to extract 185 horsepower from the 1.5-liter four using Bosch mechanical fuel injection, a flat fan, and various head and piston modifications. His abrupt departure the next spring was related to internal politics at Porsche and coincided with the emergence of the eight-cylinder motor, which replaced the venerable four in sports-car endurance and formula racing. The new 901 six engine would continue in Grand Touring classes.

The Typ 550 had begun in 1953 as a direct descendant of the first Porsche and a close relative of the road cars, but after nine years of development, the thread of connection was stretched thin. After approximately 130 550s and 550As were built, and 73 in the 718 series, aluminum racers were obsolete. The racing department by 1961 was busily engaged in the

rarified atmosphere of Formula cars, but starting grids around the world were still filled with Porsches of all descriptions, from ultralightweight specials to 356 coupes. It was these road cars that carried on the spirit of the original Spyders with the last remaining link—the four-cam engine.

"PRODUCTION CAR" GT RACING: ABARTH CARRERA GTL

In production car classes, the Gmünd coupes brought Porsche's first racing laurels, and that continued for several years. FIA GT class coupes had done well through the 1950s, but the new 1960 356B was heavier and, it was felt, uncompetitive. Lightness was the key, and Porsche decided to farm out a new "Grand Touring Lightweight" Typ 756 project to friend Carlo Abarth, who arranged for design and production of the cars in Italy. Abarth used subcontractors, and there is still some confusion about who built what, but the first svelte finished car delivered to Zuffenhausen in February 1960 weighed 100 pounds less than a standard 356 coupe with a frontal area 16 percent slimmer. It was 4.7 inches narrower and just over 5 inches lower and shorter. The Italian design was attractive, but the finish was nowhere near German standards, even for a race car. From the front, an aerodynamic sloping nose, raked windshield, and muscular rear flanks culminated in a large engine lid with louvers. That first car's small body constrained the turning of the front wheels, the entry of the driver, and the installation

Porsche's three-pronged attack in 1960: a Formula 2 Typ 718/2, a Grand Touring Abarth Carrera GT, and an RS 60 for sports racing.

LEFT: The two 356B GT 2000 Carrera GS/GT Dreikantschabers were slightly different, but both carried the new annular disc brakes. They were successful in both Europe and America.

BELOW: At the May 1963 Nürburgring 1,000 kilometer race, Hans-Joachim Walter, Ben Pon, Edgar Barth, and Herbert Linge took fourth overall in the #31 Dreikantschaber.

of the four-cam engine. These issues, as well as general build quality, were sorted out over the next nineteen cars.

Over a period of two years the Carrera GTL racked up impressive race results, beginning at the Targa Florio in May 1960. At Le Mans that year a GTL took the GT 1.6 class ahead of a 718 Spyder and a slew of DNF Porsches. In 1961 two GTLs took the GT 1.6 class at Sebring and were competitive across the country; Le Mans saw Linge and Pon take another class win. In Germany at the 'Ring in 1962 GTLs took the first two places in 1.6, and at Le Mans that year they were in seventh and twelfth overall. The cars were at venues large and small in the early 1960s, some later cars with 2.0-liter powerplants, upholding Porsche's honor among Grand Touring cars. The factory, however, had one other ace up its sleeve.

THE DREIKANTSCHABER

The idea of continuing the Abarth Carrera line became a dead end in early 1963, and an in-house project took shape to continue the already-homologated 356B GT series. An aluminum body was designed in the styling studio, where Ferdinand Alexander "Butzi" Porsche was heavily involved. Built by Wendler on Carrera 2 chassis #122991, it was ready in March 1963. A steeply sloped

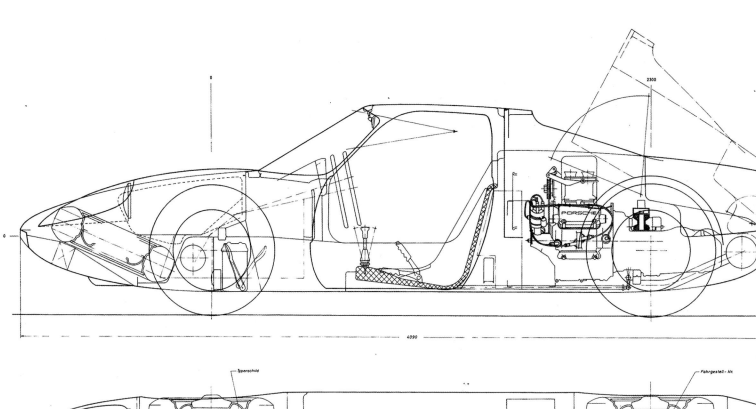

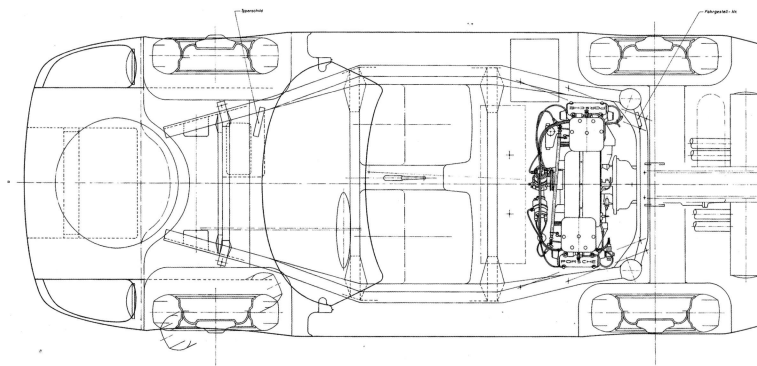

The box-member frame was unlike anything previously done at Porsche. Suspension was new as well.

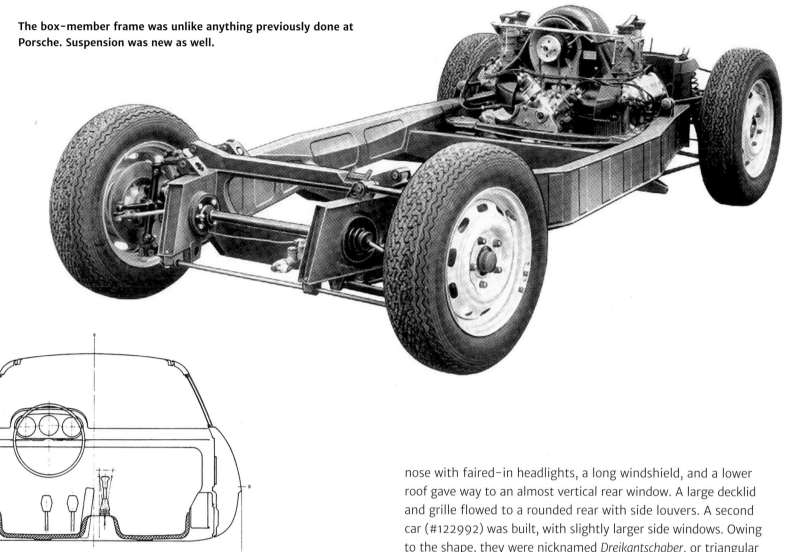

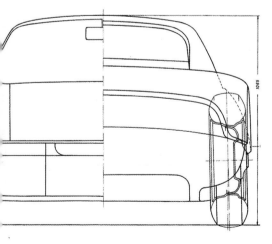

The 904 fiberglass body was bonded to the frame, which ended at the rear suspension. The pleasing shape, drawn by FA Porsche, was little modified from the original, as there was no time for modifications.

nose with faired-in headlights, a long windshield, and a lower roof gave way to an almost vertical rear window. A large decklid and grille flowed to a rounded rear with side louvers. A second car (#122992) was built, with slightly larger side windows. Owing to the shape, they were nicknamed *Dreikantschaber*, or triangular scraper. During the 1963 season the 356B Carreras had a mixed record but scored some GT 2.0-class wins in enduros and hillclimbs. At Daytona in January 1964, Barth and Linge took sixth overall and won the 2.0 class, with the other car in eighth. At Sebring in March, Ben Pon and Joe Buzzetta were the top Porsche in eleventh place, winning the GT 2.0-liter class and besting a new Zuffenhausen racer debuting there, the Typ 904.

At the April Targa Florio, Günter Klass and Jochen Neerpasch would bring chassis #122991 across the line in seventh place overall and third in class, this time following three 904s, one of them an eight-cylinder. It was the last big race for this "interim" racer. The two 356B GTs had kept the flame burning while a new Grand Touring racer was being developed. These last aluminum cars were successful beyond expectations, but the future was plastic and held more cylinders than the venerable four-cam Fuhrmann four.

CARRERA GTS TYP 904

F. A. Porsche became head of styling in 1963 after six years with the company. Late the previous year a commitment to a new GT racer had been made; it would be midengined and use the 901 engine and five-speed transmission, both under

Sold for both racing and street use, the 904 was a lovely shape. Vasek Polak had several Spyders and this 904, on display in his Manhattan Beach, California, showroom.

development at the time. A small frontal area and light weight would be necessary, but the dimensions would have to allow some usability as a "road" car, as one hundred would need to be sold for homologation.

In the last series of Spyders, the 718 coupe had proven aerodynamic and fast, as well as attractive—at least in its front half. Butzi melded attributes of that car into a shape for the new 904: a long, sloping hood; faired headlights; a large, curved windshield; and door cuts into the roof. The rear window was part of a vertical panel defining the cockpit, centered in a cavity around which the rear body sides flowed, ending in a tail sharply cut down and angled forward according to aerodynamicist Wunibald Kamm's designs. A pleasing beltline cut went from nose to tail, strengthening the form.

The design process was necessarily shortened to the four months available, and an unusual approach was taken with

both frame and body. Porsche engineers under Hans Tomala designed a frame using two "C"-section stamped steel members that ran from nose to rear axle, enclosed by flat vertical steel on the outside. Two low crossmembers supported the cockpit floor. Boxed steel lateral frames at front and rear held the suspension; in the front, wishbones and coil springs with integral shocks. The rear suspension was complicated, with radius rods from the frame rail to a single lower control arm and a reversed upper wishbone. An angled hub carrier held a driveshaft with double Nadella U-joints. Antiroll bars were used rear and front, with rack-and-pinion steering. Brakes were basic 356C discs, with alloy-center 5×15-inch wheels.

A 2.0-liter four-cam was fitted, as the new 901 six was only producing 130 horsepower. The Typ 587/3 with 180 horsepower was installed in most cars, and even the detuned street versions with air cleaners and mufflers could produce 155

Seen here at Sebring, the 904 had a frame hung from the chassis crossmember to support the transmission, muffler, and rear bodywork. Nadella half shafts and 356/901 disc brakes can be seen.

horsepower at 6,400 rpm. A five-speed gearbox with a new-style ZF limited-slip differential was used, and sixteen different gear sets were offered. Near the end of the hundred-plus-car production, about ten cars would have six-cylinder engines installed, and a half dozen would use an eight-cylinder engine.

A full-size model was completed in February 1963 and used to make molds for a glass-reinforced plastic body to be bonded to the frame by Heinkel, the aircraft maker. The effort to save time and expense was successful, but the effort to save weight was not; some of the first cars were as much as 1,700 pounds. Heinkel improved their processes, and later cars were in the 1,450-pound range. Tested at the new Weissach skid pad in August 1963, the model's first race was at Daytona in early 1964. As it was not yet homologated, "private" entries took fifth and ninth overall in a 250-mile race. In March at Sebring, Briggs Cunningham—still a Porsche enthusiast after

more than a decade—took a prototype-class win. At the Targa Florio, 904s took first and second overall, besting Ferraris and Cobras. At year's end Porsche took the 2.0-liter class manufacturer's championship. The following year it was eight- and six-cylinder 904s that took the spotlight, pointing the way to a new era of race and road cars, but the 904 had made its mark at racetracks around the world.

This was a car of firsts and lasts: The first Porsche to use a ladder chassis and fiberglass body, and to be sold as a homologated race car along with street versions. It was also the end of the four-cam era, and the last dual-purpose road/race car from the company. It is also remembered by many as perhaps the most attractive Porsche ever made.

The 356A, with an expanded product line now including the coupe, cabriolet, and Speedster, gave Porsche customers more reasons to buy. Engine choices ranged from the 1300 to the 1600 in both Normal (Damen) and Super versions. Four-cam powerplants were available for the sports-minded driver. Sales were strong enough that Reutter was under pressure to increase production even though its Zuffenhausen works were near capacity. At Porsche Werk II on March 16, 1956, assembly paused while an aquamarine-blue coupe rolled off the assembly line, the ten thousandth Porsche built. Bedecked in flowers, it

From 1956, the four-cam racing powerplant made its way to the street in coupes, cabriolets, and Speedsters. At the top of the 356A model line for 1957 was the Carrera GS/GT, a potent lightweight. Chassis 100369 was one of the first imported to Max Hoffman, and like many 356s, went through several owners over the years, suffering such indignities as a grafted-on "B" nose and cheap upholstery. Returning to Europe via Italy, France, and finally, England, it was carefully restored and today again represents the pinnacle of Porsche Grand Touring from the time.

Ferry Porsche and a flower-bedecked 356A coupe, the ten thousandth Porsche built.

was a background for speeches from Ferry Porsche, along with VW chief Heinz Nordhoff and Stuttgart mayor Arnulf Klett, both of whom had been instrumental in the company's prosperity. By the end of 1956, all the effort could be seen as worthwhile: total production had increased by 1,200 cars, or 45 percent, to 4,152, with 2,350 going to America.

"INTELLIGENT AND SENSIBLE DRIVING"

Albert Prinzing wrote early on that "the customer attaches importance to having an exclusive vehicle, but at the same time places the same demands on us as on a mass-marketed vehicle." Performance was only part of the equation; utility and longevity were also important to Porsche buyers. Any customer who reached a milestone of 100,000 kilometers was rewarded by the factory initially with a gold watch, then with a special grille badge commemorating their achievement. Today 62,137 miles is only a spark-plug change interval, but in the 1950s it was a lot. VW had such a program for years, and Porsche followed suit in the early 1950s. An original owner was required to verify mileage

through their dealer, then a cloisonné badge was mailed, along with a letter stating that it was, in part, "to thank you for your intelligent and sensible driving. In wishing you further 'driving in its finest form' with your Porsche, we remain, very truly yours."

FLAUNTING SUCCESS IN AMERICA

In the United States, Porsche's largest market by far, the man who had made it so was planning to make a statement. Max Hoffman wanted a new showplace showroom for his premier brand, Jaguar. He went to see his friend architect Philip Johnson, known for his "glass box" homes, in 1952. Johnson demurred, but suggested another architect, Frank Lloyd Wright. Hoffman and Wright met, and plans for a home in Rye, New York, began to take shape. In April 1954 a Wright-designed auto showroom was announced for Park Avenue at Fifty-Sixth Street. By the time it was completed in May 1955, the project was late and over budget (typical with Wright), and it no longer featured Jaguars. Hoffman had ended the relationship with Jaguar's William Lyons in a rancorous tiff over his taking on the Mercedes-Benz line.

ABOVE: The New York Hoffman showroom, originally meant to showcase Jaguars, had Porsches and BMWs on its rotating display table in 1955. Mirrors made the modest space look larger. Architect Frank Lloyd Wright complained that a bare BMW chassis and decorations took up too much space, but Max made the most of his showcase showroom.

LEFT: The original 100,000-kilometer badge has been reproduced several times, but in the 1950s and 1960s it represented a real accomplishment.

Using circular motifs like those of his Guggenheim Museum, which was rising a few blocks away, Wright called the showroom his "bijou," and it was indeed a small and elegant jewel. Key elements were a rotating car table with a central planter and a ramp rising along one side that ended in a cantilevered balcony. Porsches became the featured product along with BMW and Mercedes, the latter being sold there until the showroom was unceremoniously demolished in March 2013. Hoffman's new showroom was a fitting place to market what he called the "German automotive jewel."

TECHNICAL PROGRAM 2

While the 356A was enjoying critical success in the motoring press, engineers were planning improvements and additions to be in place by the biennial Frankfurt show in September 1957. Some running changes were made earlier in the year, as in March 1957, when "teardrop" taillights replaced the double "beehives." The rear license light, with integrated backup light, was moved

from above to below, and front turn signals got taller lenses. The speedometer was moved from the left to the right of the tach, to be more easily read by a rally navigator. A coupe chassis-numbering change took place, beginning at #100001. One more running change was made during the year: a new single-housing aluminum transmission replaced the "split-case" Typ 519. The new tunnel-case gearbox was given the Typ 644 designation, the number reused from the aborted 356 body modification plan of 1954. Stronger and easier to service, the new case would carry on through the end of the 356 line.

Enough significant changes were ready for the September Frankfurt show that Porsche gave the body a new designation: T-2 for Technical Program 2. Overseeing these many changes was Klaus von Rücker, new head of the experimental and technical department. A German recruited from Studebaker, he was a seasoned engineer familiar with American manufacturing processes. Ferry Porsche valued his experience and promoted him in April 1956 to replace Ernst Fuhrmann, who left Porsche and moved to engine parts maker Goetze. Fuhrmann would later come back to lead the company.

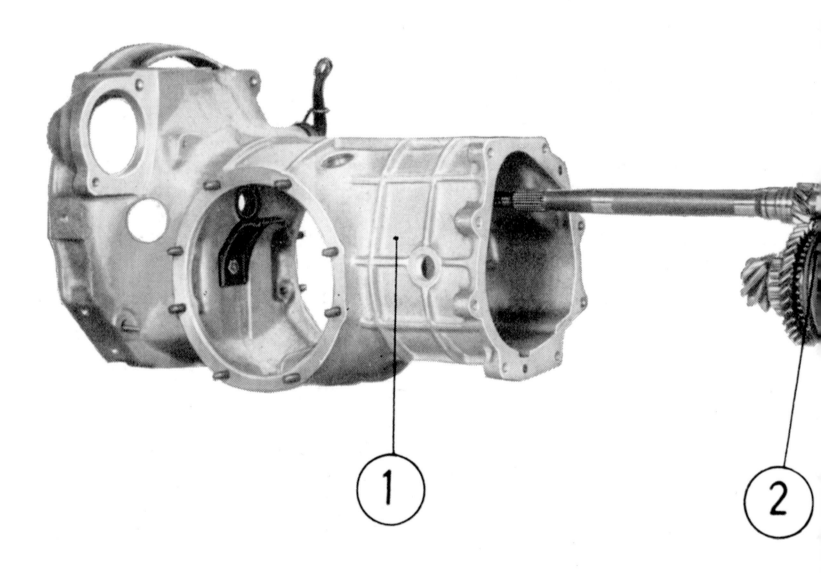

As seen in the factory lot near the gas shed, the T-2 transition was visually subtle from the outside. Cars bound for America had bumper overriders.

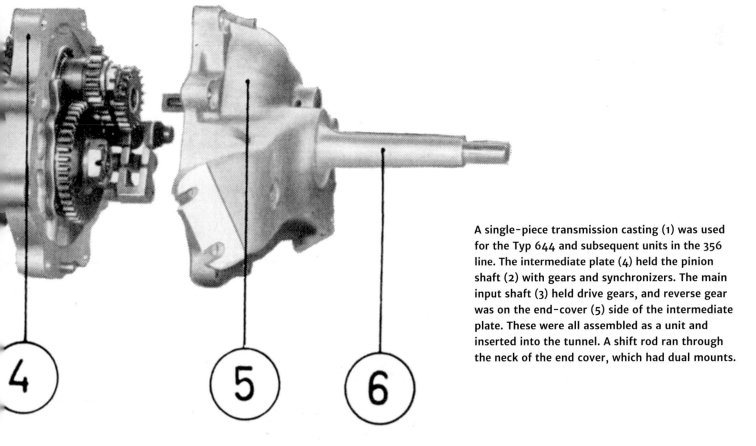

A single-piece transmission casting (1) was used for the Typ 644 and subsequent units in the 356 line. The intermediate plate (4) held the pinion shaft (2) with gears and synchronizers. The main input shaft (3) held drive gears, and reverse gear was on the end-cover (5) side of the intermediate plate. These were all assembled as a unit and inserted into the tunnel. A shift rod ran through the neck of the end cover, which had dual mounts.

THE *RENNLEITER*

Fritz Sittig Enno Werner von Hanstein was born into a noble German family in 1911. He trained in law and business, but in his twenties he began racing motorcycles, then took to four-wheel competition as a works driver with Hanomag, Adler, and BMW. He raced at Le Mans in 1937 and 1939 and, with a co-driver, won the adapted 1940 Mille Miglia in a BMW 328. After serving in the war, he lost his family estate in East Germany but continued racing open-wheelers with motorcycle engines. Huschke, as he was called, was introduced to Porsche through VW and old Auto Union connections. Moving from selling Vespas, he was hired by Porsche in 1952 in a loosely defined position as racing driver, customer service troubleshooter, and press spokesman. He also sold Porsches to his well-to-do friends. That autumn he was given dual clear titles: that of *Rennleiter* (racing director) and head of public relations.

Von Hanstein was behind the wheel of Porsches at races and hillclimbs and, memorably, took part in the 1951 Montlhéry record run. His intimate knowledge of Porsche racing machines gave him valuable insight into their strengths and weaknesses and how they should be developed to adhere to—and take advantage of—the rules set down by sanctioning bodies. He was a consummate diplomat: smiling, generous with compliments, and persuasive. An official statement by Porsche on what would have been his hundredth birthday read, "With the bearing of a man of the world and self-assured elegance, matched with a gift for rhetoric and mastery of many languages, Huschke von Hanstein achieved a great reputation in the automobile world." As the voice of Porsche for sixteen years, he knew everyone, and everyone knew him. "The baron has arrived!" might be heard at a cocktail reception or in a Sicilian village along the Mille Miglia route. In choosing races, readying cars, managing teams, and seeing to all the logistics of moving men and machines, he was a one-man dynamo. He was a cheerleader for the company and managed to hire first-tier drivers on a shoestring budget, with a handshake. "But it's an honor to drive for Porsche," he would cajole, something at which he was an expert.

Von Hanstein oversaw a staff of up to ten in his other job as public relations director. He hired a young lady named Evi Butz in 1961 to help handle advertising, which consisted of race reports that the press would disseminate. "It was made clear to us who worked for him directly, that furthering Porsche's image was what we were there for," Butz later wrote. "Getting the Porsche name in the paper as often as possible, preferably daily, was the top priority." In addition to print, with a movie camera, Huschke documented much of what happened at the track and around the factory, and it seemed he was always present to greet an important business client, vendor, or customer. Though demanding of his staff, he was also gracious,

and perhaps the only mistake he made was asking American driver Dan Gurney to give young Evi Butz a ride back to the office from the Solitude circuit in 1962. A few years later she left her job to become Mrs. Gurney and live in America.

The last year that von Hanstein actively ran the racing program was 1968. Ferdinand Piëch, son of Louise and Anton, had been very involved in the engineering of race cars since his arrival in 1963, and his goal was to run the racing program. Starting in 1969 he did, a year later giving Porsche its first Le Mans overall win. Von Hanstein transferred his skills to the Fédération Internationale de l'Automobile (FIA) as German representative, helping establish the kind of rigid rules he had so lithely danced around as race director at Porsche.

Von Hanstein gives his secretary, Evi Butz, a ride back to the office from the Solitude circuit. Female employees like Butz doubled as models for promotional photos.

The *Rennleiter* (center) in his natural element, the track. From left, Richard von Frankenberg, Masten Gregory, Carroll Shelby, Huschke von Hanstein, Herbert Linge, Wolfgang Seidel, and Helm Glöckler at the Tourist Trophy (Belfast) in 1955. Shelby drove a 550 with Gregory to a 1.5 class win, followed by Glöckler/Seidel in second and von Frankenberg/Linge in third. Huschke had a knack for bringing driving talent to Porsche, usually for very little money.

Shown in a classic German color combo of blue and red, the T-2 had the speedometer on the right and a clock above the radio. The oil-temp gauge had numbers, which were deleted on later cars. A knob for heat control was just ahead of the bent shift lever. The full horn ring was an option.

Elsewhere in management, decisions were being made about a "new" model called the hardtop: it was envisioned that some cabriolet bodies would be sold with a separate but semipermanently fixed steel top. In the end, this hardtop, with fixed rear side windows, was attached in the same manner as a soft top, so the two could be swapped with the seasons. Some buyers opted for the hardtop only, which required different rear side upholstery panels. To emphasize the model, these tops were usually painted in a different color from the body. For soft-top owners, there was a new, larger plastic rear window. All T-2 cabriolets received door vent windows for better ventilation.

Inside the T-2, new lighter seats were made from steel shells with thinner, arching backs. Porsche had consulted with medical and academic experts, not only to use their guidance but to be able to say, "With the scientific assistance of back specialists, the seats were designed to better fit the body," as *Auto Motor und Sport* reported. The shifter was moved back and given a bend, but some short drivers and passengers complained that in fourth gear it intruded on the seat. A knob controlling heat was in front of the shifter. Padded visors

replaced the dark green plastic used previously, and two courtesy lights were mounted above the coupe B-pillar, near a new rubber coat hook. New window cranks and a larger 425mm steering wheel were some of the many interior changes. A chrome ashtray was now below the radio panel. An ongoing curiosity of restorers decades later was what kind of colorful contact paper would be found as original backing to the ashtray sliding top; not every piece in a 356 came from a carefully drawn plan.

Outside, the exhaust pipes were routed through low holes in the cast-aluminum bumper overriders. New hubcaps with a center dimple and a ceramic Porsche crest were used on Supers, but available as an option to the standard "baby moons." Not seen in front was a new Ross-design worm-and-peg steering gearbox from ZF. Within the heavier flywheel was a diaphragm clutch plate. The 1300 engines became history, and the 1600 Damen now used cast-iron cylinders—heavier but quieter, as well as less expensive. There were new oil coolers, and the 616/1 Normal got an aluminum cam gear. The Super did away with the roller crank in favor of a counterweighted plain bearing model, and both engines benefited from better oiling

The original hardtop was a cabriolet with a removable steel roof. These were generally painted in a contrasting color to the body. All engines were available, including the Carrera.

and use of Zenith 32 NDIX carburetors. With these carbs a new throttle system was introduced, with a lateral shaft in front of the fan housing. Arms pivoted to the rear to each carb, improving sensitivity and minimizing temperature fluctuations.

Among several other running changes in 1958, a new transmission dubbed Typ 716 that used an improved "blocking" synchronizer system was introduced. Leopold Schmid addressed the problem of excess force needed for certain shifts—especially first gear—by increasing the number of parts in the synchronizer assembly. New brake bands within the split ring employed a servo effect to increase their ability to match input and output shaft speeds. Interestingly, even with added parts the unit was cheaper to produce and was eminently adaptable for Porsche's many outside customers who needed a transmission design.

Soon after the September Frankfurt show, production of these 1958 models ramped up, and by the end of 1957 sales were up by 22 percent to 5,073. The following year saw another increase to 5,854, almost half going to the United States, whose influence was coloring ideas about what the next Porsche should look like.

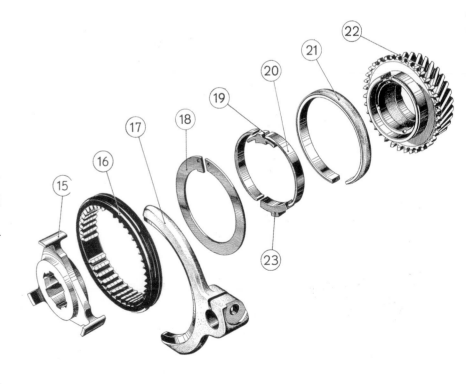

In the new "blocking" synchro transmission, the split ring was now four parts (19, 20, 23).

Speedster GT models had aluminum body parts like the coupes but already had a weight advantage. With a Carrera engine installed, it was a potent package. Bill Romig of Detroit liked the idea so much he bought two, one to race and one to keep for occasional use. Bill passed away in 1993, and his Speedster was later sold, with 7,867 miles on the odometer and no rain ever on the car. Now in Jerry Seinfeld's collection, it's an original and important piece of Porsche history.

THE GRAND TOURING PROGRAM

As the Speedster was being phased out, another model was proliferating. With the T-2 change, a special edition throughout the Carrera line was offered: a weight-saving program using aluminum doors and lids. These GT models had aluminum rim/steel center wheels, simple aluminum bumper trim (although bumpers were steel), and louvered deck lids. Aluminum frames were used for the bucket seats. The last twenty-three Speedsters in 1958 were GT models, and seven of them were built to order for America with 1600 Super engines. The spartan Speedster went out with a flourish.

LEFT: Lightweight Speedster-style buckets, vinyl floor covering, and simple door panels were used in the GT cars. This T-1 coupe has small knobs above the tach for dual ignition and a small knob left of the ignition for the Autopulse electric fuel pump.

ABOVE LEFT: An optional 80-liter fuel tank left zero room in the trunk. Even Carrera Speedsters got the cheaper canvas tire strap. Headlight grilles were common on Speedsters, both factory and aftermarket.

ABOVE RIGHT: Beside the engine itself, Carrera tails were full of wires, hoses, filters, and connectors.

TOP: The GT program meant losing weight wherever possible. Trim was deleted outside, with aluminum panels and wheel outer rims.

The new "Speedster D" by Drauz was unveiled, perhaps prematurely. The fender script was not used in the production version of this one-year-only 356A roadster.

A CIVILIZED SPEEDSTER

For the 1959 model year, there came a reckoning. Early in 1958 Max Hoffman reported that Speedster sales in the United States had declined, and his brainchild had failed to bring the same profits he saw in coupes and cabriolets. It's likely that Ferry Porsche was happy to drop the stripped roadster, but by mutual agreement an upgraded successor was planned, this time with more creature comforts.

Sales of the other 356 models were strong enough to create something of a crisis at Reutter, which was unable to increase production from twenty-four bodies a day. Porsche financial manager Hans Kern began discussions with other body manufacturers to fill the gap. Drauz in Heilbronn, some 40 kilometers north, was initially considered to take over coupe production, as the other three models—cabriolet, hardtop, and Speedster—all used similar bodies and could be concentrated at Reutter. After many discussions, in March 1959 Drauz was instead commissioned to produce two thousand "Sport Convertibles." The logistics were somewhat cumbersome, with

Reutter providing pressed parts and Drauz building the chassis and bodies. Production began in June 1958, and the first fourteen cars carried a side "Speedster" script with the letter "D" below. A change was then made to the model designation, which became simply Convertible D, with no script on the body. The Speedster was officially dead.

The new car kept the Speedster shape, but a higher windshield—still removable and chrome plated—was paired with a taller top and larger rear window. Door windows could wind up and down, and a lockable pocket in the driver's door panels gave a modicum of storage. Gone were the bucket seats, replaced by coupe-like plush recliners in vinyl. The rest of the interior and exterior, including the side spear, remained much the same, but it was a more civilized car. There were production bumps along the way, however; Drauz quality was not really up to Porsche's standards, and production costs ended up higher than planned. During 1958 and 1959 just over 450 were built, as a new model waited in the wings.

CONVERTIBLE D

On Convertible D #85692 much of the paint (5704 Ivory), the interior, and all the chrome, rubber, decorations, and so on are original as they left the factory. This is an early production car built in 1958 (approximately 192nd out of 1,331) with black leatherette and oatmeal carpeting. Owner Dick Morrison of Florida bought the car from Brumos and in 1961 spent $550 for new pistons, a special Isky cam, and associated engine parts to make his 1600 the equivalent of a Super. He removed the bumpers, storing them in the garage rafters, and went amateur racing. A not-uncommon scenario among Porsche buyers at the time, this story is different in that after its short weekend-warrior career, #85692 was carefully stored in a garage for some forty years.

In 2006 it was sold (along with the bumpers) by Morrison's family. Current owner Chuck House purchased it in 2007 and notes, "The Iskenderian race cam gave more power but makes the car challenging to drive unless you keep the revs up. The engine hasn't been apart since." Sixty years later it's still driven to Porsche events. Reflecting Porsche's ongoing quest for improvement, he adds, "This particular Convertible D has an unusual chrome lower windshield frame which differs from all other Ds and Roadsters. This is factory installed and appears to be a prototype/test installation which was not adopted for final production, making the car more unusual and rare."

First owner Dick Morrison hotted up his Convertible D engine to go racing.

The original interior has aged well. Also in top mechanical shape, it's used to attend Porsche events regularly.

Car #85692 retains its original paint and trim.

T-4 TO T-5

Responding to single issues with adjustments or updated parts was an ongoing thing at Porsche. Often a known issue would be quietly dealt with, but usually not until current inventory was used up. In contrast, Porsche "Technical Programs" encompassed large-scale changes, and a new T-4 program was begun in late 1957, even as the T-2 cars were being introduced. (T-3 was a competing program in parallel with T-2 but dropped in 1956.) Technical Program 4 would not only address mechanical improvements but respond to requests from dealers—especially in America—looking for a fresh face on the 356. In contrast, the Volkswagen already had a full decade of sameness and was using it as a marketing tool.

German automakers in general were inclined to slow, conservative changes, unlike American companies, where annual remakes were expected. Porsche was finding a middle ground, with Erwin Komenda and his staff looking to freshen the 356 and at the same time resolving some known issues. Headlights needed to be more effective, so quad bulbs were proposed for a "new" 356. American traffic demanded better bumpers; larger and higher placement was considered. Ventilation needed improvement, so vent windows would be standard on the coupe. Inside, with a new instrument panel, controls would be simplified along with a modern steering wheel, and outside, a new rear deck would use a slot instead of grilles. Under Heinrich Klie, head of Porsche's model department, these ideas were incorporated into a clay model created from designs by Count Albrecht von Goertz, a ringer brought in by Ferry Porsche. Von Goertz had been recommended by Max Hoffman to BMW, for whom he created the 507, a tour-de-force design. It was hoped he could do something as good for Porsche. The model was as far as T-4 got, however, and a new program was begun in June 1958, named Technical Program 5. Once again, steps forward would be evolutionary—at least for a few more years.

Officially underway in November, a goal was set to introduce a new 356 at the Frankfurt biennial show in September 1959. Engineer Franz X. Reimspiess led the charge for Porsche, and with drawings coming from all departments; there would be changes under the skin as well as visually. As coordination with Reutter progressed, new tooling and processes were developed even as the T-2 continued in production. Porsche sales manager Walter Schmidt walked the tightrope of meshing the old and new in the marketplace. August holidays allowed a changeover at Reutter, where once again tooling and jigs, processes, and procedures all had to be modified for the new cars. By September the assembly lines were geared up for the T-5. At Frankfurt, the 356B had arrived.

**ABOVE: An idea for a larger Porsche, Type 695, designed by Albrecht von Goertz in 1957—an early concept for what ultimately became the 911. Photo from February 3, 1958.
RIGHT: In the styling studio at Work II, Ferdinand Alexander (Butzi) and Ferry Porsche discuss ideas for a 356B bumper design.**

Ferry Porsche poses in 1960 with the latest 356B, an RSK, and an assortment of earlier Porsches. The occasion is the filming of *Made by Hand*, a promotional movie conceived by PCA president Bill Sholar and filmed by American Del Ankers. The film doesn't show the scrap metal in a vacant lot, a reminder that even after a decade of building cars, the company was still a small player on the outskirts of town.

THE 356B AND C

For the 1960 model year, the 356 was distinctly different. "It was literally a face-lift," Karl Ludvigsen wrote, "with its bumpers raised 3¾ inches in the front and 4⅛ inches in the rear to give indisputably better protection in traffic and parking." Headlights were raised to meet the fender top, which was now less rounded. The hood had a different shape and its chrome handle was larger and wider. Small grilles below the bumper aided brake ventilation, complementing the redesigned grille/turn signal above. From the side, vent windows were an obvious new touch on the coupes, and in the back, license lights were integrated into the bumper top with a backup light below. Exhaust pipes exited through the two-piece bumper uprights. Behind the wheels new larger, radially finned brake drums were used.

Inside, a new three-spoke dished steering wheel in black plastic matched the knobs, and two stalks on the column controlled turn signals and dimmer on the left, wiper speeds on the right. A stouter, hollow gearshift shaft was topped by a larger black knob. In the "back seat," the bottom pads were now 2½ inches lower, and jump seat backs were separate. The interior was a pleasant and efficient place to conduct the business of driving.

ABOVE LEFT: In 1960 Porsche built 7,559 cars, according to historian Dirk-Michael Conradt. Here an AMAG transporter is loaded with new 356s while others are prepped for overseas delivery. Open car tops were covered with plastic for the long trip. **ABOVE RIGHT:** Gone were gray and beige knobs and steering wheel—black was the standard color for the 356B controls. A radio-blank plate covers the spot above the ashtray. Radio, antenna, and speakers had always been options. **TOP:** Photographer Gunnar Mensch took carefully composed photos of 356s, marketing the images as postcards. For 1960 there was no longer a difference in bumpers for the U.S. cars, but they still used sealed beam headlamps. This sunroof coupe sports whitewalls and Super hubcaps.

Porsche 356Bs on the first test track at the new Weissach facility.

Reutter began production of the new T-5 body at a modest rate, with about two hundred units built during August. A month later the output had more than doubled, with a three-to-one ratio of coupes over cabriolets and hardtops. A needed addition to the Reutter factory was underway, with upgrades to the paint department and a remodeled gatehouse entry to the compound. Porsche itself finished the remodel of a nearby building for sales and customer service, known as Werk III, in fall 1959. In spite of more room, however, pressure on Reutter from Porsche to increase output was ever present.

WEISSACH

Testing of Porsche cars and racers was constant. Analytical measurements of speed and handling were necessary, but the autobahn was becoming too restricted for its needs, and VW's test track in Wolfsburg was too far away. In the late 1950s

Porsche had been using Malmsheim Airfield, just west of Stuttgart, as an occasional skid pad, but the company needed a dedicated venue. Mechanic and driver Herbert Linge suggested a location between the villages of Flacht and Weissach, where he lived, some 25 kilometers west of the factory. Finance director Hans Kern and Ferry's cousin Ghislaine Kaes, after an extensive search, found a 38-hectare property there. Less than prime for agriculture use, it was purchased despite being over Ferry Porsche's budget. On October 16, 1961, the boss broke ground in a ceremony driving a bulldozer.

A circular test track was built with a skid pad of three tracks with inner diameters of 40, 60, and 190 meters. In October 1962, test engineer Peter Falk, Linge, and others tested the early 901 there rigorously. The focus was on basic chassis setup, aerodynamics, and endurance tests. At first a simple hut was the only building, but over the years a large complex would grow, with Porsche development and design headquartered there after 1971.

THE KARDEX

Porsche always strove to offer a variety of color and equipment combinations, and the customer could always have whatever they wanted, for a price. In 1962 Dr. Eugene Wille ordered what may be the most-optioned 356 ever built. His wife chose a blue-green color that reminded her of the water near their home in Wai'anae, Hawaii. They sent a color sample with the order for the car and a request for several options—some twenty-five in all. Shown here is the Kardex for #19205, a Super 90 sunroof coupe.

Kardexes were simple filing cards that were meant to keep track of factory warranty claims, but for restorers they have become an important means of verifying a car's history. The VIN, motor and transmission numbers, paint color ("light green metallic" 60837 is unique), upholstery type and color, key numbers, dealer, and other info are at the top, with options listed below with the buyer's name. Warranty and maintenance records are on the bottom half.

Some Kardexes show no options. Not so with this car, which had an electric sunroof, side moldings, headrests, armrests, limited-slip differential, air horns, full horn ring, seat belts, cocoa mats, chrome wheels, fog lights, hand lamp, travel kit, luggage rack with straps, fire extinguisher, Becker radio, antenna, speakers, and, of course, custom paint (which included several cans of extra paint with the car). The car has been restored to original condition with all options (no mean feat) just as the Willes picked it up at Sonauto in Paris in 1962.

The Kardex is used by Porsche to create a certificate of authenticity for owners.

Porsche of America president Otto Erich Filius with Max Hoffman and Ferry Porsche at Zuffenhausen in 1963.

MARKET CHANGES IN AMERICA

As Porsche's largest customer, Max Hoffman had built the American market to 40 percent of total Porsche sales by 1959. His sharp-elbowed approach had generated frequent animosity among his distributors and dealers, however, and in 1955 Otto Erich Filius set up a New York office for the Porsche of America Corporation. By 1959 the company had put into effect changes that would diminish Hoffman's influence and remove him as importer. Hoffman Motors became one of six distributors in the country and for five years carried on as Northeast representative. In 1964 Max was out, but for a period of time he received a royalty on every car sold, compensation for his giving up the business he had created during Porsche's earliest days in America.

The fixed-roof Hardtop was built by Karmann, first in T-5 form, then with T-6 modifications.

The Convertible D was reborn in a T-5 body by Drauz, now called the Roadster.

Inside the Roadster, comfortable seats could recline and pivot for access to the rear area. The new B steering wheel and shifter as well as black knobs were used. No radio or speakers were offered in the kick panel, but a lockable door pocket was carried over from the D. A change was made from a knob control to a lever for heat control at the base of the shifter.

NEW CARS, LONGER SUPPLY CHAINS

A replacement of the Convertible D continued as well, with Drauz carrying on as supplier for a new model called the Roadster. It was the Convertible D in a T-5 body, with the distinctive chrome windshield, eyebrow dash, comfortable seats, and simple, unpadded top. Reutter, as before, provided most pressed parts, and Drauz built and finished the bodies. In an interesting turnabout, Drauz was tasked with producing front

panels for Reutter, which often required remedial work. This and other bottlenecks slowly were ironed out, but the issue of production capacity remained.

In spring 1960, Porsche began investigating the additional use of two other body builders. Karmann in Osnabrück was some 500 kilometers from Stuttgart, but the company was capable and experienced, having built thousands of cars for VW. D'Ieteren

Frères in Brussels was just as far from the Porsche works and also had long experience building VWs, along with Studebakers and other makes. In June 1960 Porsche contracted with Karmann to build three thousand bodies, with a fresh numbering series beginning with #200001. This would be a new model, with a profile similar to the hardtop (cabriolet), but the top would be welded in place. Production began in early 1961, with cabriolet chassis and sheet metal shipped to Karmann from Reutter. Seats were also supplied, as Reutter had become a specialist in seating, creating a division for that purpose called Recaro. From Karmann the trimmed 356 bodies returned to Zuffenhausen for final assembly. A total of 1,048 were built for 1961, then another 682 after a changeover to the T-6 body. The 1962 "notchback," as this car became known, got T-6 changes that included an external filler, a bigger windshield, and twin grilles on the decklid. The roof was no longer just a hardtop but stamped to smoothly transition the higher windshield into the roofline. It turned out to be a lot of effort for a meager return; in early 1962, owing to weak sales, Karmann hardtop production ended. Body building there switched to coupes, for which the demand was still strong. These were built on the Osnabrück line, and by the end of 356 production in 1965, Karmann was producing most of Porsche's coupes. The company later carried on as a body supplier for the 911 and 912 bodies.

END OF THE ROAD FOR ROADSTERS

Drauz quality continued to be an issue, and at the end of 1960 that relationship was ended. Roadster production was moved to D'Ieteren, where the 1961 models were assembled and finished mechanically. Unlike other suppliers, the Belgian firm drove 356s off its line. A total of 473 were built in T-5 form, and as the T-6 body change was implemented, another 249 Twin-Grille Roadsters, as they came to be known, were made before the line was terminated. Decades later collectors would covet them not only for rarity but as the last and best of the Speedster/D/Roadster line.

NEW ENGINES, AGAIN

As a new decade of Porsches began, what Ferry Porsche had envisioned as "an excellent dual-purpose car for the enthusiast"

was now mainly being marketed as a lightweight GT racer. The Carrera was too much for many drivers. But the 1600S was, perhaps, no longer quite enough. Engineers in the technical department worked toward a more potent powerplant that could be an "everyday engine." By the time the 356B was ready, so was a new engine—at least in prototype form. The 1600 Super 90, Typ 616/7, could not be delivered until mid-1960 owing to parts shortages, but then it quickly became a favorite. At a rated 90 horsepower, 15 more than the 1600S, it rode the top of the pushrod engine list for three years. Its development encompassed abundant changes—nothing huge, but rather many details that all together put a large grin on drivers' faces.

A new transmission, Typ 741, came online for the B cars, with a lower placement of the shift rod in the nose that allowed a straight-through connection from the shifter rather than the previous "monkey-motion" unit. Initially a single front mount was used, but it was changed to dual mounts in January 1960.

A suspension change was also made for the more powerfully engined cars. A rear single-bar compensating spring was connected laterally from the bottom of each axle tube and loosely pinned at the transmission. The idea was to press the inside wheel down to the pavement on hard cornering. Rear torsion-bar diameter was decreased by a millimeter, slightly softening the ride. The arrangement could be had as an option on the 60- and 75-horsepower cars as well. Brakes were upgraded, with new bigger aluminum drums having lateral cooling fins and a cast-in steel lining. Roller wheel bearings continued from the previous year on larger front spindles.

In late 1959 and early 1960 a single front transmission mount was used in the Typ 741, soon changed to double mounts. The camber compensating bar (16) was pinned via a rod to the end of each axle (17) while pivoting loosely at the transmission bottom. Rubber rebound bumpers (1) allowed increased suspension travel.

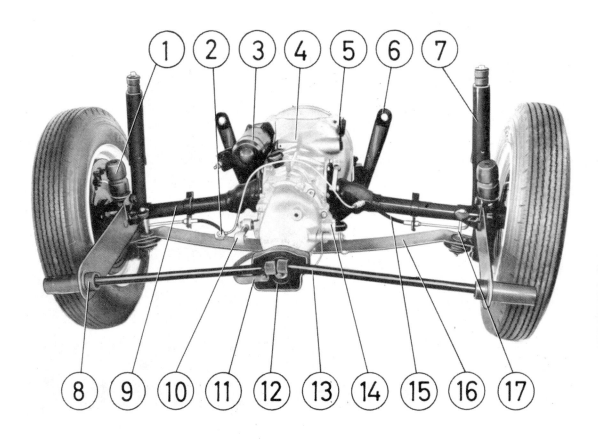

The Twin Grille Roadster had the external gas filler and squared hood of the T-6
program. Unlike coupes and cabs, no fresh air grilles in the cowl were provided.

ENGINOLOGY: SUPER 90

The compression ratio was bumped to 9.0:1 for the Super 90, close to four-cam territory, with bigger (40mm) intake valves fed by Solex 40 PII carburetors, previously seen only on Carrera engines. Light alloy cylinders had a molybdenum/steel coating called Ferral on the bore surfaces, with high, beveled dome pistons carrying three compression rings and one oil ring. Valve operation was now through a light alloy "bridge" on the cylinder head, initially made of magnesium and later aluminum.

A larger (A12) diaphragm clutch was used, in a wider recess in a new flywheel, lighter by almost 5 pounds than the 1600S. The oil pickup in the sump received a complicated makeover with a sliding centrifugal valve. The idea was that in a long, hard corner, the valve would open only to the side of the sump where oil accumulated by centrifugal force. It required a new, larger oil strainer and extra gaskets. After a few years, however, drivers would find that dirty oil would clog the valve, and Porsche would discontinue its use. An adjunct item, a ball valve in a tube, was added to the valve cover breather for the same reason: to prevent oil loss in hard curves. Clearly, Porsche felt the Super 90 would see competition, or at least spirited driving from its owners.

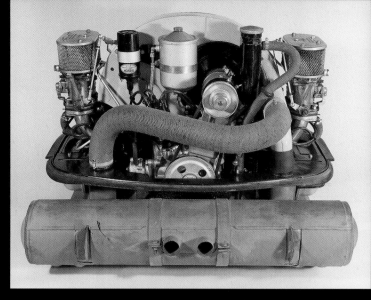

The Super 90 engine carried Solex 40 PII carbs on special manifolds, with a silver fan shroud. This engine has a European heating system.

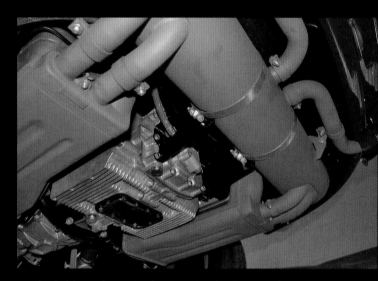

Fresh air blown from the fan housing is directed through enclosed heat exchangers, a system that was a basis for the 911 heaters to come.

A new heating system was introduced to adhere to new German regulations. The air for heating was no longer first blown over the engine. Instead, a diversion tube on the right side of the fan housing took pressurized air to two fully enclosed heat exchangers, then to the passenger compartment. As before, air gates under the car regulated this flow. It produced more heat and less chance of carbon monoxide leaks but was more expensive. Porsche chose to not use it in markets (such as the United States) where it was not required. For these legacy systems, the air channels (flapper boxes) below the engine got two flaps to increase cooling air flow at the downstream end. Upstream, air entering the fan shroud no longer passed through a convex screen. Rather, an intake funnel, or volute lip, smoothed flow into the engine shrouding. These and many of the other S-90 attributes would carry on with the next generation of engines.

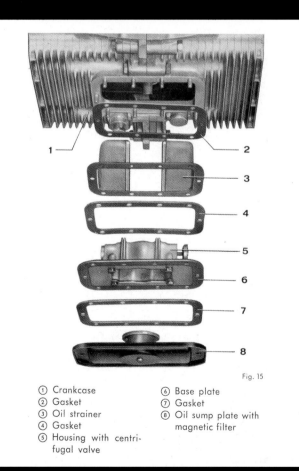

Fig. 15

1. Crankcase
2. Gasket
3. Oil strainer
4. Gasket
5. Housing with centrifugal valve
6. Base plate
7. Gasket
8. Oil sump plate with magnetic filter

The sliding sump oil pickup for the S-90 engine was later removed by many owners.

The Carrera 2 could be had in coupe and cabriolet form in the T-6 body. This C version with disc brakes shows its subtle difference from the standard car: a rear lower valance to cover the large muffler assembly. A "Carrera 2" script on the tail was the only identification.

THE CARRERA RETURNS

In April 1962 production of a new four-cam-powered street car began at Werk II. In the T-6 body a revised four-cam engine was installed, along with a number of accessories and amenities to create a true Grand Touring machine for boulevardiers that could also be utilized in competition. It was necessary to produce 100 copies of a model for homologation by the FIA—in this case, to take part in the Grand Touring under-2.0-liter class. The required number were already sold by August, and a further 210 copies were built as T-6 356Bs. After the 356C was introduced in fall 1963, another 126 found owners, according to Karl Ludvigsen.

The first series of Carrera 2—so named after the engine's displacement—in B form carried Porsche's own design of annular disc brakes, whose reliable stopping power had been proven on the company's racing cars. When the C series introduced Teves discs, the four-cam coupe and cabriolet followed suit. A rear-suspension compensating spring was standard. Double oil coolers were at the front behind lower vents with no grilles. A standard gas heater in the nose provided heat on demand.

For three years the Carrera 2 with a Typ 587/1 engine was the top-of-the-line Porsche, a "halo car" that generated

The four-cam Typ 587 was wider and a tight fit in a 356 engine compartment.

excellent reviews and set a benchmark for what the next generation of Porsches should be. It also conveniently became the homologated template for the Carrera GS-GT, an aluminum-bodied racer built to defend the GT class while an entirely new generation of fiberglass race cars was being developed.

The Carrera 2 Typ 587/1 engine had a displacement of 1,966cc, accomplished by lengthening the stroke 8mm to 74mm. Modified head spigots for the longer cylinders and some judicious machining for clearance inside the crankcase—plus smaller-diameter plain shell main bearings—just allowed the rods to spin without interference. Bore size was up slightly to 92mm, with a 9.5:1 compression ratio. New heads had a distinctive rectangular shape and gave more room around the cams for adjustment, also enclosing the small balance wheels that had protruded earlier. With taller cylinders, the engine was wider, exacerbating the service difficulty. To compensate, access panels eased spark plug changing. Large rectangular mesh air cleaners were employed. Other modifications to the oil pump, exhaust system, and other ancillaries added up to powerful and tractable engine of 135 brake horsepower at 6,200 rpm, now with torque of 120 pounds-feet at 4,600.

A racing version, Typ 587/2, was created using Weber carbs and higher-lift cams and heavier valve springs. Compression was raised to 9.8:1, and with a sport exhaust the horsepower rating was 170 at 6,600 rpm, with a redline of 7,000.

The Carrera 2 engine and 741 transmission (with dual mounts) and Porsche annular disc brakes. The engine heads and valve covers were modified, with larger reopening for valvetrain access. Note the four spark plugs, easily accessible with the engine out. That was not the case with the engine installed.

TECHNICAL PROGRAM 6

While the on-and-off with body makers Drauz and D'leteren was going on, the engineers at Porsche drew plans for further refinement of the 356. About 7,600 cars were built in 1960 and slightly more in 1961, and a freshening would keep sales climbing. Technical Program 6, begun in the summer of 1960, would affect each model, mainly with new front and rear hoods. The goal for going to market was fall 1961. When the 1962 models were unveiled in August and September 1961 there was a new look, with a squared-off front hood and a larger rear deck lid with two grilles. Coupe windshield and rear window areas were increased slightly, and for the first time an external fuel filler was used, with a door in the right top fender opened from inside the car. The new fuel tank inside was flatter and sunk into the trunk, allowing more luggage room. A larger 70-liter tank was available as an option.

On the cowl, grilles brought fresh air into the cabin. Right-hand-drive cars didn't immediately get the outside filler, owing

The 52-liter T-6 fuel tank was sunk into the trunk floor, with a formed plastic cover (not shown). The first cars had a bottom-mounted sender, changed to a top mount in the summer of 1962. The fuel cock with on-off-reserve setting was used through the end of the 356 series.

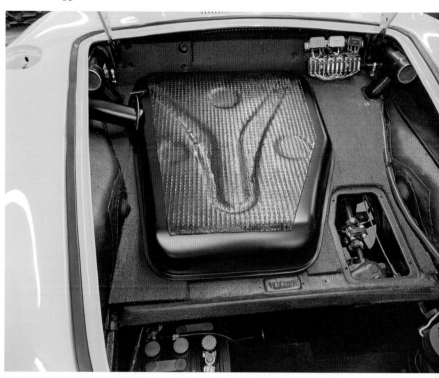

The T-6 coupe added a vent control above the clock on the dash. Three versions became available: cars with basic ventilation (single lever), cars with a blower system in the nose, and cars with gas heaters, as seen here. Note the oil-temperature gauge. In response to customer concerns about high oil temps, during the late 356A series the factory simply deleted numbers for the gauge.

On the assembly line at Karosserie Porsche, 356C coupes near the final stage.

to space constraints from the filler neck and ventilation assembly under the hood. Roadsters, carrying on a tradition of simplicity, didn't get the fresh air vents. These were well-received changes—especially the external gas filler—but the model name remained 356B.

Porsche reported at the end of 1962 that total staff was 1,315, with 800 being hourly workers; 240 salaried workers were engineers and technicians. The company produced 34.6 cars per day for a total of 8,270, with 3,100 exported to the United States. On April 3, the 50,000th Porsche left the factory.

The 1963 cars were, for the most part, unchanged from the previous year. American dealers found a silver lining in that: if a car had been in inventory while the model year changed, it wasn't that difficult to simply consider it a year newer. In many ways for everyone it was a refreshing break from the proliferation of models, with the Karmann hardtop and the Roadster now gone. Consequently, the number of cabriolets sold ticked up a bit, and those cabriolets had a new feature: a zippered rear window that could open the entire rear area of the top. Total numbers grew to 9,235 Porsches built in 1963. But for the first time, from the second half of the year, Reutter no longer built those cars.

A BLENDED FAMILY, A NEW OFFSPRING

As of May 15, 1963, Dr. Ing. h.c. F. Porsche KG was the new owner of Stuttgarter Karosseriewerk Reutter & Co. GmbH in Zuffenhausen. The Augustenstrasse plant remained with Reutter, which going forward would concentrate on seat manufacture as Recaro AG, which had been incorporated in 1957, initially to manage patents and licenses. Reutter shareholders were unwilling to take the risks of scaling up for the new Porsche model, and there were other concerns. According to Porsche archivist Frank Jung, "For serial production of the 901, as the successor to the 356, the [Zuffenhausen] facilities were outdated, the premises were too cramped and there weren't enough qualified employees." He also notes, "Owing to the first boom of the post-war period, and despite in-house training, it was difficult to find young, skilled workers."

Having been closely entwined in business for a dozen years, it's not surprising that Reutter became part of Porsche, but unlike in many commercial marriages, it was not because business was bad—quite the opposite. As Porsche took over the Reutter Zuffenhausen works that spring, sales were strong and the future seemed bright owing to a new product well along in the pipeline; the 356's successor was waiting in the wings. A few months later at the September 1963 Frankfurt show, a new Porsche was on display, called the 901. It was a prototype, literally one of one, and serial production was many months away. But the sleek light-yellow coupe attracted much attention. It was made clear that this was the future of Porsche.

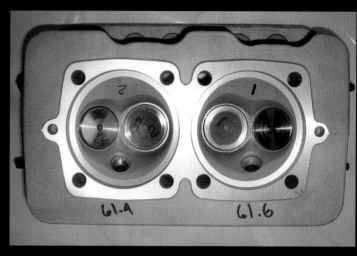

Valves for the C/SC were brought closer together in size, improving breathing.

ENGINOLOGY: C/SC ENGINES

Hans Mezger had joined the Porsche engineering staff in 1956, and after working on the Formula 1 program he became involved in the ongoing improvements for the sports-car engines. He knew that proper breathing was essential for power and efficiency, so both C (Typ 616/15) and SC (Typ 616/16) engines used 38mm intake (reduced from 40mm) and 34mm exhaust valves (increased from 31mm), with the latter sodium filled in the SC. Valves now featured three-groove keepers, and intakes used a seal at the guide top. The ports were modified "to improve cylinder breathing and volumetric efficiency," as the shop manual stated.

The C engine had gray cast-iron cylinders, a milder cam, and 8.5:1 compression with Zenith 32 NDIX carbs. The SC replaced the S-90, with 9.5:1 compression and Solex 40 PII carbs. The SC used light alloy cylinders with a Ferral coating, as used on the Super 90 and the Typ 753 Formula 1 engine in 1961. In February 1964 the cylinder composition was changed to Biral, an iron liner cast into an aluminum barrel.

The SC crankshaft was counterweighted, and cam timing was carried over from the Super 90. Heads were initially blackened à la S-90 to moderate thermal conductivity, but a service bulletin in July 1964 announced the heads were going back to bare aluminum. Interestingly, the bulletin noted the heads could all be used interchangeably.

TOP: The C interior added armrests and a lower extension for the ashtray and lighter. The headlight switch was finally moved out from behind the steering wheel. The glove box door had a magnetic catch with separate lock. A gearshift lock was available. This car had the optional deluxe horn ring.

ABOVE: Save for flat disc-brake hubcaps, there was no appreciable difference in appearance for the C/SC cars. The aluminum side spear had been an option since it first appeared on the Speedster.

RIGHT: The Teves disc brakes (rear shown here) were simple and effective. The two single piston halves were connected by an internal drilling. The shape of the cylinder seal pulled the piston back slightly when not under pressure. The rear disc was hat-shaped, acting as a drum. Parking brake shoes were actuated by cable from under the dash.

The new 356C was introduced along with the 904 and the car that would replace the 356, the 911.

Somewhat ironically, a new 356 was unveiled at the same display, the 356C. The car had a new name—in fact, two new names—but the only real visual differences were the flat hubcaps. For 1964 the 356 came in two flavors, the C and SC, replacing the 60-, 75-, and 90-horsepower units used previously.

The biggest visual change was disc brakes, built under license from Alfred Teves (ATE) with solid discs and two-piece calipers, each holding a piston. Each piston was self-adjusting, and a purging check valve in the master cylinder depressurized the system between applications. For the first time, the open-center VW-style wheel, used since the beginning, was gone. The bolt pattern was now smaller, and the simple flat chrome hubcap was initially devoid of decoration, but a Porsche crest would be added later. The rear disc was hat shaped to accommodate small parking brake shoes, cable controlled from under the dash, as before. Front discs were bolted to an aluminum hub carrier with five studs.

In the cockpit, an extension under the dash held the ashtray (a standard item since the beginning in most Porsches) along with the lighter and an optional electric windshield washer switch. Various switches switched position over the

years, but in the C/SC there was some rationalization to it all, with a clock, a radio, and headlight and fog light controls all in the dash center. Above the clock a vent lever controlled fresh air intake. Another version of the lever panel controlled air from an optional blower mounted in the nose with hoses running to the air flaps in the upper trunk, directing air to the dash or floor. A third version regulated heat from an Eberspächer gas heater behind the spare tire, along with fan speed and direction. This unit had been originally offered in the Carreras.

A rubber grab handle for passengers in left-hand-drive cars replaced the chrome piece used before. There was a day/night mirror for coupes and a new glove-box door with magnetic closure, rocker dome lights, and two door armrests, replacing the chrome pull handles. Front seats were lower, allowing more headroom, and the rear seat backs had a raised edge that, when lowered, helped keep luggage in place. Cabriolet tops now had two zippers. A 12-volt electrical system, used on the Carrera 2 models, became an option on others. In sum, there were a lot of detail changes inside, but none significant. There just wasn't much left to fix. The "German automotive jewel," as Max Hoffman had called it over a decade

earlier, had been cut, faceted, buffed, and now polished to near perfection. The C series was the best of the 356s, but the question now posed by the marketplace was, Could even the best 356 still be good enough? As the C/SC was introduced to the world at Frankfurt in 1963, the 901 provided not only an answer but an exclamation point.

The prospect of a new Porsche model caused some potential buyers to rethink their timing. Conversely, many current and future owners were motivated to get one of these "last" 356s before they were unavailable. For the model year 1964 sales were an all-time high at 10,312, but 1965 numbers were down to 1,688 as a four-cylinder version of the 901 entered the pipeline. That year 6,400 912 models were sold. The last 356 coupe built at Karmann—where the majority of C and SC coupes had been built—reached the end of the Osnabrück

assembly line on January 21, 1965. A final coupe from Reutter was completed on April 28, just before a flower-bedecked white cabriolet took its place in history, seeing the sunlight outside Werk II as the final regular-production 356. The cars on the assembly line behind it were all 911 and 912 series, and their numbers would eventually eclipse the 76,000 356s built.

An asterisk in the account books of 356s accompanies #162175. That completed 356 left the factory on May 26, 1966, the last of ten white cabriolets specially built for the Dutch national police. Apparently the Rijkspolitie were also very motivated to get a last 356—or ten—while they were still (barely) available, as the 356 was the only open Porsche at the time. When the 911 Targa was offered in 1968, the orange-and-white fleet began to move in that direction, using a total of 507 Porsches from 1962 through 1996.

The family resemblance is there, but the 901 was definitely a more modern car, both in appearance and under the skin.

THE 901'S LONG, ROCKY ROAD

A larger, longer-wheelbase, roomier, faster, and more modern Porsche had been on the to-do list for many years. From Ferry Porsche on down through the ranks of engineers, designers, and marketers at Dr. Ing. h.c. F. Porsche KG, ideas and proposals bubbled to the surface on a regular basis. Some of the players had changed, and several concepts had come and gone, but everyone knew that—in spite of Volkswagen's example—stasis was death in the car business.

The origin of what became the 901 could be traced back to 1952 when the idea of a four-seater Porsche—one that would expand the line and complement the 356—took drivable shape as the Typ 530. In 1954 the clay model Typ 656 envisioned a "new" Porsche. Instead, the 356A made its debut in 1955 as an evolutionary design.

In 1956 another generation of the Porsche family had joined the company. Ferdinand Alexander began training in the design department under Erwin Komenda. Butzi, as he was known, had studied industrial design in Ulm but left there at the suggestion of Count Goertz, with whom he then worked on a design concept for the Typ 695 project, another attempt to create the 356 successor. "For the best part of five years, Ferdinand Alexander worked in the various departments of the Porsche firm so as to get a good overall picture of our activities," his father wrote. "By 1961 he was ready for more responsibility and became head of the studio—our equivalent of a styling department." Before that happened, Typ 695 had morphed into Technical Program 7, or T-7, which was slated to be next in line after the last T-6 356.

Through the last years of the 1950s Erwin Komenda drew several ideas, from adaptations of the existing shape to much sleeker visions only peripherally connected to the current cars. Wheelbase for a four-place car of at least 2,300mm was a given, and dimensions and packaging would follow. Two issues were key: luggage space in the trunk and head- and legroom for rear passengers. In addressing these, both Komenda and

The last 356s were built a year after production officially ended. Ten white cabriolets left the factory in May 1966.

Butzi Porsche's T-7 was closer to the final form for the 901, which went through three years of gestation and several false starts.

FA—"Porsche Jr.," as he was referred to in the company—evolved independent ideas for what was to be a larger Porsche. By 1961, of the two, Porsche Jr.'s design was accepted for further development.

THE PROTO-911

If this was to be the separate "big" Porsche, what would replace the 356? In November 1961 a two-seater project was begun, called T-8, essentially built on the 356 chassis. The car's exterior would be similar to but not duplicate the T-7. Space in the trunk would be made by moving the fuel tank to the back seat area, with storage above it accessed by an opening rear window. As it was narrower and lower than a 356, designers expected an aerodynamic gain, which was proven in a wind-tunnel model test. But the car's original concept changed when, in early 1962, the prospect of a two-tier product offering suddenly dimmed. Plans

for a bigger Porsche were dropped, and the T-8 became the main focus of planning. In March it was given the Typ 901 designation. Karl Ludvigsen explained the reason: "In the early 1960s Porsche was more closely integrating its sale, parts and service operations with Volkswagen. Porsche part numbers, therefore, needed to become compatible with those used by VW." The larger company's only unused numbers were the 900s, which were then used by Porsche for its line of cars and parts.

A new chassis was needed; its project number, Typ 754, had begun under technical director Klaus von Rücker in late 1959. Suspension for the new car would have to leap forward by decades from the VW front trailing arms, and engineer Helmuth Bott, who came to Porsche in 1952, was instrumental in developing new ideas for the front. A strut design showed the most promise for saving space, and Bott worked to develop it from concepts of Wolfgang Eyb's work in 1952, using longitudinal torsion bars with a lower A-arm. For steering, a

TOP: An early 911 and a late 356SC at the factory. The 356 series lasted seventeen years, but its successor would continue for decades, produced in numbers only dreamed about in 1965.
ABOVE: Erwin Komenda's T-9 take on a new Porsche was prototyped in 1962.

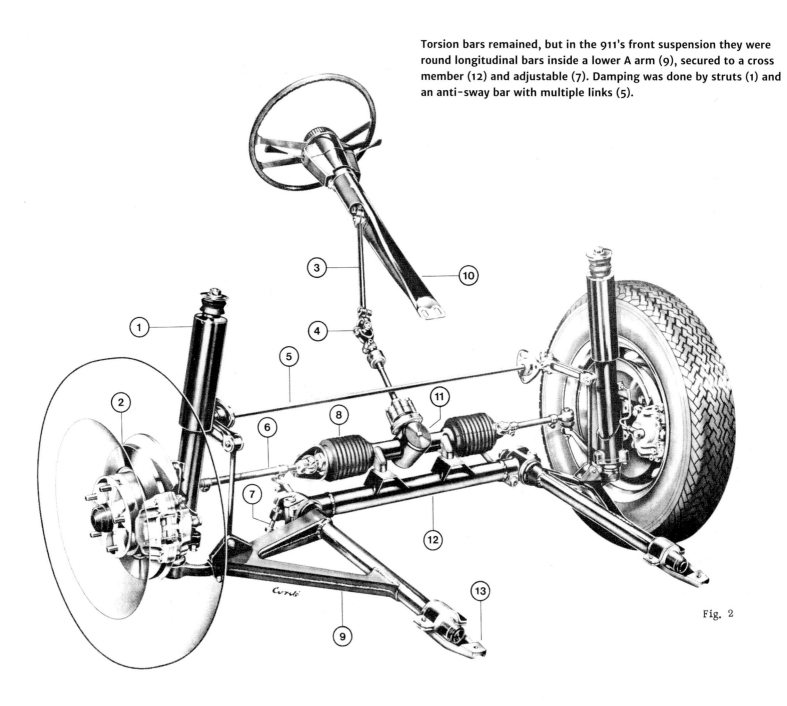

Torsion bars remained, but in the 911's front suspension they were round longitudinal bars inside a lower A arm (9), secured to a cross member (12) and adjustable (7). Damping was done by struts (1) and an anti-sway bar with multiple links (5).

Fig. 2

central rack and pinion was simple and inexpensive; it would allow control from either the left or right side, and its offset jointed steering column was a safety feature. The 356's rear suspension was used when, on September 14, 1962, a prototype 901 body was delivered from Reutter to Porsche and mechanical assembly began. On November 9 Bott made the first test drive. The 901 was less than a year away from its public debut, but much work needed to be done, including development of a completely new engine.

A SIX FOR THE FUTURE

In the middle of 1959 work had begun on a 2.0-liter six, Typ 745. With four main bearings and two cams driving pushrods,

it was an unusual design, but by the end of 1961 development was abandoned. A new approach to six-cylinder design was begun with Typ 821 as the calendar turned over to 1962, and after a year's worth of design and testing the formula was fixed: a single overhead chain-driven cam on each side of the flat engine topped six individual heads and 80mm-bore cylinders. A total of seven main bearings held a counterweighted crank solidly, with a 66mm stroke for a displacement of 1,991cc. Dry-sump oiling used a separate oil tank in the right rear fender.

By early 1963 Hans Tomala was now technical director, von Rücker having left for BMW. Leopold Jäntschke was in charge of production engines, and Hans Mezger came to the group from the racing side when the Grand Prix eight-cylinder project was shelved. It was a good team facing a formidable task with a short amount of time.

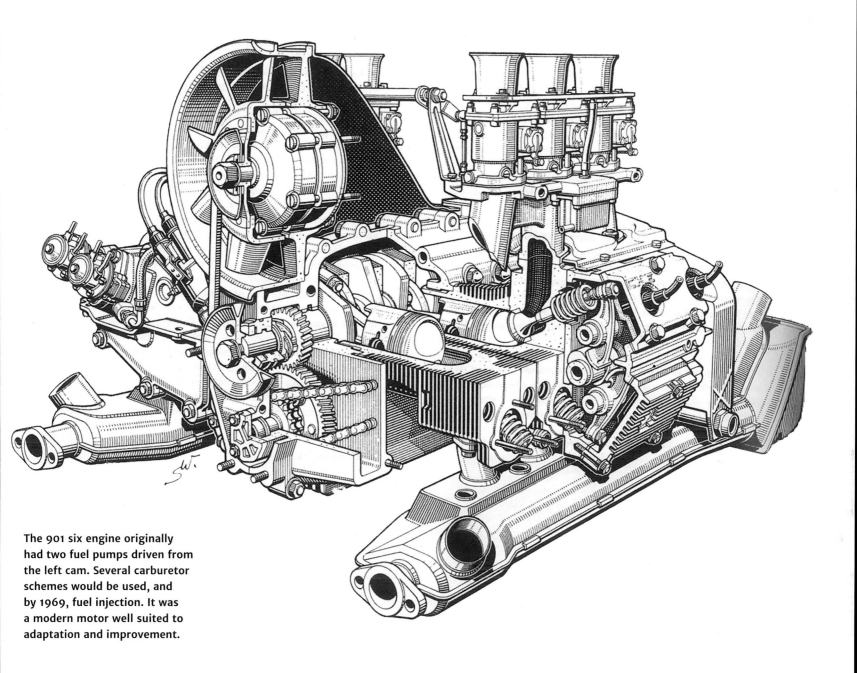

The 901 six engine originally had two fuel pumps driven from the left cam. Several carburetor schemes would be used, and by 1969, fuel injection. It was a modern motor well suited to adaptation and improvement.

Joining them in March 1963 was Ferry Porsche's nephew Ferdinand Piëch, bringing a recent engineering degree. Working with Mezger and several other engineers, Piëch helped develop the 901 engine for the production car, but with an eye toward racing as well. It was needed to replace the four-cam in the new 904 GTS. Testing continued for many months after the car's debut in Frankfurt, with modifications made to many systems.

With a new five-speed transmission using universal joints, the powertrain was finally tested and ready, and the 901 went on sale in fall 1964. At the Paris salon in October it was on display when Peugeot representatives challenged the nomenclature; that maker used a three-digit number with a middle zero for its own cars. To avoid legal action, the easiest solution for Porsche was to insert a 1, and thus the car became the 911. Soon a less expensive variant was offered: a 911 body with a slightly modified

356 SC engine, called the 912. It outsold the 911 through its final year of 1969.

Within three years Ferdinand Piëch became head of the experimental department at Porsche, advancing the company's racing efforts to new heights. When all Porsche family members left active management in 1971, he would go on to lead Audi and, later, the entire Volkswagen Group. His cousin Butzi later founded Porsche Design, creating stylish and functional items for industry and consumers alike. The Porsche family would continue to be influential in the European auto market for decades to come.

THE OTHER PORSCHES

The original Porsche design consultancy was called a "design bureau for motors, automobiles, airplanes and watercraft construction." Some of the first work done was for truck design in 1932, and during the next decade airplane engines, bus chassis, wind generators, tanks, jet engines, and a wide variety of other projects brought the Typ numbers to over three hundred by war's end. The company had prospered through German government contracts, including those for the Auto Union Grand Prix car, the people's car, and another pet idea

Ferdinand Porsche's vision ranged from automobiles for the masses to tractors for the small farmer. His son Ferry made that idea a reality through partnerships with Allgaier and others. One of the specialty tractors built was a P-312 "orchard" version designed for coffee plantations in Brazil. The bodywork was not aerodynamic, but rather intended to keep the tractor from snagging fruit branches. The wide range of products and inventions by Porsche engineers contributed greatly to the company's success.

A Typ 312 at Gmünd. Lugs in the rear wheels, conceived by Karl Rabe, could be moved away from the tires on smooth ground.

A poster to remind buyers of the tractor's origin: "Everything from one head. Every construction a worldwide success."

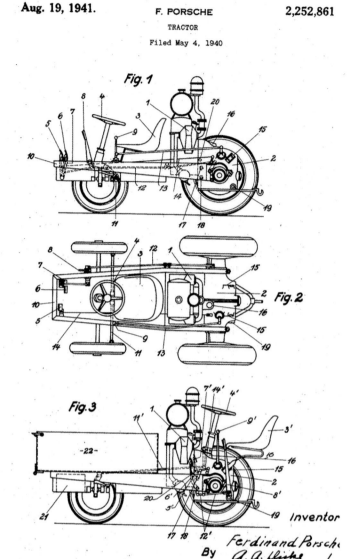

Aug. 19, 1941.   F. PORSCHE   2,252,861
TRACTOR
Filed May 4, 1940

A 1940 U.S. patent granted to Ferdinand Porsche for a tractor shows controls that can be moved from front to back, for "general uses" (towing) or "farm tractor" (plowing). Interestingly, the patent describes at length its possible military use for carrying weapons and driving in columns.

from Hitler: a *Volkschlepper*, or people's tractor. Ferdinand Porsche felt that German farmers, as well as motorists, should have an inexpensive and efficient conveyance. Beginning with a 1937 mandate from the government, Porsche refined its tractor Typ 110 design several times. The Typ 112 *Volkstraktor* was a developed version, with a larger engine and suitably adapted transmission. A plant for producing tractors—similar to Fallersleben—was planned at Waldbröl, Nazi leader Robert Ley's hometown. It was designed and financed but did not have enough priority for completion as the war continued.

While in Gmünd, however, Porsche engineers had time and incentive to focus on other agricultural products. A water turbine and tractor were part of the 1947 deal with Piero Dusio to design

Badged Porsche-Diesel, the Mannesmann-built tractors ranged from the four-cylinder Master, left, to the single-cylinder Junior, right.

In the United States, Porsche sold about a thousand tractors from 1958 to 1963. Roland Lohnert was a factory rep who would deliver tractors and instruct new owners. At a trade show at a Boston hotel in 1958, he rode a crane cable to the second floor, then drove the 6,000-pound Master into the display hall.

The agricultural equivalent of a Porsche Taycan, the fanciful Mission E tractor.

his Grand Prix car. That Typ 323 tractor wasn't built, but a few years later the Allgaier company contracted with Porsche for the AP 17. In production beginning in 1950, the AP 17 was the first of some twenty-five thousand units built through 1955. Porsche could not build tractors directly, owing to an edict the Allies imposed after the war: only manufacturers that had built tractors previously could continue postwar. Allgaier would build the air-cooled diesel units under license, including one-, two-, three-, and four-cylinder models, all with interchangeable cylinders. A similar contract was made with Austria's Hofherr-Schrantz. This arrangement remained until 1956, when, in a bid to expand production, the licenses were transferred to Mannesmann, a large industrial conglomerate that refurbished an old zeppelin plant near Lake Constance to build tractors.

In a deal brokered by Dr. Prinzing, Porsche-Diesel Motorenbau GmbH Friedrichshafen was formed, and in 1958 the line included a one-cylinder, 14-horsepower Junior priced at just DM 4,980 ($1,180). The other models were the two-cylinder, 25-cylinder Standard; the three-cylinder, 38-horsepower Super; and the four-cylinder, 50-horsepower Master. Production continued until 1963, by which time competition in Europe and a change in NATO policy combined to close the plant. The Friedrichshafen factory was needed by MTU-Daimler to build diesel engines for NATO tanks, a more lucrative business. Over 125,000 tractors had been built there, and a deal was made for Renault to service Porsche-Diesel tractors going forward.

Despite a hiatus of fifty-five years, it became clear that Porsche never forgot its agricultural history. On April 1, 2018, the company announced the 700-horsepower Mission E electric tractor. "Porsche is confident that the combination of tradition and innovation—and enough power to set a pretty good lap time on the Nordschleife—will make the Mission E Tractor a runaway sales success." We can't wait to see it.

PORSCHE
INFORMATION
PORSCHE
1,6 Ltr. Flugmotor
Typ 678/3
Startleistung 52 PS n_M = 3200 U/min
Dauerleistung 50 PS n_M = 3150 U/min
ohne Untersetzungsgetriebe
Doppelmagnetzündung Bosch 12 V
Handanlassvorrichtung
Mustergeprüft
Dr. Ing. h.c. F. Porsche KG. Stuttgart-Zuffenhausen

The 678/3 was marketed along with other Porsches at auto shows.

OFF THE GROUND

Ferdinand Porsche's résumé included aircraft engines going back to before the First World War. The company returned to this field of flight in the late 1950s using an off-the-shelf unit, the 356 engine. Industrial versions of the engine were introduced in 1954, the first ones based on the 1500 Normal. An offshoot of this industrial business was airplane engines, beginning in 1957 and designated Typ 678. After some development, three models were available. Typ 678/3 was a basic 1600 52-horsepower engine without reduction gear and with shrouding that let the airstream cool the unit. With two carburetors and magnetos, it was hand cranked to start, although an extra-cost starter and dynamo could be had.

Typ 678/1 was rated at 65 horsepower, again with airstream cooling but with a choice of four reduction gears. With a single downdraft carb, customers could choose either dual coils or magnetos. Electric start was standard. The 75-horsepower 687/4 had dual carbs, 9.0:1 compression, and, again, choice of gears, magneto or coil ignition, and electric start. All engines had dry-sump lubrication and twin plugs per cylinder, with silencers built into the exhaust pipes. The 687/4 had 356-style shrouding for installation in planes such as the Rhein Flugzeugbau RW-3, with a midships engine and a propellor slot in the tail.

ABOVE: A restored 678/4 on a custom stand. Zenith 32 NDIX carbs were warmed by lower shroud air. The dry sump tank is below with lines from the oil pump. All systems are redundant, including the coil and distributor ignition.

BELOW: The Gyrodyne XRON could transport a man for observation or be dropped behind enemy lines for rescue.

The glider-based Pützer Elster used for the engine's civil inspection tests in 1957 had carburetors that would allow rolls, banks, and loops. Many engines were sold to individuals, but it's unlikely they bought them for aerobatics.

HELICOPTERS

In 1952 Peter Papadakos's Gyrodyne company of New York offered an additional military opportunity, although an unusual one. The one-man helicopter design was meant for reconnaissance or assault, using counter-rotating (coaxial) rotors driven by a light, air-cooled engine—in this case the Porsche 1.5 industrial engine, mounted vertically. Fifteen copies of the XRON Rotorcycle were evaluated by the U.S. Marines and Navy in 1955–1956. Both wheeled and float-equipped versions were made. Although very maneuverable owing to a unique rotor tip "brake," the manned unit idea was not adopted by the navy. Later, prototypes were built using both single and double

Porsche engines, carrying a torpedo in a radio-controlled drone version for the navy in antisubmarine work. In final form with a Boeing turboshaft engine the QH-50 served for a decade.

THE NEXT JEEP

During the Cold War, the United States was the big spender in military equipment, and new ideas were proposed constantly. The Mid-American Research Corporation (MARCO) in Kansas City was interested in developing a lightweight truck for "vertical envelopment operations," i.e., deployment by helicopter. Prototypes of the MM-100 were built by 1953, aluminum bodies over steel tubular frames weighing under 1,500 pounds dry. These used a front-mounted Porsche 1300 developing 44 horsepower. Some issues arose, but the main problem was having a foreign engine in a Marine Corps vehicle—something that was not permitted by the government. The vehicle, named "Mighty Mite," was eventually built by American Motors using its

The MARCO "Mighty Mite" never got beyond prototype stage because of its German engine.

GERMAN ENGINED "AIR-BORNE" JEEP

ABOVE: Wendell Fletcher thought he had a good idea with his Porsche-powered Flair and Commando. The army didn't.
RIGHT: The first industrial engines were based on the 1500 Normal.

108 V-4 air-cooled engine, which used chrome-plated aluminum cylinder bores, probably influenced by Porsche. Typical of military projects, the Mites took until 1960 to go into service.

Californian Wendell Fletcher's similar idea was to provide the army with the small utility vehicle it wanted: one that could ford streams and would be light enough to be carried in an airplane. His aviation company had some expertise in aluminum, and a prototype was built using a Porsche engine, adapted to use Fletcher's "jet cooling" as a propulsion in water. With four-wheel drive and high clearance thanks to reduction gears on the rear hubs, the four-place vehicle, called the Flair, weighed in under 1,500 pounds and was reported to reach over 60 miles per hour on land. Its movement in water, however, ultimately depended on its rotating wheels and was just over 2 miles per hour. The plan was to have Fletcher build all components under license, thus skirting the "no foreign parts"

INDUSTRIE-MOTOR TYP 546/1

rule, but it was all moot since the army declined to pursue the project. Part of the agreement with Porsche was to sponsor its Carrera Panamericana entries, from which Porsche benefited in the last two of those races.

WORKHORSE POWERPLANTS

Entering a lucrative market in which VW already took part, the first Porsche Industrial engine was the 546/1 in 1954, based on the pre-A 1500 Normal engine. The principal differences between the Industrials and automotive engines were magneto

ignition standard and distributor, coil, and generator for battery operation optional. Speed was governed, usually set around 3,000 rpm. A single central carburetor fed long intake pipes à la VW with heat pipes from the exhaust. With cast-iron cam followers, lighter valve springs on early engines rode on cast-iron rocker frames, all sufficient for low-rpm use. Hand cranks were used for starting, with a starter motor optional. A larger crank pulley gave more cooling air at low revs. Compression ranged from 6.5 to 7.5:1.

Basic engine design was much the same for all uses. In 1955 the new three-piece case engine was used (616/3), with a Solex single-barrel BIC carb. Through 1964, variations included

A variety of applications included a combination water pump/ generator (with fuel tank above, so no fuel pump is needed).

Combined water-pumping and power-producing unit. Capacity 30,000 watts/hour

The Devin D (for Deutschland) would take a VW engine, but a Porsche 356 engine was the way to go. This thoroughly Californian concept was inexpensive, sexy looking, and fun.

Typ 597's transaxle (left) was a special tunnel trans with reduction gearboxes. In the front (right) was an on-demand differential and long-travel suspension.

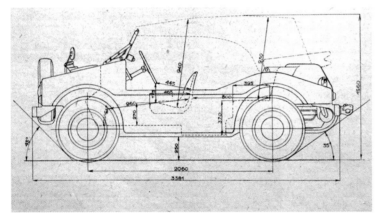

A well-designed and quality-built military vehicle, Typ 597 was simply too good, and the army chose a cheaper, simpler design.

A Typ 597 Jagdwagen at an auto show in Ohio, 2008.

higher-horsepower units with Zenith 32 NDIX carbs. In 1963 a 1,680cc unit came online. Some of the last built in 1964 used C/SC heads with alloy rocker stands (#616/33-1).

Ancillary equipment, shrouding, and gearbox connections were custom-made for each application, which included generators, pumps, welders, and irrigation and dredging equipment. Mobile applications included snow-track vehicles, air boats, amusement-park train engines, and even harvesting machines. These engines were sometimes retrofitted into VWs in Europe, and by the late 1950s engine swaps were becoming popular.

Porsche also sold replacement 356 motors. Bill Devin of California had created a light fiberglass body with a tube-frame chassis for a VW engine, and a logical next step was to install a Porsche engine. Devin would sell you a body, body and chassis, or complete car with a 356 engine for $3,350. These were lighter and faster than a 356, and the factory men took notice, quickly restricting the flow of engines to dealers supplying Devin and other builders. Industrial engines required enough modification for street use that few found their way into Porsches or VWs until recent decades, when finding a brand-new or low-use engine became almost a holy grail. Today they're seen in Bugs, buses, and, of course, 356s.

TYP 597 HUNTER

In late 1953 the German Bundeswehr was rearming in the face of Soviet threats, and Porsche heard its call for a German (and later NATO) jeep-like vehicle. Having created the Kübelwagen and its variations, the company's engineers were no newcomers to the concept. Porsche was one of three makers—along with DKW and Goliath (Borgward)—to propose concepts, its project dubbed Typ 597. Overseen by Franz X. Reimspiess, a boxy unibody was welded at Reutter, with watertight joints. Final assembly was done at Porsche next to 550 Spyders using an

TOP: The first Beutler-Porsche had styling that Erwin Komenda didn't like. A similar cabriolet was built to order, then five cars on stretched 356B chassis.

ABOVE: In May 1960 replacement chassis #13069 was used to build a coupe for Bill Jones with Porsche trim and styling cues. Although slow sellers originally, the surviving cars are well cared for.

RIGHT: The lemon-yellow 356B four-seater built for the son of the Wendler company owner, pictured around 1961 in Reutlingen.

industrial-like 1500 engine. A tunnel transaxle with reduction gears at each end had five speeds, the first being ultra low. A driveshaft ran forward to a single-speed differential that the driver could disengage to freewheel. Torsion bars gave long travel, and 16-inch wheels were used. The first units were planned to have propellors, but that idea was soon dropped. Body construction moved to Karmann, with new ribs on the sides for strength and a slight wheelbase change to 2,050mm.

Like other Porsche introductions, it appeared at the biannual Frankfurt show in 1955. It was capable and durable and looked the part, but it was more expensive than either of its rivals by far. The money and effort had not won a contract. Ferry Porsche decided to rebrand the vehicle for civilian use, calling it the Jagdwagen, or hunter car. Its target market was outdoorsmen, but the idea of a premium off-road vehicle was several decades ahead of its time. By the time production ended in 1958, twenty-two had been built for evaluation and another forty-nine for civilians. Perhaps twenty survive today, examples of a concept that could be described as too much, too soon.

THE BEUTLER PORSCHES

Almost from the beginning of production in Stuttgart, Porsche had been pursuing the idea of a larger, four-place car. In 1958 the company contacted the Beutler brothers in Thun, Switzerland, about producing such a vehicle. The Beutlers did custom work for many clients and had assembled the first 356 Gmünd-chassis cabriolets ten years before. In the 1950s they built a number of aluminum-bodied sedans and cabriolets on VW chassis and, for customers who desired it, offered Porsche power. In 1958, in cooperation with Porsche, they embarked on a quest to create a fresh body on a Porsche 356A chassis, which they lengthened by 250mm. When complete at the Zuffenhausen factory, it was well received, although Erwin Komenda felt the style was not "Porsche" enough. Carl, Duke of Württemberg, ordered a similar car in a cabriolet version after seeing it at a Geneva show. Five more cars were built, these on the new 356B chassis, lengthened as before. These were Porsche replacement and prototype chassis numbers, using 60-, 75-, and 90-horsepower engines. They were closer to Komenda's idea of a Porsche, with a less angular nose and tail using 356B bumpers, taillights, and segmented B hood handle. The cars were expensive, but at least one was exported to Brumos in Florida, and another was ordered in 1960 from Beutler by Porsche dealer Bill Jones with Porsche Cars Southwest, one of the regional distributors.

By 1962 Porsche was again considering its own four-seater with Typ 695, and disagreements over whether Beutler could sell directly or through the Porsche network brought the end of the Beutler-Porsche. It was a stylish and modern take on the existing Porsche, but modern restorers have found that

bimetallic corrosion between the steel chassis and aluminum body may have led to many problems. Perhaps it was best that this Swiss-German connection was short-lived.

Other body builders were anxious to make a connection with Porsche. The owner of Karosserie Wendler built a 356 four-seater for his son that looked very much like the standard cars. It was a one-and-done in 1961, however.

ENGINEERING FOR VW

Returning to the concept of the original Porsche design consultancy, it should be remembered that Porsche actively sought outside work, and many of its in-house creations made more money through licensing than as part of its own cars. Everything was patented, or applications made. Even dead-end projects such as some of those noted above led to useful inventions. While there was only one "pure" Porsche with those seven letters on the nose, there was a little bit of Porsche in all kinds of machines—especially those made by Volkswagen, the company's largest engineering customer.

A project starting in 1950 sought to expand the VW's appeal by using a diesel engine. This Typ 508 powerplant was in development for two years, but its noise, vibration, sooty exhaust, and lack of acceleration caused VW chief Heinz Nordhoff to pull the plug after two test cars were built. In 1948 two VW transmission concepts with synchronized forward gears were created using Leopold Schmid's split-ring design. VW passed on the idea, forcing Porsche to find its own manufacturing source for a 356 version. A front suspension using a strut/shock connected to a single trailing arm was developed for the VW and tried on a 356 in 1952. Wolfgang Eyb designed the unit; he would go on to be a principal suspension engineer with the company.

Typ 534 for VW was described as a "Kleinsportwagen," with a 356-like 2,100mm wheelbase in a two-door unit body. Reutter built a prototype body in the summer of 1952; a similar notchback version was put on paper and designated Typ 555. These were some of many ideas to expand the line or even replace the Typ 1 Beetle, but in the end, the original VW just kept selling and few Porsche designs were implemented. Ferry Porsche wrote, "In fact, between 1950 and 1970 we produced numerous prototypes for Volkswagen, always with the object of bringing it up to date; but all these drawings and modifications were set aside since the Beetle business continued to prosper year after year, without the need for major modifications. Wisely, the company took the position that no drastic change was needed. Most of the improvements were matters of detail." In other words, if it ain't broke, don't fix it.

Typ 534 was an idea for an all-new Volkswagen sports car that clearly had Komenda's influence. About this time discussions were underway between Wilhelm Karmann and Luigi Segre of Ghia in Italy that would result in a different VW sports car, which would surpass half a million built over a decade.

356s have a place of honor at any Porsche gathering, and there are more events to chose from each year. The premier celebration of Porsche's racing history is Rennsport Reunion, held every three or four years. Rennsport IV took place at Laguna Seca Raceway in 2011 where competition Porsches from every decade strutted their stuff in front of huge crowds. Three cars thread the corkscrew, led by Ernie Nagamatsu in the #7 Speedster, a car that has been racing consistently since 1965.

THE 356, A CAR FOR THE AGES

The seventeen-year 356 era was a time of roaring success, occasional failure, and constant effort to improve—sometimes slowly and sometimes in huge leaps. The final 356 series, the C/SC Porsches, was as near perfect as the aging design could be. How perfect? Author Karl Ludvigsen notes that warranty claims in 1965 amounted to $8.38 per car. In May of that year, when the last of some seventy-six thousand production 356s left the line, the House of Porsche was moving on to new cars, new technologies, and expanded aspirations in the world of racing. The 911 made the 356 obsolete, but enthusiastic owners continued to drive their "bathtubs" for years, even as the 911, 912, and 914 eclipsed them in the marketplace.

The 356 may have been declared dead after 1965, but a funny thing happened after the funeral. Interest in the cars, especially the earliest ones, waned over two decades; following a familiar pattern, their values went down as well. Few people were willing to do extensive rust repair or scrounge scarce parts for cars that nobody cared about. At the end of the twentieth century, that began to change, however, and a new appreciation of the old used sports cars took hold. There was a new awareness, but also a slowly

Dennis Aase raced 911s for years and, along with his brother Dave, ran a Porsche wrecking yard in Los Angeles. In this 1990 photo, it's clear that 356s were not worth spending a lot of money to repair. The upside was there was a good supply of used parts. Porsche carcasses like these are coveted today.

building network of vendors re-creating parts that had been no longer available. At the same time, new specialist craftspeople stepped up to fill the void left by retired mechanics. The driving force behind it all was admirers who had rediscovered the aesthetic beauty, the ergonomic grace, and the simple "just right" feel of a 356. A new generation had fallen in love.

CHECKERED FLAGS TO THE HORIZON

Porsches were never common on the street, but racetracks were a different story. Both pushrod and four-cam 356 racers were a mainstay in SCCA for many years after 1965. Air force general James Kilpatrick campaigned his No. 7 Speedster from 1964 to 1996 in California, putting over 55,000 racing miles on it and almost always finishing in the top ten. After his death it was sold to Dr. Ernie Nagamatsu, who continues to drive it in vintage races, a career of almost sixty racing years for the car—so far. It retains its red livery and, save for some safety

upgrades, still looks like it did in 1964, a rolling, roaring museum piece for future generations to enjoy.

Vic Skirmants began racing a 356 in 1965, soon leaving his engineering job to work on 356s exclusively—which supported his racing. He made his eight hundredth start in a 356 fifty-one years later and has added to that number since. No stranger to SCCA and vintage racing podiums, he also provides expert engine and transmission rebuilding services to 356 owners and racers, keeping the cars on the road and in the public view. Skirmants also owned two Gmünd coupes and an America Roadster when they were just forgotten cars. Those—which he flat-towed home behind another 356 coupe—are now in museums and other private collections. In 1974 he connected with Jerry Keyser through small ads in *Road & Track* magazine to form a new club focused exclusively on the 356 series. So began the Porsche 356 Registry, and almost fifty years later the organization remains dedicated to "the perpetuation of the vintage 356 series Porsche." Other 356 clubs around the world have followed, with tens of thousands of members gaining mutual support in their enjoyment of the first Porsches.

LEFT: Swap meets are social events and the traditional way to find parts that are no longer available. As late as 2006, at this L.A. event, old parts were casually laid out, open to offers. Today, both presentation and prices are to a higher standard.

BELOW: "The General," as Jim Kilpatrick was known to all around the racetrack, did his own engine work, logged meticulous records, and competed for three decades in his #7 Speedster.

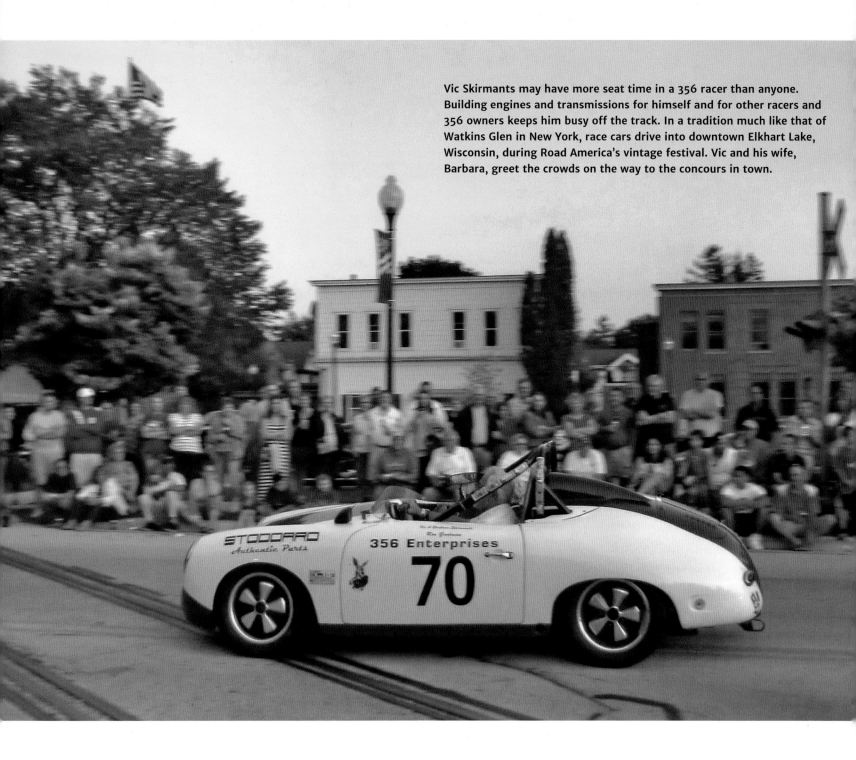

Vic Skirmants may have more seat time in a 356 racer than anyone. Building engines and transmissions for himself and for other racers and 356 owners keeps him busy off the track. In a tradition much like that of Watkins Glen in New York, race cars drive into downtown Elkhart Lake, Wisconsin, during Road America's vintage festival. Vic and his wife, Barbara, greet the crowds on the way to the concours in town.

THE SINCEREST FORM OF FLATTERY

The Porsche Speedster and 550 Spyder are the most commonly copied classic automobiles, with over a hundred manufacturers churning out plastic clones around the world—with varying degrees of accuracy and good taste. It's easy these days to simply write a check for a lookalike, but for some individuals that isn't enough. Building their own is the only way to scratch that Porsche itch.

Erwin Komenda's shapes are evocative even after decades, and Dave Miller, a metal crafter in North Carolina, found himself smitten by the Rome-Berlin Typ 64. After five years of work—from a wooden buck to metal shaping and welding the panels—he built an aluminum re-creation on a modified VW

chassis. In 2017 the finished car went to the A2 wind tunnel in Mooresville, where the drag coefficient was found to be an astonishing 0.17. Komenda's "eyeball" aerodynamics from the 1930s were proven correct, eighty years later. Miller has driven the car cross-country, as have Michael Barbach in Austria and Jörgen Andersson in Sweden, who have built their own Typ 64 facsimiles. The allure of what some consider the "first Porsche" continues to call across the ages.

A young man in rural Minnesota was similarly smitten by the honest simplicity of Walter Glöckler's VW postwar specials, which predated the 550. Armed with only basic tools and a vision, Chris Runge hammered aluminum sheets to re-create a

ABOVE: Rennsport Reunions bring together street and race cars from every year of Porsche production. Here, as always, 356 era racers share the front rows at Laguna Seca.

LEFT: Originally planned to compete in small-bore land-speed competition, Miller's finished car was tested in a NASCAR wind tunnel. The tunnel operator remarked he had never seen an early car produce such low drag numbers.

Over five years Dave Miller crafted an inner and outer aluminum shell, then combined them for a sympathetic re-creation of the Typ 64, mounting the body on a modified VW chassis.

midengined "Frankfurt Flyer," then built several more on tube frames with Porsche and VW power. His latest creations are polished aluminum riffs on Porsche's RSK, which have found willing upscale buyers for their collections.

A bit simpler is building a car from premade parts, which these days are readily available. While it used to be that builders could purchase floor pans and rocker panels, the rest of the complicated 356 sheet metal was a DIY project. Today, Restoration Design in Toronto offers every part of a Speedster chassis and body in steel, by the piece or as a complete assembly. On the mechanical side, along with brakes, wiring, interiors, and even instruments, almost all the engine components have been reengineered and manufactured—no more welding cracked heads or flywheels. If the 356 ever goes away, it won't be because of lack of resources.

A WALK ON THE WILD SIDE

Like almost any other make, 356s have been customized at times. Perhaps the best known is a 356C coupe owned by

singer Janis Joplin. Custom-painted by her band roadie Dave Richards, it had a hard life after her death in 1970 but was restored and repainted at the Denver Center Theatre Company in the 1990s. Sent to the Rock and Roll Hall of Fame in Cleveland in 1996, it toured for several years. In 2015 it was sold at auction for $1.76 million. If Janis were still with us, she surely would say, "Oh Lord!"

In the 1980s Californian Gary Emory had an idea: if you're going to restore an old Porsche, why not personalize it? At a time when beaters were plentiful, no one questioned his taking liberties with fender shapes or unusual paint schemes on a restoration project. Ultimately, his modifications turned heads and got the thumbs-up from many 356 fans, although the purists considered him an "outlaw." Embracing the term, Gary had Outlaw badges made, to be bestowed upon the chosen few who shared his approach.

By 1998 Rod Emory had joined his father and drove a "Special" they had created to the Monterey Historics with his young wife and infant son; even the baby seat was custom-made. Rod opened Emory Motorsports in North Hollywood a few years later and has to date built over 170 Outlaws, both

The light and smooth racers built after World War II by Glöckler were like a siren song to Chris Runge, and he built several, improving his skills as he went along. No. 4 proudly shows its hand-hammered shape in bare aluminum.

ABOVE: The factory and its dealers gave up supplying body parts decades ago, but today you can replace virtually any piece of a Speedster. Other 356s and 911s also benefit from a wider range of replacement parts thanks to vendors like Restoration Design.
ABOVE RIGHT: Seen at the Grammy Awards in 2011, Janis Joplin's 356 Cabriolet has become a cultural icon.

Gary and Rod Emory have built many cars with a "wow factor," including this Special from the late 1990s. Their creations pose the question, "What would Porsche have done if the 356 line carried on?"

356 and 911, and done restorations of several significant Porsches. One of those projects was ironic: rather than customizing a stock car, they brought a much-modified old Gmünd racer back to completely original condition.

GMUND SL 356/2-063

After its class win at Le Mans in 1951, Porsche #356/2–063 took part in the Liège–Rome–Liège Rally (where it took tenth overall), then ran at Montlhéry (where three international speed records were set). It was then sent to America, one of three SL race cars that went to Max Hoffman. Next #063 went on to California, where John von Neumann painted it red. After races at Pebble Beach and Golden Gate, von Neumann found it too heavy and the brakes inadequate. His solution was to have Culver City Indy car builder Emil Diedt turn it into a roadster, smoothing the rear deck and fenders. With upgraded brakes, the topless racer began to win, but new Porsche racers were coming on the scene. A few owners later, it was for sale in 1957.

That year, twenty-two-year-old Chuck Forge was in graduate school at Stanford, just beginning a career as an electrical engineer. An avid sports-car fan, he considered several makes, including an old Porsche he had heard about. His friend Llew Kinst recalled, "Once he found out that the local Porsche dealer would sell parts at a discount if you had a race car while other dealers wouldn't, he figured he had to at least take a look." One test drive through the old Golden Gate Park race course and he was sold. For $800, #063 went home to his parents' orchard in Cupertino (when there were still orchards in Silicon Valley), where it became his autocross car and fun street car. Forge focused his attention on racing a VW and other Porsches, very successfully.

For a while #063 languished; it was offered for sale in the 1960s for $1,500, but there were no takers. But when vintage race organizer Steve Earle announced Porsche as the featured

VW and Porsche four-cylinder engines can be tweaked for more power, but a serious outlaw needs a serious engine, like this Emory-Rothsport Outlaw 4, based on a 911 3.6. Perhaps Porsche would have done well to adapt its own six decades ago.

Chuck Forge drove the Gmünd "roadster" mostly at the Monterey Historic Races each year. It was a familiar and popular entry, and many fans miss seeing it there.

marque for the Monterey Historic Races in 1982, Forge had metal work and new paint done, completed the night before the Laguna Seca Raceway event. That was the first year of many appearances there, and over the decades new generations of Porsche fans came to appreciate #063's significance as an early Porsche racer. While Forge was aware of the car's history, his friend Harlan Halsey notes, "We looked several times but could find no clear chassis number." The Porsche Museum in Zuffenhausen had on display another Gmünd coupe wearing the number 46 and representing the Le Mans class winner from 1951.

Chuck Forge passed away in 2009, and the red car was sold to Porsche collector and vintage racer Cameron Healy of Oregon. Healy and restorer Rod Emory suspected there was more to the story; Cameron scoured the Porsche archives while Rod inspected every part of the car. They unearthed important archive documents and found significant evidence of repairs and subtle marks that corresponded to the Le Mans car's racing career. Now confident the red roadster had in fact taken the checkered flag in 1951
in France, Emory embarked on a restoration that was high-tech yet old-school. Using lasers to measure two other Gmünd coupes, he built accurate wooden bucks and carefully crafted new panels by hand. With traditional tools, the car was returned to its original shape, authentic, yet not overrestored.

In this condition, #356/2-063 made its debut at Porsche Rennsport Reunion in 2015 and was later driven onto the lawn at the Pebble Beach Concours, just a few miles from where its American racing career had begun. Porsche's first racing winner was back on the world stage.

Brought back to its 1951 Le Mans configuration, 063 makes the rounds at Porsche events, arguably one of the most important historic Porsches extant.

KEEPING THE FAITH

The first Porsche club was formed in Germany in 1954, and in the United States the Porsche Club of America began in 1955. The latter's annual Porsche Parade brings members in the United States and Canada together, and other clubs offer events around the world. Most countries in Europe have dedicated 356 organizations, and they host one another at an International Porsche 356 Meeting each summer. In North America the 356 Registry and some twenty-five regional groups have regular gatherings that give members a driving destination, face time with friends, and a chance to compare notes and show off their rides.

While some events, like the European Pre-A Meeting, are tightly focused on a few years' production, a recent event series is a sort of hybrid. Luftgekühlt was the brainchild of Porsche driver Patrick Long and creative director Howie Idelson. With a definite Southern California vibe, this unpredictable happening is as much about a cool venue as the air-cooled Porsches it celebrates, spanning fifty years of Porsche production. A movie studio backlot, a harbor loading dock, an English bomber airfield—where will the next one be? It's an inside secret until the last minute, but be sure of this: it will be a good time.

In 2001 Porsche Cars North America created an event to honor its motorsport tradition. The first Rennsport Reunion at Lime Rock Park in Connecticut was so successful that two more were held, at three-year intervals, at Daytona International Raceway in Florida. Rennsport was moved to Laguna Seca in Monterey, California, for 2011, 2015, and 2018. With attendance of 81,550 for the 2018 event, it was an over-the-top experience for Porsche fans, who could see the largest selection of historical Porsches ever in one place, their favorite drivers from today and yesterday, and racing action over several days.

The entire 356 series represents around 2 percent of all Porsches built to date, but even in a sea of Porsches—like this parking lot at Rennsport in 2011—a Speedster will turn heads and stand out.

The first Porsche Club of America parade drew a crowd, including many owners of the new Speedster model. Held outside Washington, DC, in 1956, it was organized by club founder Bill Sholar.

Luftgekühlt 5 used a Los Angeles wholesale lumber yard as its venue, drawing hundreds of cars and an appreciative crowd.

An active 356 group in Japan has regular "Holidays," featuring interesting cars like this Zagato re-creation of the car built on a Speedster chassis for Claud Storez in the 1950s.

THE EVERGREEN AUTO

The 356 resides at the intersection of exclusive and everyday. Porsche strove to build cars for which "exciting" and "dependable" are not mutually exclusive terms. Just ask Guy Newmark, who has driven his 356C coupe over 1 million miles. Working in the Los Angeles area, Newmark has logged 1,015,000 miles over several decades and as of this writing is still going. Ergonomics, economy, and simple driving pleasure have been his mantra for all those years.

The dedication of enthusiasts has helped this blossoming of interest, but the little bathtub-shaped cars speak for themselves. Even among newer, faster, more sophisticated, and more exotic Porsches, a 356 stands out. The appeal is clearly there; whether it's because of simplicity, the smooth shape, a nostalgic bent, or some intangible, the first cars from Zuffenhausen speak to people. Owners lavish time, effort, and money on their cars, but most recognize they are not really owners but just custodians—caretakers of a line that now spans three-quarters of a century. Ferry Porsche created a special automobile that has already charmed several generations, and hopefully, it will continue to put smiles on drivers' faces for years to come.

Guy Newmark and the 356C that has taken him over a million miles around California.

The 356 Registry Holidays attract hundreds of members to locations across the country twice each year. This group enjoyed the lawn at the Biltmore Estate in Asheville, North Carolina, in 2003.

ACKNOWLEDGMENTS

A book covering more than 75 years of history requires contributions from many people, and I am fortunate that so many experts and enthusiasts pitched in. First and foremost, I must express gratitude to Karl Ludvigsen, the dean of Porsche historians. His tomes on the marque have been inspiring, entertaining and invaluable in the writing and publishing I've done over the last thirty years. Material by additional authors provided the groundwork for this effort, and I thank Frank Jung—who in addition to writing Porsche 356 by Reutter— is also head of the Porsche Archives.

Other writers deserve thanks as well. Brett Johnson's books on 356 authenticity are without peer; Phil Carney is a tireless researcher and insightful scribe; Sean Cridland's excellent writing is matched by his photographic eye; Dirk-Michael Conradt's 356 book is a treasure of details; and Randy Leffingwell has given us several editions of wonderful words and photos about Porsche. It is an honor to be in their company.

A key element in telling any story is the visual, and Jens Torner at the Porsche archives has answered my call, once again, for historical images. I am indebted to him not only for help with this title, but for several decades of providing material for 356 articles and books as well as gracious and memorable archive tours. Many others at Porsche AG have given their time, and I thank Paul Gregor for arranging these interactions.

Aside from the archives in Zuffenhausen, a significant institutional memory exists in the membership of Porsche 356 Registry. Story and photo contributions by the group over my 26 years editing the club's magazine gave me a sizable foundation on which to build this book. The thousands of enthusiasts who make up the club represent every possible area of 356 expertise, and they willingly share that knowledge. I thank them all

sincerely and encourage each one to "keep the 356 faith."

Special thanks to those behind the camera lens for images old and new in this book: Shep Adkins, Frank Barrett, Gregg Blue, Gianni Cabiglio, John Calamos, Kristina Cilia, Sean Cridland, Gerry Curts, Alex DeJonge, John Eaton, Wolfgang Franke, Dennis Frick, Skeet Gifford, Chris Greenwood, Alan Gruening, Jerry Haussler, John Hearn, Chuck House, Ken Ito, Prescott Kelly, Roy Lock, Roland Lohnert, Sean Lorentzen, Bob McCarthy, Dave Miller, Laurent Missbauer, Dennis Molnar, Thomas Lloyd Meyer, Freddy Rabbat, Chris Runge, Eric Simpson, Tony Singer, Bruce Sweetman, Henry Walker, Stefan Warter, Tom Wheatley, Walden Wright, Ted Zombek, Michel Zumbrunn and Chris Casler, Nick Clemence and Ted7 at European Collectibles.

Assistance of all kinds came from long-time friends, acquaintances and some people I was referred to, all of whom helped get this book off the ground. My thanks to all: Audi AG archives, Automuseum Prototyp-Hamburg, George Batcabe, Peter Bodensteiner, Michael Branning, Sam Cabiglio, Andy Daugherty, Gary and Rod Emory, Alex Finigan, Dennis Frick, Cameron Healy, Cam Ingram, Llew Kinst, Ray Knight, Franklin Lock, Rex McAfee, Gunner Mensch, Jacques Mertens, Bernard Moix, Ernie Nagamatsu, Guy Newmark, Reinhold Plank, Lee Raskin, Paul Russell, Ron Roland, Peter Schaeublin, Vic and Barbara Skirmants, Myron Vernis, and John von Nolde.

I am grateful to my editor Zack Miller and project manager Brooke Pelletier for steering me gently but firmly through this project.

My wife Lonnie has spent decades patiently waiting while I worked on one Porsche project or another. To her, I dedicate this book with all my love and appreciation for her support.

PHOTO CREDITS

All images courtesy Porsche Historic Archives except the following:

Shep Adkins: 248 (middle)

Automuseum Prototyp Hamburg: 72, 100 (bottom right), 150 (top), 151 (top)

Matt Bleything: 209

Gregg Blue: 232 (bottom)

Markus Bolsinger: 111 (bottom)

Brundage Family collection: 103

Gianni Cabiglio: 55 (top), 194, 195 (middle, 2)

Tom Countryman: 80

Cunningham Family photo collection: 83 (bottom)

Jerry Curts: 213

Daimler Benz Archives: 15 (2)

Ken Daugherty: 112

Alex DeJonge, Restoration design: 245 (bottom left)

John Eaton: 206 (top)

Courtesy Rod Emory: 246 (center)

David Epstein, courtesy Tony Singer: 23, 141, 189

European Collectibles: 117, 128 (top), 130, 136, 192, 195 (top, middle), 200 (bottom right), 206 (bottom), 213 (bottom), 216 (top left)

Jayson Fong, courtesy Simon Bowrey: 184

Wolfgang Franke: 17 (top), 21 (top), 36, 37, 147 (right), 227 (top)

Dennis Frick: 133 (bottom)

Skeet Gifford: 250

Michael Gray (Wikipedia): 227 (bottom)

Chris Greenwood: 246

Alan Gruening: 182

Jerry Haussler: 100 (top)

Cameron Healy collection: 247

John Hearn: 29, 81, 82 (bottom), 144, 238, 248 (bottom left)

Robert Heintz: 128 (bottom), 129 (top, bottom right)

Chuck House: 197 (3)

Brett Johnson: 69, 100 (top)

Prescott Kelly: 187 (bottom)

Ken Ito: 248 (bottom right)

Mathilda Larson: 6

Roy Lock: 245 (bottom right)

Roland Lohnert: 227 (bottom)

Sean Lorentzen: 249 (top right)

Gordon Maltby: 4, 21 (bottom), 32, 126 (bottom), 215, 240, 241 (top), 242, 248 (top)

Courtesy Rex McAfee: 118, 119

Gunner Mensch: 202

Courtesy Jacques Mertens: 10 (top left)

Thomas Lloyd Meyer: 108 (bottom right), 124, 145

Stan Michael, courtesy Tony Singer: 42 (middle)

Dave Miller: 243 (bottom), 244

Laurent Missbauer: 224

Dennis Molnar: 137 (top)

Courtesy Ernie Nagamatsu: 241 (bottom)

Reinhold Plank: 95 (top, middle), 68 (4)

Freddy Rabbat: 193 (top)

Courtesy Sue Ramage: 44 (top)

Courtesy Lee Raskin: 162, 163

Road Scholars: 55 (bottom)

Courtesy Ron Roland: 82 (top), 83 (top)

Chris Runge: 245 (top)

Paul Russell: 77 (top)

Eric Simpson: 243 (top)

Courtesy Tony Singer: 12, 43, 98 (left)

Jim Smeltzer: 249 (bottom)

Bruce Sweetman: 148, 176

Hans von Nolde: 108 (top), 109 (2)

Henry Walker: 234 (bottom)

Stefan Warter, Corporate Archives AUDI AG: 9

Thomas Wheatley: 58

Walden Wright: 2

Ted Zombek: 110 (bottom), 111 (top), 113 (2), 233 (bottom), 246 (bottom)

Michel Zumbrunn: 54 (top), 100 (bottom)

INDEX

Page numbers in *italic* refer to captions.

Quarto

First Published in 2023 by Motorbooks, an imprint of The Quarto Group,
100 Cummings Center, Suite 265-D, Beverly, MA 01915, USA.
T (978) 282-9590 F (978) 283-2742 Quarto.com

Motorbooks titles are also available at discount for retail, wholesale, promotional, and bulk purchase. For details, contact the Special Sales Manager by email at specialsales@quarto.com or by mail at The Quarto Group, Attn: Special Sales Manager, 100 Cummings Center, Suite 265-D, Beverly, MA 01915, USA.

26 25 24   2 3 4 5

ISBN: 978-0-7603-7737-6

Digital edition published in 2023
eISBN: 978-0-7603-7738-3

Library of Congress Cataloging-in-Publication Data

Names: Maltby, Gordon, 1950- author.
Title: Porsche 356 : 75th anniversary / Gordon Maltby.
Description: Beverly, MA, USA : Motorbooks, an imprint of The Quarto Group, 2023. | Includes index. | Summary: "Porsche's first car, the 356, entered the market in 1948 and celebrates its 75th anniversary in 2023. Porsche 356: 75th Anniversary celebrates this iconic sports car that launched one of the greatest brands in automotive history"-- Provided by publisher.
Identifiers: LCCN 2022042134 | ISBN 9780760377376 | ISBN 9780760377383 (ebook)
Subjects: LCSH: Porsche automobiles--History.
Classification: LCC TL215.P75 M34 2023 | DDC 629.222/2--dc23/eng/20221004
LC record available at https://lccn.loc.gov/2022042134

Design and Page Layout: www.traffic-design.co.uk
Hardcover Image: Jayson Fong, courtesy Simon Bowrey
Jacket Images: **Front:** Porsche 356 at Duxford Airfield, Cambridge, United Kingdom. Photo by Kristina Cilia. Kristina Cilia is an automotive and car culture photographer. She resides in Northern California. www.kristinaciliaphotography.com **Back:** Top left: Porsche archives; Top right: Thomas Lloyd Meyer; Middle right: Porsche Archives; Bottom right: European Collectibles
Endpapers: **Front:** Porsche Archive; **Back:** Stu Watson

Printed in China